# Dedication

*For Gary and Elizabeth, my family,
and Ann, my friend. I also dedicate this book
to my interns, students, and all those who have
encouraged me to share the fascinating career
of photo styling. And to Nicole Potter-Talling,
my editor at Allworth Press, for recognizing that
a definitive book about photo styling was needed
and giving me the opportunity to publish it.*

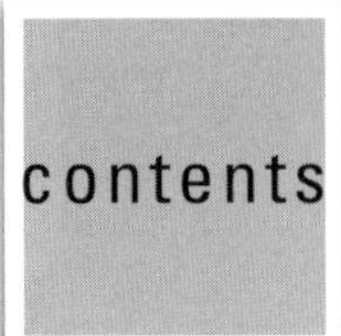

# contents

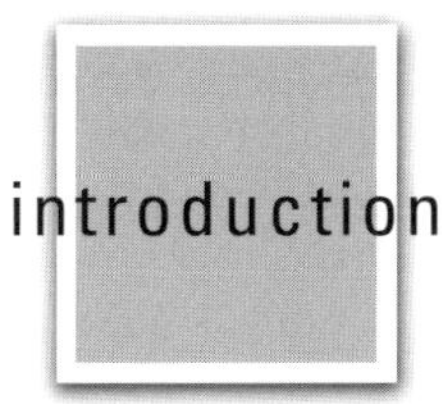

# introduction

**HOTO STYLING IS AN "INVISIBLE CAREER."**
The goal of the stylist is to create the illusion of naturalness in a photograph. We make a stack of sweaters look as if they were casually placed. We make a dining room look like the residents just walked out of the room. We make a model look like she is casually walking down the street in an attractive outfit. In reality, all these scenarios take a great deal of preparation, planning, adjustments, and precision. That is the job of the photo stylist.

Secondly, the career is "invisible" because not much is known about it outside of the photo industry. Little has been written about the career. Most of us come upon the field accidentally through graphic design, as I did, or as my fortunate interns have done, through college fashion programs. However, no formal education is required.

This career manual explores the numerous directions photo styling can take. The book provides new and working stylists with information on all these specialties. The stylist can take on various roles; production, casting, and location scouting are a few. In this book, the photo crew, etiquette, creating a portfolio, and marketing are explored in depth. The aspiring stylist must learn how to develop and maintain a freelance career. Business forms such as proposals, invoices, and vouchers will give stylists a head start on building their own freelance businesses.

Dirty little secrets of the trade are revealed. Challenging and hidden aspects of styling, such as merchandise returns and re-tagging garments, are discussed. Interviews with professionals introduce stylists to real career stories.

When models, art directors, and photographers understand the work stylists do, everyone benefits. The outcome of the photo shoot is greatly improved. Three final chapters advise these professionals on how to work with stylists to enhance their own careers. Knowledge of the work stylists do helps the team create effective photographs, whether for catalogs, advertising, stock photography, or magazines.

Photo styling touches nearly every image we see, except for the raw portrayals of journalism. From the self-conscious primping for snapshots to the most exacting attention to details in commercial photography, styling makes a visible difference in the world around us. Though some might say "It's not rocket science," the skills of a photo stylist have an effect on all the images we see.

Styling is a tremendous opportunity for creative and organized individuals to express themselves. What adds to the excitement is that one can continuously draw on life experiences and accumulated practical skills to energize this intriguing career.

# Introduction to Photo Styling

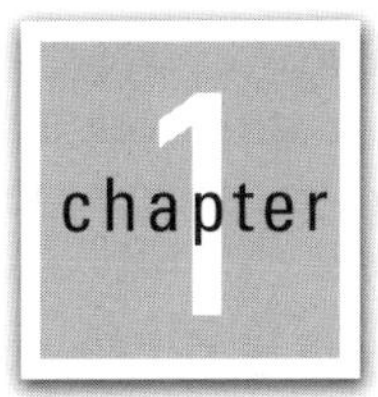



# chapter 1

# What is a Photo Stylist?

**P**HOTO STYLING IS THE LITTLE-KNOWN ART OF MANIPULATING and controlling all the physical elements in a photograph to create an effective image. It takes a creative and organized person to be a good photo stylist. Many artistic people find styling to be a more practical outlet for their creativity than a career in the fine arts.

And now the word is out about this behind-the-scenes career. Many young adults have heard of styling, perhaps because of reading about celebrity stylists in magazines, and it has become their dream job. This glamorous image of styling, though, is not wholly accurate. Knowledge and understanding of the interdependent fields of photography, graphic design, and marketing are important to success as a photo stylist. Long hours, physically demanding work, thorough organization, and business management skills are as crucial as creativity.

As Boston stylist Ann Fitzgerald says, "Becoming a good stylist takes time; to build resources, train your eye, and learn to beg, borrow, and steal in the nicest way possible."

## DESCRIBING WHAT YOU DO

The goal of styling is to make a photograph look as though there wasn't a stylist involved. So it's no wonder most people don't know about photo styling. They see photographs in catalogs, magazines, and advertisements and have no idea of the amount of work involved in creating them. As a stylist, you can explain that you make everything in a photograph look just right. But there are people who hear the word "photograph" and stop right there. Even after the explanation, they may say, "Oh, so you're a photographer?" Then you bring out a catalog and describe the process—how you stacked the T-shirts so that one might see every color, making them thicker with batting, like the kind used for quilting, tucking in the sides, lifting the top one with cardboard held up by a brick; how you adjusted and readjusted the stack so it would look perfect. The response will be, "Oh, I had no idea every photograph took so much work!"

The preparation—and expense—involved in a fashion shoot on location will amaze them even more; the weeks of planning, scheduling, booking models, prop shopping, the travel to locations, hotel rooms, meals, and steaming the merchandise. The response then may be, "All that, just for a background that you can hardly see?" "It's the light," you'll say, "and the local landmarks we include in some shots for atmosphere." They won't believe you, but who's complaining?

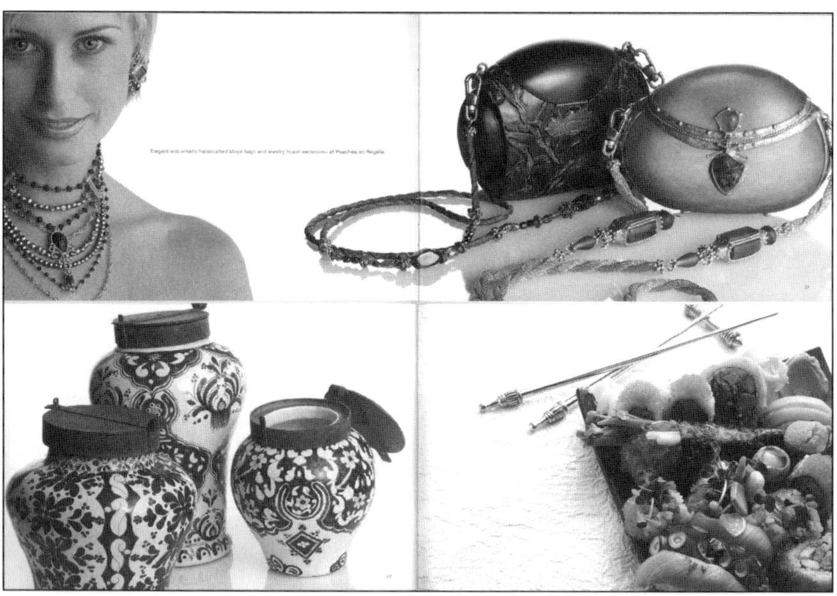

Four pages from a holiday catalog showing different types of styling. *Photographer:* Tim Mantoani. *Art director:* Cindy Cochran. *Styling:* Susan Linnet Cox. *Hair and makeup:* Claire Young. © Tim Mantoani

## Discovering Styling

What leads one to discover this fascinating hidden career? Most stylists just "fall into it" as a career. One of the interns I trained, Veronica

Guzman, said she wished she had known there was such a thing as a stylist during all those youthful years when she was cutting photos out of magazines.

Conversely, New York fashion student Tiffany Olson says, "I am one of the few who have been interested in it from the start, since my mother is a catalog art director. Growing up, I used to sit for hours at my mother's photo shoots just watching and knew it was for me. Now I'm looking for an opportunity to learn more about styling."

Generally photo stylists emerge from creative fields like fine art, graphic design, theater, or fashion. Many have a college degree in these fields, but what is really required is a visual aesthetic and an independent spirit, along with an organized and practical nature. Most stylists have a desire to create something visually pleasing, while earning a good income.

## THE REAL LIFE RÉSUMÉ

When you create a résumé, you don't tell the whole truth. You only tell the good parts, the skills and accomplishments that qualified you for your present goal. You're not hiding the truth when you leave out the various forks in the road and side trips that you've taken in your life; you're just getting to the point. And as you grow, you will take more side trips—that is, if you're adventurous. And if you are reading this book, you probably have a penchant for adventure. It is not an easy job—it's never easy to work for yourself, to wonder what job you will work on next, to work long and hard, and to have responsibility for your part of the project. But it is still the best career in the world.

All those trips you've taken won't be wasted. The dead ends can teach you skills that will surprise you later. The long hills…the potholes…even after the crashes you learn that you have experienced the worst that can happen, and you survived.

You meet people that turn up again later in your life. You find out you weren't wasting your time fishing when you know the strengths of various monofilaments and where to find them. Your brief interest in embroidery, your study of perennial plants, your experience driving a motorcycle, your time in nursing school—they all come back to you in your styling career with some useful knowledge or skill. Because in this field you don't *only* deal with fashion or gourmet food. You work for clients in such diverse enterprises as pet stores, window blind companies, software designers, nursing homes, fork lift manufacturers, or ice cream shops. The more you know, the better you will understand why they need a photograph taken and how it can help them sell their products.

So your "real life résumé" is mysterious at times and confusing at others. The older you get, the more you will accept your path and realize it was all really worth the trip.

## My Background

I wish I had discovered styling earlier. I think I would have had a delightful adult life as a photo stylist. Instead, after finishing a fine arts degree, I put in thirteen years of waitressing, off and on. It was a job I could always find, with ready cash. At the same time I owned a house-plant store in Kent, Ohio, in the 1970s, the decade when young people were rediscovering their grandmothers' house plants and placing them in macramé plant hangers. I was able to live for five years on an initial investment of $50, supporting quite a few employees as well.

I was a substitute art teacher in the Akron Public Schools. I sewed clothing for a small designer in Venice, California. I sewed one-of-a-kind shirts for a Melrose Avenue boutique. I made custom lingerie for Trashy, a famous private-membership store in Los Angeles—but it was a small room in a shoe store at the time, and I had a sewing machine set up between the shelves in the back. I held a job in a fabric store. I worked part-time in a darkroom for my brother who was making copy prints of old photos. I started a mail-order T-shirt company with another woman. We sold sushi T-shirts from our ad in the now-defunct *Wet Magazine* in New York and Los Angeles. I designed the ad and didn't even know I was doing graphic design. I drew the silkscreen design of the sushi by hand on seven sheets of tracing paper, which all fit together to print seven different colors. I sewed and marketed soft sculpture TVs and guitars out of satin.

## A Few Dead Ends

If all of this sounds like I flitted from success to success, it is not true. There were lots of dead ends. That is why the waitress skills kept coming in handy. The economy in Northeastern Ohio grew steadily bleaker in the late 1970s. I gave up on the beloved plant store. California beckoned me, as it did many of my generation and I found myself in luxurious Montecito, near Santa Barbara. It was the home of a rock star friend and I was able to camp there in a guest room for three months—too long. It is not as it sounds. I literally spent my last dime while helping his wife shop for antique furniture with royalties from a major album. I found another waitress job and then the lingerie opportunity in Los Angeles. I left that job to start my own line of silk lingerie, Suzy, which I took to Beverly Hills boutiques. I didn't get an order. It was around that time that I met a photographer from Kent who shot for "girlie" magazines. He told me there are people whose job it is to actually shop for the props and other items that are used in photo shoots. A stylist! I was amazed but never imagined it would later be my profession. First I had a different road to travel.

## The Long Road

I found a waitress job in a jazz club in West Los Angeles. I spent my days roller-skating at Venice Beach and worked at Snooky's at night. It was the best job I'd ever had. There were famous musicians playing and a real nightclub atmosphere. The cash was good and my boss, Gary Cox, became my husband. We fell madly and truly in love, and I left my job to stay home and be a newlywed. Eventually I got serious and started to face the idea that I was about to have a child who was going to need my support and I didn't even have a sensible career yet!

After my daughter was born, she enthralled me. Fortunately, I didn't have to leave her and go to work full-time like many mothers do. I did want to do something, though, and worked part-time at a day-care center where we could be together. At night I parked cars for an all-women valet parking service. What a contrast!

Finally when Elizabeth was three, I found the career I'd been looking for and that career led me to styling. I became a graphic designer. When I was in art school, "commercial art," as it was known then, was somewhat repugnant. It was selling out. We all wanted to be artists and had no idea how that might support us. The art department didn't offer much practical help.

## The Florida Years

We had moved to St. Petersburg, Florida. Gary worked in developing property, and I was hired by one of those chains of TV and appliance companies that have a big ad in the newspaper several times a week with lots of little boxes showing all the microwaves, refrigerators, and televisions, and their prices. I sketched out the ads and the newspapers designed them. The company advertised "Christmas in July," and I got to be involved in a TV production. The owner was dressed as Santa and sitting in a sleigh with a group of children, including my own darling daughter. While helping him with his costume I searched for a pillow to fill in the jacket and found a throw pillow in his office that was embroidered with a Jewish star and I used that. It was my first real styling experience and I enjoyed the irony.

After another graphic design job, I was familiar with the tools of the trade, an X-Acto® knife, T-square, triangle, and waxing roller. We sent copy to typesetters and printed halftone photos in the darkroom. When I was hired it was assumed I knew the basics of graphic design, having done all those complex ads, but my lack of experience with these tools was nearly my undoing. Luckily, my coworkers trained me and I repaid them by going out on my own after a year! Now I was getting somewhere. I had clients and loved the process of graphics, designing ads, brochures, and catalogs.

## One Step Closer to Styling

Next, we moved to Portland, Oregon, so my husband could continue his equally indirect career path. He had returned to the field of education and was hired as a counselor in a middle school. I found a freelance position with a major catalog company, Norm Thompson. I liked being there and they liked me and I was hired just as computers were being introduced. The computer training was hard—we were all pretty attached to our X-Acto knives.

Soon the company had cutbacks due to postal increases (we'll talk in chapter 3 about the ups and downs of the catalog industry). To my amazement I remained employed. Typically when there are layoffs, the remaining employees do the extra work of those let go. We had to find someone who could art direct the fashion photo shoots. My family and I had just returned from a Christmas trip away from the rainy weather to Mazatlan, Mexico, which had reminded me how much I love travel. So I willingly agreed to direct a shoot in Miami, just to see if I liked it.

I have never done anything in which I instantly felt so competent. With no training, I knew to stand behind the photographer to get the right view of the model. I could see what background would end up in the shot. I understood that the reflector would bounce sunlight back into the model's face. I knew what I was looking for when the photographer passed me a Polaroid print, and how many shots we could get done in a day. I loved my new world behind the camera.

## Life as an Art Director

I also felt sort of guilty. I was flying out of the gloomy climate of the Northwest every six weeks or so and leaving my husband with all the responsibilities of a home, a daughter, and a dog. I was leaving my child. But I also loved my job, even with the long exhausting days and the pressure of bringing back photos that sold the merchandise. Sometimes Gary and Elizabeth visited me on location and that helped. The tension in our family was growing, though, and I had to find another way. So after three years of this, I decided to move on. Elizabeth had only five more years before growing up and moving away, and I didn't want to miss any more of her life.

Besides, I was ready to embark on three new ventures. I was going to model for the older model market. (I found an agent but ended up with just a few bookings.) I was designing a cookbook but the chef authors never completed their recipes and the project fell apart. And I was planning to art direct photo shoots on a freelance basis. However, I hadn't done my homework—there wasn't much opportunity for that. Most companies in the area used in-house staff for art direction, as with my Norm Thompson position.

It wasn't all a waste of time. I started another plant store, something I'd dreamed about, feeling even more competent at store design than the first time. I did freelance preproduction planning for Norm Thompson's photo shoots. And I had my first styling job. I was asked by a photographer to style "laydowns" of Adidas clothing for a catalog. Most of my art direction had been on location shoots of models, not in studios, but I knew the look the client was after. I thought that batting and foam would probably fill the garments enough to give them a good shape when the photographer shot them from above. I jumped in.

After one more rainy winter we moved to San Diego—we all missed the sunshine and were ready to be Californians again. There I found enough freelance graphic design and art direction jobs to meet quite a few people and progressed nicely in my career as my daughter completed high school and Gary worked in special education.

## More Valuable Experiences

I also worked for a photographer as a studio manager. I thought that going to work in a photo studio every day might be pretty heavenly. And it was—I got to do styling and find props; I built my portfolio. I found out that what I did *not* like was doing estimates, answering the phone, monitoring the status of my employer's jobs and stock photography sales. I observed the art directors and clients, who spent time on the phone instead of watching the shoot and I brought their coffee and ordered their lunches. That was hard. I held back from giving advice about their photographs: if you move over this way a little your background will be better, maybe a slightly higher camera angle. One photo assistant referred to me as "the secretary," and I decided the styling opportunities weren't worth the rest of the job.

Next, I spent the better part of a year in the in-house graphic design department of a software company. There I experienced the security and give-and-take politics of the corporate world.

I took a position as senior art director of an Orange County catalog company. I watched the stylists I hired and had to hold back from doing their jobs—I was one level up, I was the art director. I directed the fashion shoots and had more foreign travel but I felt unable to use my creative experience to refine and improve the rather stodgy catalogs.

The following year I spent as a model agent. This difficult field gave me more appreciation of the work that both models and agents do. (In chapter 14, I'll address the world of modeling.)

## Making the Leap

During these few years I maintained one wonderful client, a home-products catalog. The art directors regularly came to San Diego for their spring and summer photo shoots. I started out doing a little prop shopping for them. There would be a few things they needed and if I was working I'd just drop them off. This was my first steady client. Soon I worked on complex prop shopping expeditions and did all the styling on these shoots.

When I stopped working as a model agent I finally had the courage—and the portfolio—to stop procrastinating and be a serious stylist.

## Types of Styling

At this point in my career I had experienced many types of styling. In the coming years I'd learn even more.

I had a call a few years ago from a Minneapolis-based "production designer." He wondered if I could assist him with a month of work for a window-treatment company. I learned an immense amount from him about renting furniture, carpets, and accessories. During that project I had a chance to work on a couple of days of video, and styled a bubble bath.

I'd always wanted to work on a car shoot to see what a project of that scale was like. I had an opportunity to work on a series of photos for Buick, and found out about the water trucks that wet the street and about shooting on streets at night. I didn't style the cars. My role was wardrobe styling for a family that was out of focus in the background of one shot, and decorating the front of a boutique in the night shot. I also got to drive my Jeep up and down the street, carefully shining the headlights onto the Buick's side while the photographer did a long exposure.

There is no absolute description for each type of styling; there are regional differences, different terms, and different job descriptions. When I was called to style for a Tampa, Florida, catalog company, I was told I'd be doing two days of "fashion." So I brought my styling kit for models to the studio the first day, and waited for the makeup artist and models to arrive. It turned out that what they called fashion was what I called "wall styling." (You'll read more about wall styling in chapter 7.) I spent the days quietly styling dresses and Capri sets on a vertical board. Luckily, because I'd had lots of experience with this type of styling for other clients, this was not a problem for me. I still did not know what to officially call the technique of forming life-like clothing on a wall.

Your own life history will come into play in many ways as you develop a styling career. You'll find what type of styling appeals to you and what you're most comfortable with. Here is a summary of the six most common areas of photo styling.

## FASHION STYLING

For years I looked at magazines trying to figure out who put those fabulous clothes on the model and never could find a listing for the stylist. The photographer, the makeup artist, and, sometimes, a prop stylist would be listed on the pages, but never the stylist. The image that many of us have of what a stylist does, dressing all those fashionable models in magazines, is not called a stylist at all. This is a fashion editor.

### Fashion Editor

Fashion editors create the fashion stories in magazines, from start to finish. The role is universal: fashion magazines from many countries have fashion editors who analyze the new styles and trends by attending the major semi-annual runway shows, develop photographic stories relevant to their readers, produce and style them, and even write about the fashions. Newer and smaller magazines are more likely to use freelance stylists for these roles. The big-name magazines have the coveted positions in which an editor can become a well-known name.

### Commercial Styling

Styling clothing for fashion advertising, the kind you see in the same magazines, can be well-paying work. The designer clothes are the star; the model, photographer, and stylist work to create a photo that will make the buyer want them. They may be creating a mood or identity for the brand more than featuring the fashions. It's a natural step for an editor who knows the fashion world inside out.

### Catalogs

Styling for catalogs that market clothing may not be cutting-edge fashion, but it provides a great deal of work for stylists. The resources are limited to what is available for sale, rather than pulling together garments from many designers into an exciting new combination. Though catalog styling may be referred to as either fashion *or* wardrobe, we include it with fashion styling here.

### Runway Shows

Another role in fashion is styling fashion shows. The major designer shows in Milan, Paris, London, and New York involve concepts in styling and makeup. Exhausting and stressful to execute, they are an extraordinary opportunity for a stylist. Local, smaller scale events can be good practice.

### Celebrity Stylist

A consultant who advises celebrities on fashion and provides the clothing they wear in public appearances is a celebrity stylist. A major part of the stylist's role is finding resources that will loan the garments in exchange for free publicity. (These careers will be described in chapter 5, with a focus on magazine and catalog fashion styling.)

## WARDROBE STYLING

Wardrobe styling and fashion styling can easily be confused. Wardrobe styling may seem a little less creative. Indeed it is more practical—finding clothing to be worn in advertisements, commercials, and other photographs, which may not be made for selling clothes. For lifestyle photography, the stylist is dressing the talent in generic items so as not to distract from the featured product or concept. Or perhaps the stylist is replicating an historic period for a video or commercial. The effect should be just enough that the clothes work but do not distract.

### Lifestyle, Advertising, Stock

A lifestyle shot depicts real-life situations and people for an ad or for stock photography. The people portrayed in advertisements usually look real and approachable. Lifestyle is often also the theme of stock photography. Stock photos are available for clients to use for a fee, as opposed to photography commissioned by a client for a specific project. Since stock photographers may be paying for the shoots themselves, they often don't use a stylist.

People in non-fashion advertisements may be interacting with a product or enhancing a lifestyle concept for a specific company or brand. In these cases, as well, the wardrobe should not distract from the lifestyle being portrayed.

## Video, Commercials, Film

There is some crossover between video styling and still photography styling. The fields are not so different; a stylist can move back and forth between the two. Skills learned in one can be useful in the other. Here the wardrobe may need to be generic, historic, outrageous, or anything else that's required for the commercial or video.

The world of movies, however, is more complex than the world of video. There are particular resources available for the movie industry, as well as unions and other protocols to be aware of. The wardrobe team is larger and the duties more exact. Wardrobe for film, like set design, would be a fascinating and exciting career.

(Chapter 6 will describe styling for wardrobe, and provide information on shopping, organizing, and prepping garments, working with models to provide wardrobe options, and how to manage it all.)

# STYLING OFF-FIGURE

In discussing styling off-figure, we will be looking at techniques for styling clothing that is not being worn. Presentations range from showing natural-looking folded items to imitating gestures of the human body.

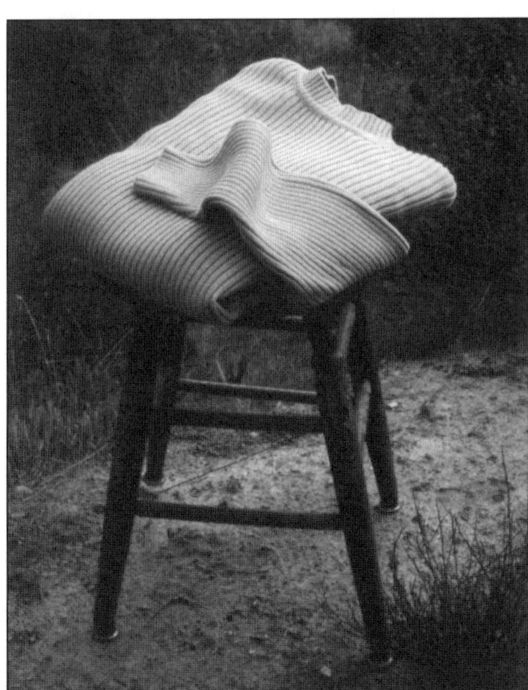

Folded sweater shot on location. *Styling and photography:* Susan Linnet Cox. © Susan Linnet Cox

### Stacks, Hangers, Mannequins, Laydowns, and Wall Styling

There is a variety of techniques stylists use in working with clothing to show the details of garments, color selections, and the texture of the fabric. It may be folded and stacked on a tabletop in a studio, hung on hangers to show a selection of colors, dressed on a mannequin, laid down flat and shot from above, or arranged on a wall in a manner that suggests the human form. Most often this work is done in the studio environment, but it may be styled on location.

(In chapter 7, you will learn the basic techniques for styling clothing all five of these ways. Understanding what fabric does and how to manage it, can enhance your skills in all other types of styling.)

## PRODUCT STYLING

Rarely will a stylist work exclusively with either clothing off-figure or products. We are making distinctions here because there are different techniques that stylists use, depending on the product styled. Some stylists may excel at one or the other, having a preference for the draping qualities of fabric, or adeptness with setting up dishes.

Photographers do many product shots without the need for a stylist. For simple items in a catalog, presenting a smaller budget to a client may result in more volume of work for the photographer. You wouldn't want to style some of it anyway. Endless variations of hammers, office supplies, or electronic components might make you feel like you're working in a factory.

Other items are much more fun, especially when props are needed, or there is the challenge of making a handbag strap drape in mid-air.

### Tabletop

Products may be handbags, accessories, beauty products, dishes, or other household items. Often a background surface needs to be selected, as well as other props that will give a sense of scale and create a variety of levels. Sometimes the term tabletop is used to describe product styling.

### Shoes

Styling shoes is fun, but there are standards for showing aspects of shoes that present their own challenges. A surprisingly large part of styling work, footwear may be shot on location or on a tabletop in studio.

### Jewelry

You may find jewelry styling, which requires working on a much smaller scale, inspiring. When shooting an item so close, clean jewelry and clean backgrounds are important. Challenges arise from positioning the items in a variety of arrangements, with the photographer carefully controlling reflections.

(In chapter 8 I will share useful techniques for working with varied products, and hints for propping these shots.)

## FOOD STYLING

In a world full of mysterious techniques, the food stylist has a unique kit and set of specialized skills. Except for propping the shot, the food stylist operates in a separate world, not as a jack of all trades like many other stylists. An appreciation of cooking is important even though the styled food may not always be edible.

(An interview with a professional food stylist will shed light on this field, as she reveals some tricks of the trade in chapter 9.)

## ROOM SETS AND BEDDING

The photographers who work in this area are architectural photographers. They are skilled at lighting and shooting a large area without distortion; they see the big picture. As a stylist for room sets, you too will be thinking big. Furniture, rugs, curtains, and the props that make a room look like home are all part of the stylist's responsibility.

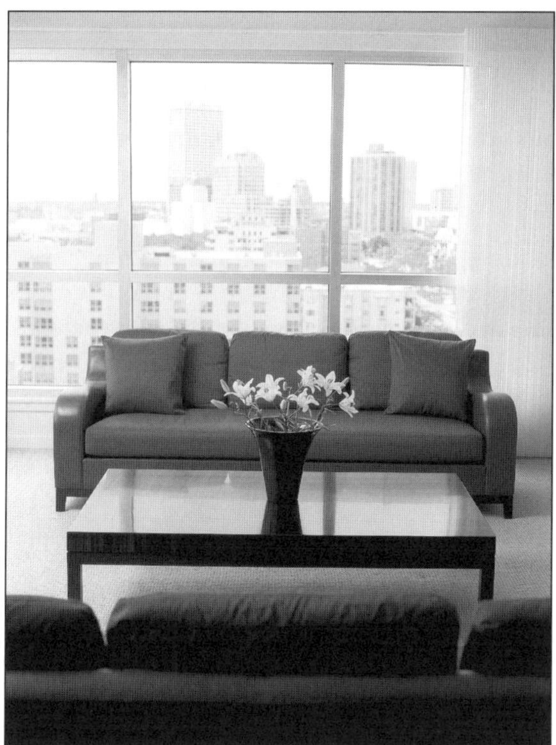

An architectural image of a living room includes what is inside and outside the windows. *Styling:* Colleen Heather Rogan. © *Milwaukee Magazine*

### Production Design, Advertising

Many projects the architectural photographer/stylist team works on are advertising images. Typical clients might produce kitchen cabinets, appliances, windows, window coverings, or grills. The product is the feature and the environment, like wardrobe, is there to enhance it.

## Home Magazine Editor

Like a fashion editor, an editor for a home magazine produces visual stories for magazines. The subject is homes instead of fashion. The editor may find the home, pitch the concept, style the shots, and write the article.

## Linens

Bedding, blankets, curtains, towels, and other linens make up a large part of the catalog industry. Stylists use special techniques to make these products beautiful and inviting. The stylist is again thinking big, and decorates the whole room, or the constructed set.

(Specialists in several of these areas will provide insight into their careers in chapter 10. You will learn from their techniques for creating the big picture.)

# PRIMED TO IMPROVISE

What is so fascinating about the world of photography is how it touches every other field. What other career could bring you into contact with everything from running shoes to auto parts to edible flowers? Once I participated in a casting for an instructional video on forklift safety. What I learned from that experience has come in handy in more than one catalog warehouse.

The techniques you will learn in this book are practical and useful. You will have the tools for folding sweaters and styling a room. You'll know what to do in a photo studio and on location. You'll know who everyone on the crew is and what their responsibilities are. But no matter what I teach you in this book, you will invariably run into some unexpected challenges. Each styling project can be completely different. No two photo shoots are alike. And there are no absolute rules for photo styling. You'll solve each challenge as it comes. Your kit will grow to include new tools and materials. And you'll participate in one of the most unique and intriguing careers in the world.

# The Photo Shoot

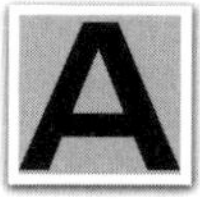**S YOU HAVE ALREADY LEARNED, THERE IS A GREAT DEAL OF** variety in the field of photo styling. There is almost no such thing as a typical day. But I will try to describe for you a day in the life of a photo stylist.

There are three days that might be described as being typical in this career. One of them is working on a photo shoot. The second is spent catching up on all the aspects of life that get out of control while one is working long, focused ten- to twelve-hour days. The third day is when there are no projects coming up, and the stylist gets a panicky feeling and wonders, "What if I never work again?"

You'll get a further look at a typical photo shoot in the six chapters on styling specialties. Every adult is familiar with the practical second type of day, and the third will be addressed in chapter 11 on marketing yourself.

First we'll start with some basics you need to know before you get to the photo shoot.

## WHAT TO WEAR

One might think, in the exciting world of photo shoots, that the crew would be fashionably dressed. The makeup artists would have flawless makeup and the stylists would be wearing some very cool fashions. While stylists tend to be creative dressers, most photo crews are dressed for work, not style. I've heard more than one makeup artist say she hadn't even bothered to put on her own makeup.

There are two reasons for this. The crew is not the focus of the shoot, and they work too hard to be anything but comfortable. Very early call times don't allow for much morning primping either. The priority at that point in the day is usually remembering everything you have to bring to the shoot.

## Your Wardrobe

Exactly how nicely to dress depends on where you are shooting. If you're shooting in an upscale restaurant, country club, or hotel lobby, it would be disrespectful to dress too grungy. If you're on a golf course, you might avoid jeans and T-shirts. But for the most part, your wardrobe can consist of anything comfortable.

Since the days extend from early morning to high noon to dusk, it's good to have several layers with you. Even in the studio temperatures can vary. Some areas of the studio are warm because of heat-producing lights in use there, whereas other unheated or air-conditioned parts of the studio may be chilly. Have layers handy. Sunscreen is probably the most important thing you can wear when you are outdoors all day. Keep it in your kit and share it with the crew.

## Comfortable Feet

Shoes that allow you to stand comfortably and move quickly are important. I even bring along an extra pair, which feels wonderful to change into in the middle of the day. Sometimes, in the studio the set up is on "seamless" paper, which is white or colored paper on a roll, pulled down to make a smooth background. To keep the paper clean, you'll have to remove your shoes when you go onto the set. Then it's good to have shoes that are easy to slip in and out of. Or you can use hospital booties for covering shoes; some photo studios keep them on hand.

Essentially your work clothes are the same as your everyday clothes. You can be creative as long as you don't scare your clients; but mainly, be practical. From New York to California, stylists expect to climb around sets or work on the floor, and dress accordingly. Some stylists do dress fashionably; it's really a matter of personal taste. But remember, no one is really going to be looking at you.

## THE CREW

The photo crew is a tightly organized group of people, working together to create the needed photographs. All members work hard to fulfill their own roles but also contribute to help the others. They have fun together while performing as an effective team.

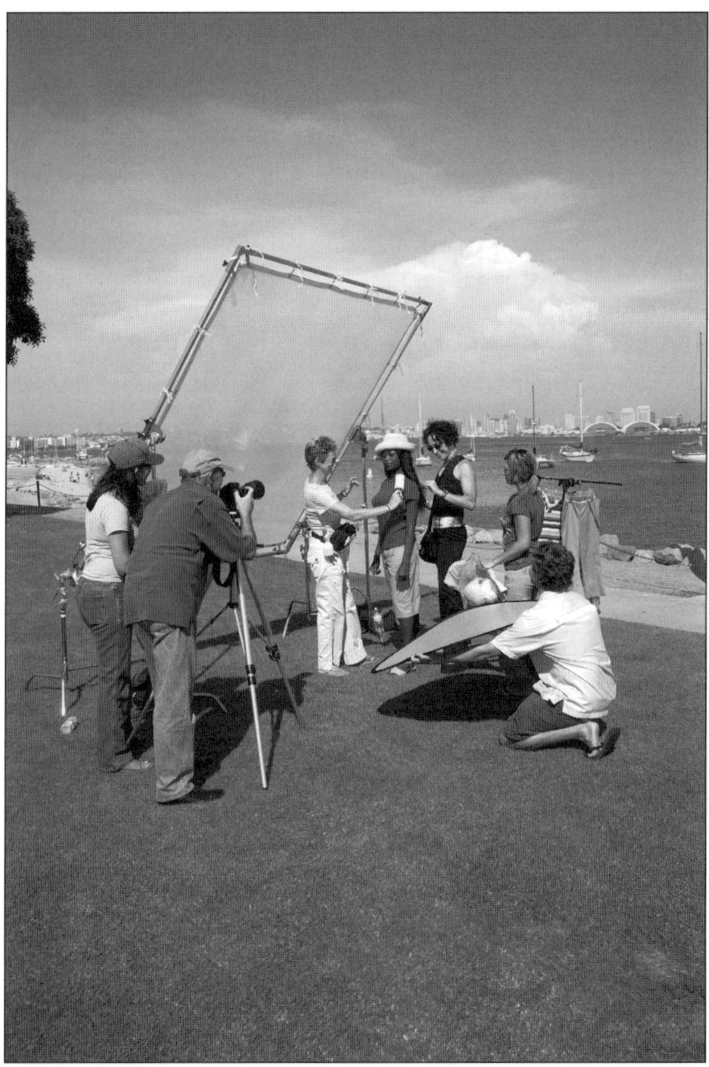

Crewmembers doing their jobs. From left, art director (Heather Neibert); photographer (Michael Christmas); stylist (Susan Linnet Cox); model (Jolie Benoit); hair and makeup artist (Claire Young); assistant stylist (Michelle Siscon); and assistant photographer (Marty Carrick). © Michael Christmas

**The Photographer** is the person behind the camera who has experience with all aspects of creating photographs and is ultimately responsible for making the shot happen. A good part of the photographer's time is spent marketing to get new business and estimating potential projects. The photographer's business also includes learning about new techniques and equipment, purchasing equipment, and managing a studio.

A photographer may employ a studio manager or other staff to take care of some of these tasks. Marketing may be handled by a representative (or "rep" as they are commonly known). In any case, there is more to the photographer's business than shooting images.

**Assistant Photographer** is a photographer in training. He (often a male, but less and less frequently) helps the photographer with equipment and lighting. Photography assisting is one of the few classic apprenticeship situations in our world today. In the days of Michelangelo, artists were trained for many years by assisting an established artist. They learned from the artist and performed many of the more difficult tasks for which the artist was given credit. Throughout history, workers in many fields were trained this way, but nowadays most career learning occurs in schools.

Assisting is the next step after photography school, according to San Diego photo assistant Taylor Abeel. He says one big advantage for the assistant is the freedom from responsibility for the shoot. This period of time also gives assistants time and income to purchase equipment for their own careers, such as cameras and lights. Assistants participate in all aspects of the photographer's business. Like a good internship, it can be an opportunity to acquire the skills of a practicing professional. And assisting a recognized photographer can add prestige to the assistant's new career.

For a complex shoot the photographer may hire two or more assistants. There is usually one assistant who works regularly with the same photographer and is familiar with the studio. Responsibilities include setting up the lighting and trouble shooting any technical problems, as well as anticipating the photographer's needs. The assistant can also take the blame for anything that isn't working, Abeel says, helping the photographer look good in the client's eyes.

Assistants often carry equipment on location, hold reflectors and other light-modifying devices, and are a valuable part of the team. As a stylist, you will get to know many assistants and see their careers progress; some will become photographers themselves. They are great contacts for collaborating on test shoots, because they too are in the process of building their portfolios.

**Producer, or Production Manager**, coordinates the details and logistics of a photo shoot, generally on location. This function is sometimes filled by the art director or the stylist, so this may or may not be an additional member of the crew. A producer is more likely to be hired if the project is complex and involves travel. (Production duties are explored in chapter 4.)

**Art Director** is ultimately responsible for approving the look of the photographs. He or she may have a graphic design background and may be the designer of the printed piece. The art director may be employed by a catalog company, an in-house design department, an ad agency, or be a freelancer. Sometimes it seems the photographer and art director are the "mom and dad" of the crew. They share the responsibility for the best photos being created and have more control over the budget and expenses.

**Client** is a representative of the company financing the photo shoot. As an employee of the company, the client may be an executive or merchandise buyer. If the client is not very experienced with photo shoots, he may frequently consult with the art director to achieve the best result. A client, while financially responsible for the entire shoot, can sometimes slow down the process. During the early steps of setting up a shot, the stylist may not have adjusted the model's dress and the lighting is not yet refined. The client wants to feel a part of the project and draws these problems to the crew's attention. Be patient—this is your boss for now.

The art director, whether staff or freelance, also could be considered "the client," because she represents the company that commissioned the photograph. There is no client shown in our crew photo, but the art director would be considered the client.

**Stylist** is you, the one who makes all elements within the photograph have the look your client needs.

**Assistant Stylist** may be hired in a more complex shoot—one involving models and wardrobe or lots of props—to help the stylist by performing multiple tasks, such as steaming clothing and dressing models. While not as established a tradition as the photography assistant, being an assistant is excellent training for styling. In fact, assisting is the ideal way to learn about the field. As an assistant, you may spend most of the shoot steaming garments or keeping track of merchandise, but you are there. You have an opportunity to watch, listen, and learn. It is considered improper to solicit work by handing out your card or promotional materials—you are there only to support the stylist.

**Makeup Artist and/or Hair Stylist** may be a single person who styles hair *and* does makeup, or there may be separate specialists. This specialization, and the budget for it, is more common in larger markets. The makeup artist/hair stylist takes up to an hour preparing the model at the beginning of the shoot and makes sure the model continues to look good on set.

Describing her duties during the shoot, makeup artist Mary Erickson says, "I am like a waiter in a fine restaurant, hovering and watching to see if there's anything I need to do. As soon as there is, I'm in there."

**Talent** is a generic term for the person being photographed, whether professional model, child, famous person, or lifestyle actor. In a product shoot, of course, the makeup artist and talent are not included in the crew.

Another member of the crew, if you are shooting in California, is a **Set Teacher**, also known by the union term, **Studio Teacher**. By state law, a certified set teacher must be present any time people under the age of eighteen are working, with a few exceptions. Responsibilities include checking children's work permits and providing some educational guidance.

There may also be an **RV Driver** if a production vehicle has been rented. The driver knows where the vehicle can be parked and will run the generator on request throughout the day so there's power for prepping clothes, drying hair, or air-conditioning. The driver will keep an eye on merchandise in the RV, and will occasionally be an extra hand for carrying things. Often, the driver will provide catering services such as coffee and snacks.

## A TYPICAL DAY IN THE STUDIO

Here's a very basic day styling in the studio for a catalog. Having packed your kit and all your supplies the evening before, you'll arrive on time, or preferably, earlier. Enjoy a cup of coffee and a muffin now, because you won't stop moving until lunchtime. You will go over the shot list with the photographer and the art director. Make sure you are clear about the look and styling of the shots, how the merchandise is organized, how much time can be spent on each shot, and in what part of the studio you'll be working. Become familiar with the studio, and if you need any materials or an electrical outlet, the photo assistant will know where to find them. Plug in the steamer if you're using one, so it gets hot. Pull together and organize your products, along with any props you're using.

### Now You're Working

Exactly what you do next varies according to the styling project; possibly you're shooting models or stacks of sweaters. Keep your work flowing and be aware of what's coming next so you can be prepared. Maybe you can begin to stage the next shot while this one's being refined. Always be available to make any changes and adjustments to the products or clothing. Be cautious with all the photo equipment around—you may have to bend and reach into some pretty awkward positions to style your items. You'll be on your feet a lot.

Try not to make personal phone calls or to read magazines. Some cell-phone usage during the day is to be expected with freelancers, but your main focus is on the job at hand. If you are really meant for this career, you'll be so interested in the shoot you won't want to miss a moment.

The day goes like this until lunchtime, with maybe a snack or a bottle of water. After a quick lunch in the studio you wash your hands and get back to work. The afternoon progresses the same way—more styling, more shots checked off the list. You may get a sense of how the catalog is coming together by reviewing the photographs.

## Music and Humor

Two consistent elements in photo shoots help keep the atmosphere light and fun: humor and music. The people you're working with are intelligent and creative, and so are you. Conversation and jokes are part of what makes the shoot day fun, and they make the models comfortable. Don't get so involved in talking, though, that you are distracted from your work or that you distract others.

In a studio, there is almost always music playing and a selection of CDs to choose from. When appropriate on location, music can add to the relaxed atmosphere. Sometimes you'll see a dartboard or a basketball hoop in a photo studio, but I have never found that there's time to use them.

## The End of the Studio Day

When the day ends, help the other crewmembers with any cleanup that needs to be done. Make sure your job is finished and that you are free to leave. Unplug the steamer, thank the photographer and the art director for a good day, review your call time for the next day if the job is continuing, stretch, repack your kit, and go home.

## LOCATION DAYS

When your location is outdoors, the call time usually is early, as the photographer typically wants the early morning light. The photographer may also want to capture the warm glow of sunset. The sun at midday is usually too bright and high to get the best shots. You're carrying your kit and merchandise to and from vehicles, and moving more quickly.

If you're shooting in a private home, you'll probably move furniture and other décor; everything needs to be put back in place and returned to the way it was when you arrived. Sometimes it helps to take a Polaroid or digital image of the room at the beginning of the day; remembering where things were placed is harder than you expect. You might even need to vacuum the areas where you shot or worked. Load your car, then take one more look around.

By the time the location day ends, you still have to travel back from the location, unload, and get reorganized. But you've had a great time working and lots of fun with the crew.

## THE "POLAROID PROCESS"

This is my own term, left over from the days before digital photography. A special "Polaroid back" is attached to the camera so the photograph can be previewed. An image is taken through the actual camera lens and exposed on Polaroid film instead of on regular transparency or negative film. The image is the size of the film, so if 35mm is being shot the image is small— a rectangle about one inch by one-and-a-half inches. A larger image is created by 120mm film, and 4 × 5 film actually is four by five inches. The photographer pulls the Polaroid film out of the camera and hands it to the assistant, who times development for about sixty or ninety seconds. When it is developed, the assistant looks at it and hands it to the photographer.

Here they are both looking at the lighting of the shot and may get to work on making some changes. The photographer may use a "loupe," which is a small magnifying glass, to check for focus and other details. Unless they see a problem that they can quickly resolve, the art director is next to see the Polaroid.

### The Art Director Views the Polaroid

The art director also looks at aspects such as composition, overall color, depth of field (how much the background is in or out of focus), background elements, and whether this image represents what he or she wants. The art director will look for anything odd or distracting, like a horizon line going straight through a model's head. For a product shot— a sweater laid down against a white background, for example—critical elements would be the overall shape of the featured item, and whether the folds and shadows are too deep.

The art director then discusses these details with the photographer or the stylist. As they make more improvements to the image, they take more Polaroids. This film is expensive and used to be a significant part of the expense of photo shoots. It is not unusual for dozens of Polaroids to be shot before the image is considered ready to be photographed.

## The Next Step

If a client is present at the shoot, he views the Polaroid next. Here, the art director should remind the client (probably her boss) that this is only the first look at the photo. With no client present, the stylist is next in the chain of command. You have waited on the sidelines until it's your chance for a close look at the Polaroid. This is really your first opportunity to see what the shot looks like through the camera, and it may surprise you.

The art director will point out improvements that you can make to the product or wardrobe. You may notice some improvements you'd like to make in addition to those suggested by the art director. She will appreciate that you have the experience and dedication to improve your work.

On a fashion shoot the makeup artist would like to see the image and be sure the makeup and hair look right. It is optional to share the Polaroid with the talent at this point. It may be helpful for a model to see how the shot looks, how it's cropped, and if the positions look natural.

## DIGITAL PHOTOGRAPHY

With the use of digital photography, the cycle of the Polaroid is a rarity. Previewing of the image takes place not on Polaroid but on a computer monitor. I wanted you to understand the way it used to be, so you can appreciate how easy it is now to see and revise your styling. But the etiquette still applies. You don't want to put your head in front of the monitor until the photographer

### The "Polaroid Process"

This is the order in which the crewmembers view a photograph in progress. The image may be a traditional Polaroid preview of the shot in actual film size, if film is being shot. Or it may be a digital shot viewed on a computer monitor. In any case, the sequence is a matter of etiquette and respect in a photo shoot.

1. Assistant photographer

2. Photographer

3. Art director

4. Client

5. Stylist

6. Makeup artist, Hair stylist

7. Talent

and art director have had a chance to see what the shot looks like. In addition, there may be lighting or composition improvements that will change everything.

Once it's your turn to make styling revisions, it is fine to ask the photographer to take another view of the image since no costly Polaroid film is being wasted while you make adjustments. The benefits of digital photography are obvious when the stylist is working on a product shot, since you don't have to worry about exhausting the talent. The product waits to be perfected.

## The Flow of Film

Having directed fashion photography during the days of silver-based film, I can see a great deal of difference when shooting fashion digitally. With film, there is a rhythm to the shoot. The model can hear the automatic winding of the camera as a roll of film is shot. Experienced models build a series of moves based on this cycle. Often, the first half roll of film is just for warming up. The photographer shoots dozens upon dozens of rolls, or sheets, of film; the art director will have five to ten really good shots to choose from.

Some photographers still prefer to shoot film on location. There is less equipment to transport; maybe the camera, tripod, film bags, reflectors, scrims, C-stands, and sandbags, but not the computer equipment. And it can be hard to view the image on the monitor in bright light.

## The Model Stands Alone

And then there is the spontaneity and the flow of the traditional film shoot, once the Polaroid is accepted. With digital photography the flow is interrupted—the model is often left standing alone while the crew goes to look at the monitor. When they return to the model on the set, she needs to resume modeling. And hope they weren't criticizing her look or technique over at the monitor.

The photographer may use a digital camera on location and simply view the images on the LCD display on the back of the camera. But when the photographer pauses to look at the image, it still changes the pace.

Only "old school" people like me notice the difference now. Newer models may prefer digital photography because they get instant feedback on the success of the shoot. They like looking at the monitor to see how they're looking, instead of the guesswork of Polaroids.

The advantages of digital photography far outweigh the altered rhythm of a fashion shoot. There is little doubt that the ideal shot has been captured. No more editing countless strips of film. And the technical processes of graphic design and printing are integrated. The image files can be placed directly into the designed catalog, brochure, or other material. When the printer receives the files, everything is in place.

## COMMUNICATION

While the talent is being shot, it's best if one person is designated to communicate instructions. Usually this will be the photographer. It can be confusing for the model to hear suggestions from several voices at the same time.

### The Spokesperson

The chain of command takes effect again. A good art director is near the photographer at all times, watching the shot from behind the camera, and can make comments when necessary. The stylist and makeup artist clear it with the photographer or art director before "going in" to make adjustments. If they see something they would like to improve, they can quietly tell the art director, who will decide if it's worth asking the photographer to pause for them. It's distracting for the photographer, too, to be addressed by various crewmembers while shooting.

When the photographer uses a long lens—to put the model in focus while making the background blurry—the model may be thirty feet or more away from the crew behind the camera. That makes it especially difficult to communicate. I have been on shoots when the model was so far away, a walkie-talkie was used to communicate with her. Walkie-talkies were more commonly used in the days before cellphones, but are still used sometimes. They also help the crew communicate when the equipment and vehicles are far away, as is often the case on location. A walkie-talkie-enabled phone now can take care of all these situations.

## WORKING WITH CHILDREN

When children are being photographed, the shoot becomes more complicated. It's harder to determine who is the designated communicator. The parents, stylist, and photographer may all be trying to get the attention of a small child who doesn't understand what all the fuss is about. All this takes special skill on the part of the crew.

No matter how much experience children have had with photo shoots, they are still unpredictable. Weariness, hunger, boredom, and tense parents all play a role. Photographers who work with children may have some squeaky toys or music to capture the child's, or even infant's, attention. As a stylist, you'll spend more time on the floor styling the little ones.

## The Child's "Entourage"

When children are modeling, the shoot tends to become crowded with family members. In addition to one or two parents, there are likely to be siblings, aunts, uncles, grandparents, or nannies. Some are there to bring the children, others for the excitement. In addition, several children may be scheduled for the same time period, and often a backup model is hired in case the first one is less than cooperative. Try to have a comfortable and separate area where the other children not in the shoot can wait, with all the extra family members. If there is a set teacher in attendance, that person can greet families and help herd the extra talent.

Be patient. The excitement will end soon, and you can look back at how adorable the children were and how hard they tried to be young models. The older ones will have learned to thank you and shake your hand.

## The Set Teacher

If the shoot is in California, the client needs to be aware of the law requiring a set teacher. The purpose is to protect the health, safety, and morals of minors on film sets or still photo shoots. The set teacher also checks to make sure children and teens under eighteen have a current work permit. With a few rare exceptions, a certified set teacher must be present any time people under the age of eighteen are working, whether it is during school days, evenings, or weekends. I have seen cases where a client chose to ignore the requirement to save that expense on their shoots. The producers are responsible for informing out-of-town clients of such rules, but they cannot force clients to follow the regulations.

The term "teacher" may be somewhat misleading. While some set teachers do provide learning activities, assist school children with homework, and they must be certified teachers, their *presence* at a shoot is the primary requirement, not that they come equipped with lesson plans.

Other states have their own rulings, and there are also federal regulations protecting child workers. To find information on other states' child labor laws, go to the Screen Actors Guild Web site, *www.sag.org*. Listed in Resources is a "Young Performers Database" with pertinent regulations for each state. Eventually more states will increase restrictions for child performers. Anyone working in photo shoot production should keep up to date with these regulations.

## WORKING WITH ANIMALS

With the popularity of pets, some models are of the canine or feline variety. Several competing national chains of pet-supply stores create a good deal of advertising. It's not hard to find pet owners who are happy to have their darlings model, but some jobs call for more professional pet models. In the film industry, there are professional animal lovers working to provide all sorts of trained animals. These trainers are available to the photo industry, too, and are known as "pet wranglers." If you can find someone in your area to provide this service, you'll have experienced animals for your shoots; otherwise you can do your own talent search.

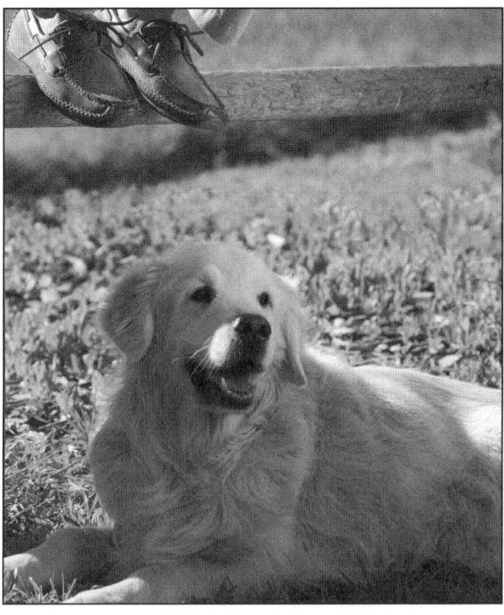

Jake modeling at the feet of a shoe model. *Photographer:* Michael Christmas. © Michael Christmas

Pets, particularly dogs, make good props for photos, as nearly everyone responds favorably to them. My golden retriever Jake accompanied me to many shoots and was very good about looking at the camera and smiling. He would work in exchange for a grooming.

Lighter-colored animals photograph better than dark ones, whose eyes and noses blend into their fur. Often on location or in a home, a good model dog will appear and his owners are always happy to have him included in a shot. In some cases a property release is needed to use a pet's image. It's a good idea to have one signed, just to be sure.

## PHOTO SHOOT ETIQUETTE

A stylist who is a pleasure to work with, in addition to doing great styling, will be remembered. You've eagerly done your share of the workload and been considerate of others on the crew, including help with tidying up the studio or location. You've been energetic and happy to be working with them. You remembered to say thanks for lunch, and at the end of the day, said goodbye to the crew and especially the art director. You might also mention how much you enjoyed working with the art director, that you hope the photos turn out great, and that you hope to get a chance to work together again.

## Networking

Be sure to hand everyone on the crew your business card or promotional card, so they can find you again. And get theirs too, so you can follow up later. You will especially want to contact the art director when the photographs are printed to request some "tear sheets," or samples.

One exception to this networking is when you are the assistant stylist. In this case, you are working for the stylist, and you don't want to bypass your employer by trying to take away a client. As a matter of ethics, don't promote yourself when assisting: it's just a time to learn. (The photo assistant should follow the same protocol.)

## A Follow-up Note

It's also thoughtful to follow up with a written note, or at least an e-mail, to the art director and the photographer. I designed and printed a note card on my desktop computer system with a sample of my own styling on the front and my contact information on the back (along with a credit to the photographer who had shot the front image). Pre-folded note cards can be purchased at office supply stores for your desktop printer; they even come with envelopes.

## The Photographic Equipment

One final item that is important to mention is your respect for the expensive camera and lighting equipment used on the photo shoot. The photographer has a great deal invested in these treasures. The assistant knows the equipment well and has complete access to it. You, however, do not: always ask before even looking through the lens and try not to touch the camera. It may not be placed at a convenient height for you, so ask for help seeing through the lens. Don't "help" the assistant with the lights, power packs, or meter readings unless requested.

It might seem fun to take some snapshots of the shoot with your own camera. Always ask the photographer before doing this. Your flash can trigger the photographic lights to flash, and possibly cause damage. Although you're likely to get cooperation, you must respect your co-workers who may not want to deal with your photographic hobby in the middle of a shoot.

## AFTER THE SHOOT

Since the crew works so closely together during the shoot, it seems strange that it is disbanded afterwards. One week you are spending all your time together working toward a common goal. The next you've all gone your separate ways. Art directors are back at the office; photographers are starting other projects. And you, after the postproduction returns and you've invoiced the job, are putting on a different hat. It's time to get ready for the next project, market yourself, or take some time off. You *will* work again!

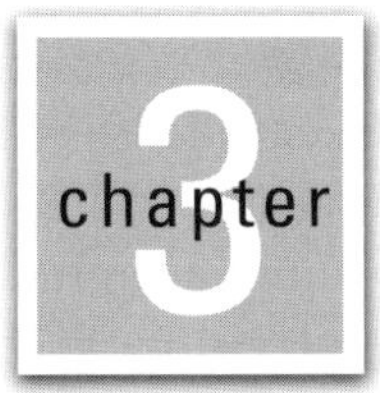

# Styling Basics

**I**F YOU HAVE GOTTEN THIS FAR, YOU ARE INDEED SERIOUS about your styling career. Let's say you have already done a couple of projects that could be considered styling. You're not sure if they qualify you as a stylist yet. Aside from the childhood project of setting up Barbie dolls and photographing them, the first time I actually styled a photograph was for my sushi T-shirt business, and I was also modeling in the photograph. I brought a pair of chopsticks as a prop and the male model was plucking at one of the sushi on my shirt. I didn't realize till later I was styling.

Looking back you will realize the creative things you've already done that have prepared you for the exciting career of photo styling. Somewhere along the line, you heard the term photo stylist and a description of the career. It piqued your interest. You're ready to get started.

## GETTING STARTED

You are not going to be a stylist overnight. Remember the bumpy road and all the experiences I described in chapter 1 that led me to styling? The most important advice is to observe and learn. The more you understand about styling and photography, the more skilled you will be.

## Education

There is no official degree or certificate program for photo styling. Some fashion schools do offer classes in styling. Most styling courses at the Fashion Institute for Design and Merchandising (FIDM) in California focus on wardrobe for film, television, and video. Some schools, such as Fashion Institute of Technology (FIT) in New York, offer one or two courses on styling for photography.

The styling classes are generally part of larger programs such as fashion design or merchandising. They are intended to give fashion designers background on promoting their own designs, or to teach merchandisers about marketing fashion. By and large, what you learn about styling is going to happen on the job, and by keeping your eyes and ears open.

Even workshops are hard to find, so I began offering my own styling workshops a couple of years ago. The weekend workshops include one Saturday of dialog and discussion on the business of styling, personalized to answer the needs and questions of the students. And on Sunday there is a day of hands-on participation when students style tabletop products and clothing on a model. Much of the information presented in this book is compacted and condensed into the workshops. Now I've developed a program of online workshops so that students from all over the world can study the career of styling in-depth at *www.photostylingworkshops.com*.

The response from my workshop attendees is the reason I wrote this book—there is so much to learn and absorb. I've listened to students and had e-mails from new stylists all over the United States, and hope to provide answers to their questions.

## Internships

The chance to work as an intern with a stylist is rare. I had arrived at the mentoring part of my life with much to share about the career. After contacting Mesa College, a community college in San Diego, to see about providing internships, I found three wonderful young women in the fashion program there. I initially thought an intern would help me get some filing and marketing work done, but was surprised by their eagerness to get busy learning the field, not filing. They each inspired me too, with ideas for test shoots we could arrange together, and with all of their questions.

One intern, Veronica Guzman, is now a professional wardrobe stylist; Jessica Sanchez has suspended her career in store display to go back to college to study fashion merchandising and international business; and my first intern, Paula Tabalipa, found a position with an upscale department store in charge of window and store displays as well as producing fashion shows. Some day, I'm sure Paula will be a fashion leader in Italy, which is her long-held dream.

If you can find an opportunity for an internship with a photo stylist, you'll amass hands-on knowledge of the career. But interning with a magazine, model agency, ad agency, fashion merchandiser, photographer, or any other related business would also yield a bounty of useful knowledge. Whether or not you receive pay for your internship, the time spent will be well worth it.

## Expose Yourself to Shoots

Any chance you get to be around a photo shoot is going to help you learn. You might volunteer to assist a stylist for no pay, or a nominal amount, so you can be on a shoot. If you know photographers, or photography students, you can offer to help them with any of their projects, even if you're merely carrying equipment. If you see a photo shoot going on, stop and watch. Listen to what the photographer and assistant are saying. Watch what happens when they open a reflector and bounce light back onto the model. See what the art director and the stylist are doing.

The more you know about photography, the better you'll do your job. A basic photography class can introduce you to f-stops, exposure times, light meters, and tripods, along with the language and terminology of photography. You'll understand that raising the camera a few inches will completely change the composition of the shot. And by observing, you'll know the clothing looks so good because of all the clips in the back.

You may at this point decide that you want to *be* a photographer, which is wonderful. If you find you're not the least bit competent with a camera, you'll still have learned valuable information that will come up again and again in your career as a stylist.

## Looking at Photographs in a New Way

Now that you've been introduced to styling, you'll never look at photographs the same way. You'll see the difference it makes whether the background is focused or the model is in shade or full sun. You will see good techniques and things you'd do differently. You'll analyze even more carefully the fashions and accessories used in magazine editorials, and observe how the makeup is used to enhance the theme.

Looking at catalogs, I try to identify the locations and models. After getting to know many locations, such as Miami's South Beach, Charleston

(South Carolina), Mexico, Hawaii, and nearly every spot in San Diego, I can't help trying to identify locations. Sometimes I think I look at backgrounds more than foregrounds. Maybe I will recognize a model, and if not, I try to see why she is an effective model. The trends in faces, ethnicity, hair length, lips, and nose shape all distract me from looking at the merchandise. I look for misplaced shadows of scrims that should have been obscured. I see if there are any folds in the model's sleeves that I would have treated differently.

When you see print ads, you'll know the stages the photographic concept has been through. Hiring the crew, dealing with the agency art director, the storyboard (a preliminary sketch), props, and styling are all elements you may not have been aware of, and now you know about them. It's a good exercise to look carefully at all these details, though you'll never again have the simple pleasure of merely flipping through a catalog or magazine.

## THE ROLLING RACK

The collapsible rolling rack is the most basic and universal piece of equipment used by stylists. You are certainly going to have more to transport than you can hold in your arms, and you want the items to remain unwrinkled, so you need to use a rolling rack. The racks hold more than just clothing; you can place boxes and your kit on the bottom rails, and hang accessories and bags on the extenders on either end of the top rod.

### Setting up the Rack

If you want to look like you know what you're doing, you need to practice setting up the rack. Since the rack is collapsible, there are points in its assembly when it wants to collapse; you're briefly fighting gravity. It's much easier if two people work together, but sometimes you may be on your own.

In my workshops, everyone has a turn at this humiliating exercise. Attendee Rebecca Fabares said it was the only part she did not like. But she soon found herself working as a wardrobe assistant on a three-day shoot and successfully put up the rack by herself—on a hill.

The rolling rack may be your own, or may belong to the client or studio. Most racks are the same style, and are affordably priced at store fixture suppliers. Look up "store fixture supplier" to find one near you, or search online. My own has extenders that slide out too easily and are always getting in the way. Some racks are more manageable than others, but watch out for unpredictable extenders.

The following illustrations show the components of the rolling rack, assembly with two people and the challenging process of setting it up alone. At the end of the day, remember to lower the top bar to the lowest button before reversing the procedure and collapsing the rack. This is a little easier to do on your own, thanks to gravity lowering the sides for you. Just make sure they fold down side by side, like they started.

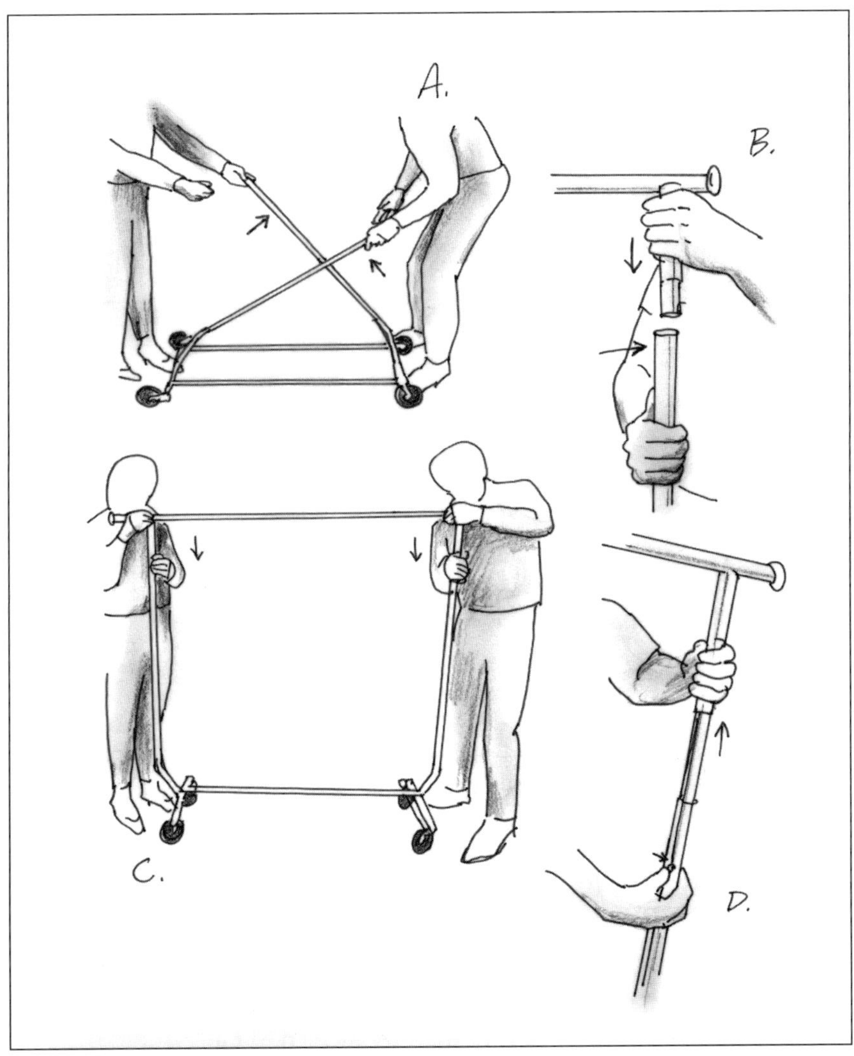


Setting up a rolling rack with two people: (A) Lift the side posts at the same time. (B) and (C) Pulling outward on the side posts, insert the top rod. (D) Push button to raise rack, while holding base of top bar.
© Susan Linnet Cox

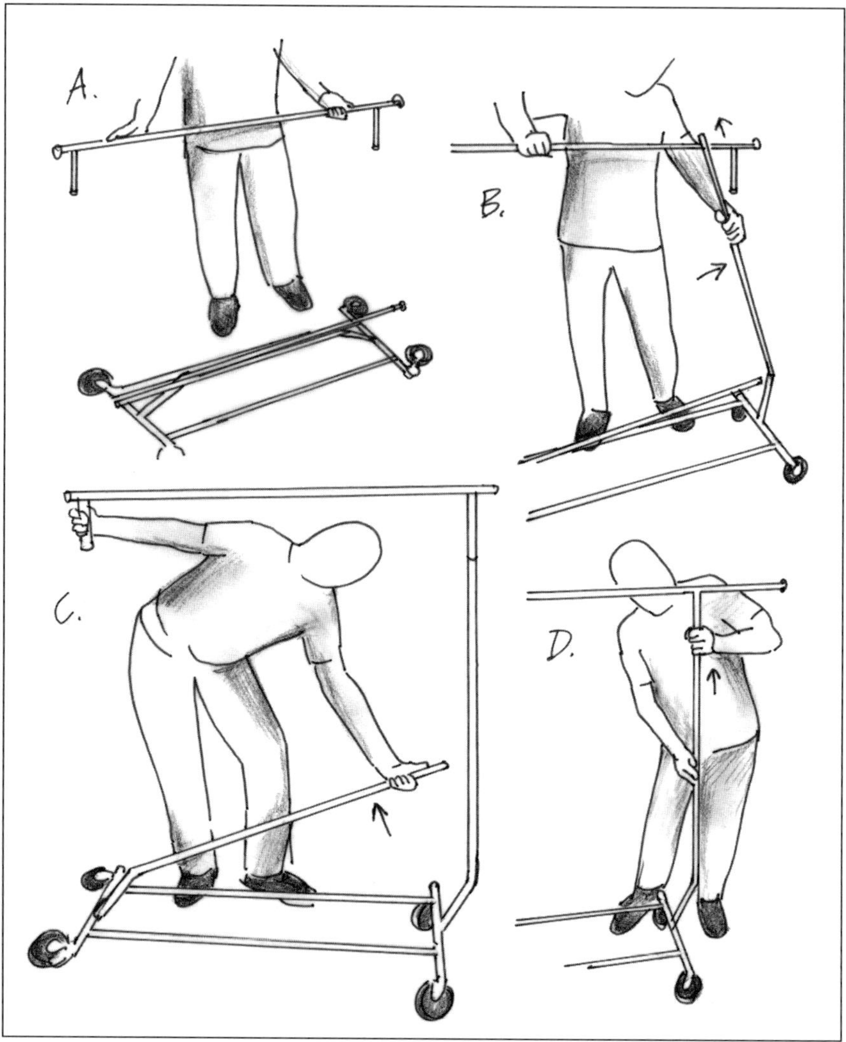

Setting up a rolling rack alone: (A) Pick up top bar. (B) Prepare to insert top bar by raising side bar. (C) Carefully hold top bar while lifting second side bar. (D) Gradually, one side at a time, push button to raise rack, while holding base of top bar. © Susan Linnet Cox

## THE STEAMER

The steamer is another piece of equipment familiar to all stylists. If you have your own steamer you can bring it to shoots, after confirming whether there is one available. Having your own is a mark of a true professional—along with knowing how to use it and doing great styling, that is. To be effective, the steamer has to be a professional-quality model with at least a one-gallon water capacity and a removable bottle (see illustrations on pages 38 and 40).

I have tried portable hand-held steamers and they just do not work. Maybe if you've never used a professional steamer, they might seem to work, but certainly not well enough to use for photo shoots. I'll share some hints, though, for steaming with a spray bottle on location. You can probably find a selection of steamers at the store fixture supplier where you bought your rolling rack.

## Using the Steamer

Among the first tasks upon arriving at the shoot are 1) finding a place to plug in and use the steamer, 2) filling it, and 3) turning it on. Once it's warmed up, you can turn the steamer off again until you use it, but the process will be quicker if the water in the chamber is already hot. Ask the photography assistant about available outlets in the studio. If you're on location, make sure you don't overload circuits that have other equipment, such as the computer or lights, plugged in.

The steamer bottle can be filled with regular tap water; no special water is needed. Find a sink with enough space to fill the bottle. Sometimes it won't fit under a bathroom sink faucet.

At the end of the day, unplug the steamer and let it cool. Unless you're coming back to the same place tomorrow, empty the bottle, pull the steamer to the sink or take it outdoors, and empty it out completely.

## Fabrics for Steaming

The steamer can be used on most materials, including some vinyls and plastics. Test these materials first to make sure the steam won't warp them. I had this happen to a shower curtain that had some serious creases; fortunately, I was able to obscure the irregular parts, but I felt bad about it. I have used steam without any problems on vinyl raincoats and patio umbrellas.

On most fabrics, the steamer works as well as an iron and, in my opinion, is easier to use. Some stylists prefer to iron, but I use the steamer whenever possible, unless the item is a shirt that needs to be very crisp. Test the steamer in a less visible place like the bottom back hem to see how it works on each item. If you are steaming a sweater, it may stretch a bit temporarily; give the garment some time to dry out afterward.

## Steaming a Blouse

First, a safety reminder; don't touch the head or put your hand directly into the steam.

Let's look at a woman's blouse as our first example (see the illustration on the next page). It's on its plastic swivel hanger, hanging from the steamer's top loop. We'll start with the bigger areas, the front and back, before getting to the sleeves and collar. Assume that the whole garment will be prepped—it is better if it's all smoothed out, unless you are sure the shot is a detail of one specific area.

Unbutton the blouse. With the steamer head inside the blouse facing out, work it down from the shoulders while gently pulling downward with your other hand. Work in downward strokes along both front panels and along the back, then do the same down the side seams from the armholes to the bottom, to eliminate the creases down the sides.

Steam along both sleeves, front and back, while holding each cuff. Then eliminate the sleeve crease by pulling the steamer head sideways down the outside of the sleeve (A). It's standard in styling to get rid of the distracting crease on the outside of the sleeve. Check the underarm for any creases and smooth those.

Touch up the collar from inside the neck area (without getting your other hand in the way), lifting the collar to smooth out that fold (B). With the steamer head held sideways, go inside the cuffs and smooth out the edges (C). Do the same with the bottom hem.

Go back to the shoulder area last, to smooth out any new wrinkles that may have occurred there. Use the steamer head on the inside of the blouse again, going over the shoulder and down, front and back. Inspect the blouse for any new problems that may need another touch-up and you're done.

## Steaming a T-Shirt

Now that you've steamed the blouse, a T-shirt is going to be a snap (see the illustration on page 40). This is a perfect candidate for the steamer, although if you're doing a laydown of a T-shirt you may really want it flat, as only an iron can do. Be sure to place tissue paper over any screen imprints when ironing, so they won't melt and smear.

When you are steaming a T-shirt, work the steamer head in the same downward motion on the inside of the front and back (A), being sure to steam out the side creases (B). Check under the arm and go down the sides, front, and back again. Steam the sleeves from the inside, softening the side edge. Go along the hem of the sleeves and shirt with a sideways motion to make the hem flat (C). Finally, touch up the shoulders and neckline, being sure to soften the creases along the shoulders.

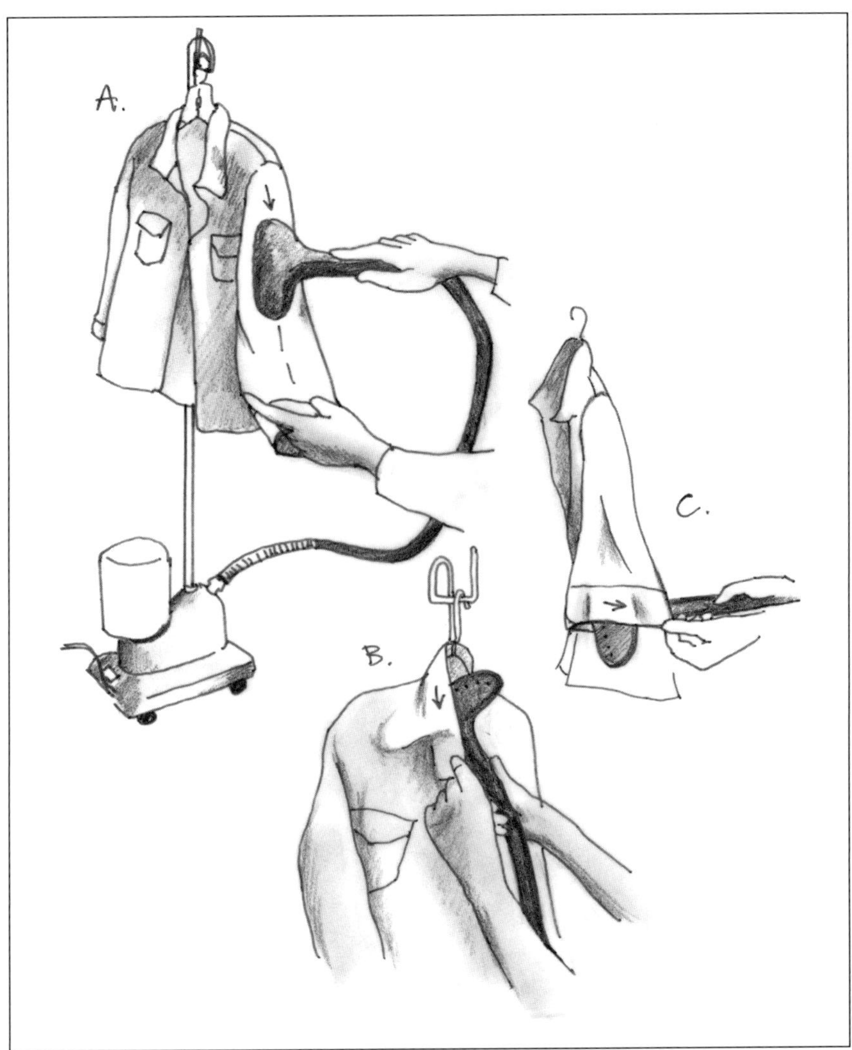

Steaming a blouse: (A) Hold steamer head sideways to smooth sleeve crease while holding bottom of sleeve. (B) Lift collar to soften fold. (C) Steam inside of sleeve cuff. © Susan Linnet Cox

## Pants and Slacks

Steaming pants is essentially the same process, except that you'll be steaming them from the outside only. Fasten the button and zipper and hang them straight across a plastic pant hanger with clips. Since the pants hang down longer from the steamer's loop, you'll end up squatting on the floor. Steam downwards, holding the pant leg gently at a lower point, and working your way down the leg. Go around the hem from the inside with the steamer head held sideways.

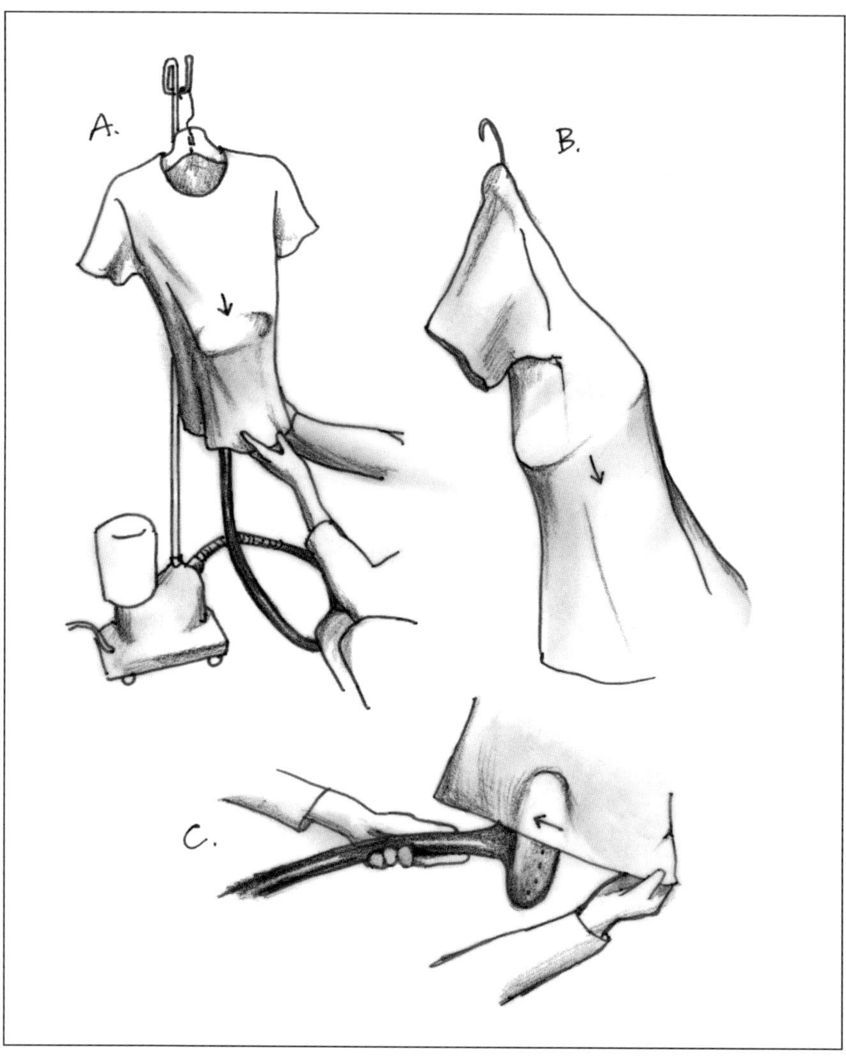

Steaming a T-shirt: (A) Move steamer head down inside of front and back of shirt. (B) Smooth side creases by moving down from underarm. (C) Hold steamer head sideways to smooth hem of shirt. © Susan Linnet Cox

You can soften the top of the crease in the pant leg but for the most part, leave it in. Steam down the top part of the pants, working into any pleats there. Steam the seat too and into the crotch where the legs meet. Watch for any folds that have developed on the sides near the pockets. Unfasten the hanger clips, one side at a time, and smooth the waistband.

A skirt will be a similar process, but you can work from the inside. If there is gathering or pleats, work into them by holding the steamer head sideways.

## Household Items

If you are styling bedding for a catalog or advertisement, you'll be working with an iron on a large scale. But for a quick prep of sheets and bedding you can use the steamer with the sheets right on the bed. It's a quick and convenient way to get out folds created by the packaging. Simply place the fitted sheet on the bed and run the steamer along the surfaces, and do the same for the top sheet and blankets. However, if the shot is a close detail and you need the top sheet to be very crisp, you will have more success with an iron.

Towels, tablecloths, throws, and other large household items can be attached to clip hangers and stretched out on the rolling rack. First steam one side, then the other. Or they can be touched up right on location in a similar fashion to sheets.

## Water Spots

It's bound to happen sometimes that your steamer will drip or spit some water droplets on the garments. I've never seen this cause a problem, and they usually dry by the time you need the item on the set. Try to work ahead to allow time for the drops to dry.

## Steaming with Water and Sunshine

The first time I saw this done I was really impressed with the stylist's ingenuity. I was art directing a fashion shoot that I arranged on a "no frills" Russian cruise line. But that's another story. The important story here is that we got off the ship near the shore of Belize in Central America, got onto a smaller boat, went ashore, got off, and had six hours to photograph the garments that the stylist and his assistant had carried ashore in big zippered bags.

I knew they'd be pretty wrinkled, but I was not the stylist, so it wasn't totally my concern. Before I knew it, the assistant stylist had the merchandise spread out on rocks all over the beach and was spraying the items with water from a spray bottle. They were then placed on hangers and hung from palm trees to dry in the tropical breeze. By the time we needed them to shoot, they were perfectly prepped.

I have used this technique myself as a stylist, and it works very well even when the model is wearing the apparel and wrinkles occur. Temperature is the key element; it works best on a hot day. It can be awkward if the model is standing in a water-soaked outfit and it's time to shoot.

## THE STUDIO ENVIRONMENT

These studio scene and the finished boot shots (see page 43) can give you an idea what the studio environment is like. When customers look at an

H.S. Trask & Co. catalog and see these boots, they will envision the room they appear to be photographed in. It's a medium-sized room, possibly in a cabin or a farmhouse. The rough flooring and paneled walls indicate that it may be a back entryway or mudroom, where the owner stores his fishing tackle and removes his boots. That was our intention in creating this full-page photograph.

Note the bare-looking area in the upper left quarter of the finished boot shot. It was purposely left empty for overprinting copy describing the boots.

## The Real Scenario

In the studio scene, you see the real scenario. This "room" is in fact a fairly small tabletop set placed on sawhorses and held with clamps. The set is surrounded by five lights, including a "model light" and a "soft box", which is a large light that stands above the set at head level to illuminate it.

Six "C-stands"—adjustable, three-legged stands for attaching equipment—surround the set. One, just to the left of the set, is holding a small cardboard oval to create a shadow in one area. The lights are attached to C-stands, and the poles that hold the lights extend out on opposite ends. Cords extend across the floor to power packs, which provide power to the lights to make them flash when triggered by the camera. At the rear of the set are several power packs on the floor.

The camera isn't shown. It's attached to a massive stand with three wheeled legs and a vertical rod for moving it up and down. There may be a stepladder if the camera is raised. There is also a very important cable running from the camera to the computer. The computer is on a moveable desk not far away.

To look through the camera, clear it with the photographer first, of course. Then climb the ladder, if one is being used, and look through the lens without touching the camera; it's tricky if you and the photographer are different heights.

## Studio Hazards

You can see that no matter how large the studio is, the area around the set can become very crowded. You, as a stylist, spend much of your time moving in and out of the area, and can easily collide with some of these obstacles. You must be aware of what is behind you or over your shoulder. In addition to avoiding bumps and bruises, you wouldn't want to knock any equipment over. Waitress work was good training for me. I was

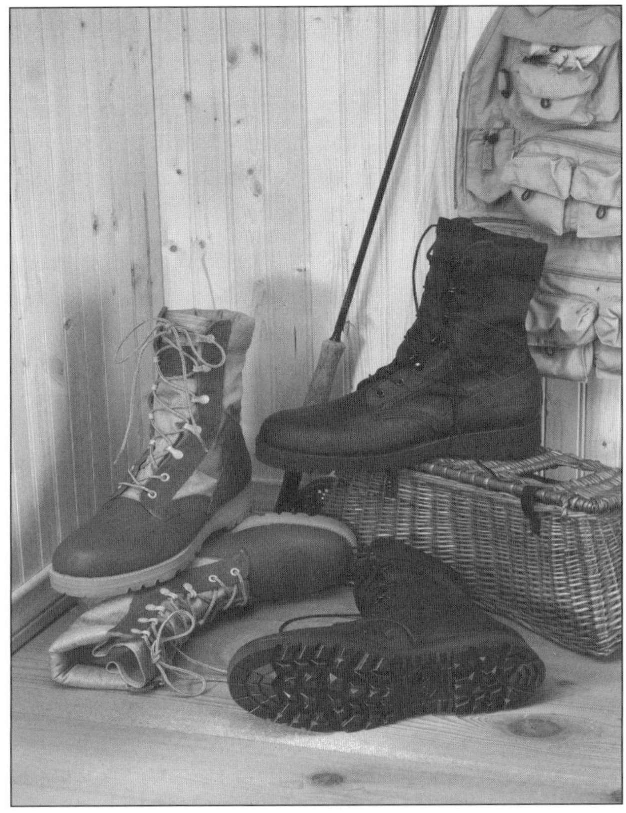

Finished photograph of boots, as seen in H.S. Trask Co. catalog. *Photographer:* Michael Christmas. *Styling:* Susan Linnet Cox. © Michael Christmas

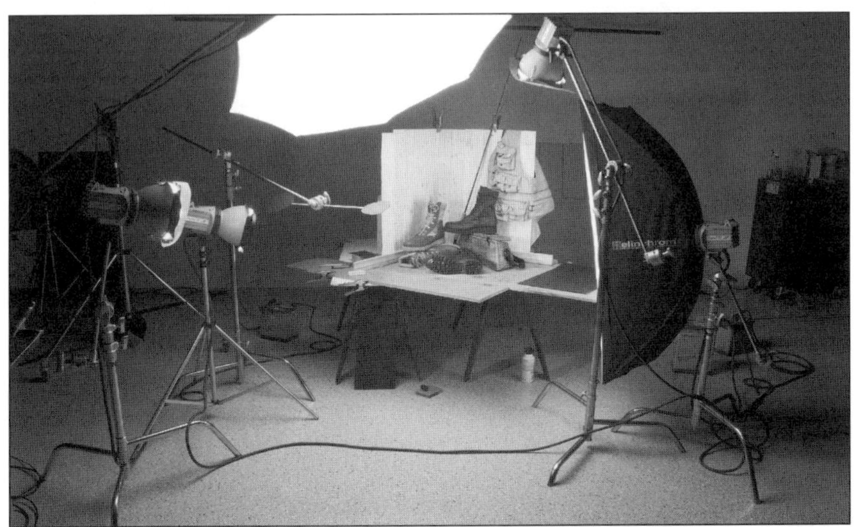

The studio environment the boot photo was created in. *Photographer:* Michael Christmas. © Michael Christmas

already accustomed to looking over my shoulder before I make a move, from years of carrying loaded trays.

Now that we are in the digital age, you won't be likely to run into darkroom chemicals. If you handle a developing Polaroid, however, there are processing chemicals to be aware of and avoid. Wash your hands if you come into contact with this gel-like material.

We have already discussed the risks of using the steamer and the rolling rack. Remember to keep them in mind. Also, you need to be aware of very hot lights, which could burn you if touched accidentally.

## SAFETY ON LOCATION

On location there are hazards too. There are C-stands weighted down with sandbags over the legs, as wind can easily blow them over. The stands may be holding a large "scrim," which is a piece of thin, translucent fabric for softening the sunlight, stretched onto a lightweight framework. In some cases, there may be lighting, power packs, and a generator used outdoors to supplement the natural light.

Be sure to use sunscreen on location; you'll be outdoors for many hours and may be too busy to remember to apply it. You can share it with the other crewmembers too—the rest of the crew may forget and will appreciate your looking out for them. A hat is a good idea, as well as plenty of water.

I almost always finish an outdoor styling project with a few bruises from carrying and moving products and my equipment, loading the car, or hurrying too much. You do need to be prepared to lift some weight and keep moving for extended periods of time.

### Shadows and Reflections

It may seem obvious, but always be aware of where the camera is so you don't find yourself standing in front of it. Not so obvious is the possibility of casting a shadow into the shot. Your position can interfere if you are near the reflector and get in the way of the sunlight bouncing onto it. In a tightly controlled, meticulously lit studio I've even found that wearing white or black clothing near the set can affect the shot. These colors can reflect or absorb light, which can actually lighten or darken the shot.

In a room shoot, your reflection could also show up in a window or mirror or on a piece of jewelry. The best plan is to always be aware of your surroundings when you're on a shoot.

# PREPPING FOR YOUR STYLING BUSINESS

Now that you have learned the roles of the crew, techniques for putting up a rolling rack, and prepping wardrobe with a steamer, it's time to think about building your business as a stylist. It's not enough to know what to do on a photo shoot. You need to know how to manage self-employment, find the styling projects, get paid for them, and earn enough income to live and enjoy being a stylist.

Unless you find a job as a staff stylist or a magazine editor, you are working for yourself. You have a lot to manage: record-keeping, finding clients, your portfolio and promotional materials, test shoots, health insurance, budgeting your money, and your actual styling work. No one will remind you what needs to be done. It's a common misconception that working for yourself gives you a lot of free time.

## Self-Employment

I grew up in a somewhat unusual situation in the 1950s. My father didn't go off to a mysterious job every day, like the classic dad; he had a home-based business. He was a court reporter who went to depositions and hearings in downtown Pittsburgh, and came home to transcribe his stenographic notes into a legal record. He usually was home, but when he wasn't, I answered the phone for him and learned the importance of taking thorough messages. My mother, who wasn't the classic 1950s parent either, was perhaps annoyed when she found grocery lists he set out for her.

## The Home Office

It was fun for me to have cabinets full of office supplies on hand. I could always find a stapler, cardboard, carbon paper, and paper clips, and use the big hand-pull adding machine. Friends and I would spin on office chairs. To this day, one of my favorite activities is shopping for office supplies.

I've been self-employed for most of my adult life. Even when I held a job, I always had some sort of home-based business. It's like an addiction, setting up a home office, keeping receipts for business expenses, marketing myself, and filing a Schedule C (self-employment tax form) with the Internal Revenue Service.

Of course, nowadays the home office is centered around a computer, not a supply cabinet. Your home office can be a desk in your bedroom, a corner of the dining room, or a spare room. You'll need a place to check e-mail, research the Web, invoice clients, work on promotional materials, and keep records of expenses. When you're in the middle of a project—

organizing merchandise, wardrobe, or props—you'll want to stage those somewhere so you can view your work.

The IRS has strict guidelines about exemptions for home offices. Seeking the advice of a tax accountant can help you claim a valid deduction. To get a tax deduction, your home office must be a room or portion of your home or apartment that is not used for any other purpose. Based on square footage, a percentage of your rent or mortgage may be a legitimate business expense. Measure the space of the home and your work area so your accountant can help you calculate the portion exclusively used for business.

You will also need to store your steamer, rolling rack, kit, and props you've accumulated. Perhaps you'll need to rent a storage space, especially as your supply of props begins to grow.

## Variety

What's nice about being a stylist is that every day is different. Just as no two styling days are alike, there is a great deal of variety in your daily life as a self-employed person. I love coming off a week of focus on a studio styling project, when there isn't even time to pay bills, and then having a day or two to get my life back in order. In addition to financial duties and laundry, I might also include an afternoon coffee or a pedicure. Then I should fit in a test project to be creative and improve my portfolio as well as my relationships with others in the business.

## Economic Changes

As the years go by, you're bound to observe the effect the economy has on your workflow. National and worldwide economic changes ultimately end up cutting advertising budgets. When companies have less to spend on advertising, there is less work for graphic designers, photographers, stylists, and other creative professionals. Ad agencies seem to be one of the least-secure work environments—their revenues change drastically based on their clientele.

Catalogs feel budget pinches when customers have less to spend or are worried about politics. Some other factors affecting the catalog industry are paper, postal fees, and other shipping costs.

Technical developments like computer graphics and digital photography have also touched everyone in the industry, especially photo labs. More people with fewer skills are able to do their own creative work cheaply, resulting in less work for professionals. There will be more changes in the future you will need to be aware of.

These fluctuations are natural. Pay attention, develop a backup plan for your income, and save money when you can.

## The Three Client Rule

Sometime in your career you might find yourself in this enviable circumstance. You have a new client, and you're glad because there hasn't been much work lately. Maybe the new client is a retailer that advertises every week in newspaper inserts, and the art director loves your styling portfolio. You are hired to do a shoot and it goes well. There is so much work that they would like to book you for two weeks of every month for the next year. You are set: you'll never have to market yourself and worry about work again.

In fact, it is not a perfect situation, though it seems so. The problem is that you've taken yourself off the market and are relying on one client. This great work situation could disappear, but it probably won't, will it? Yes, it probably will.

Here are some things that could take away your bread and butter client. The company could go bankrupt, leaving you unpaid for recent work. The art director can be fired, or accept a new job, and be replaced by someone who has her own favorite stylist. The company might decide to revise its entire advertising plan without informing you that a change is about to take place. A retail chain that has its own photo department in another city might purchase the company.

Those situations are always possible in our industry and may even be considered normal. It would be all right if you had three regular clients, and one went away. You'd still have work with the other two while you find a replacement for the third. You'll have some extra time to work on your marketing, but you'll also have some projects coming up with the other two.

If you've turned down new work because of your full-time client and maybe let go of another client that called occasionally, you are in the same situation as someone who was fired—but without the benefit of unemployment compensation. The work may have been worth it if you have prepared for it to end.

Let's hope you had the foresight to save some of the money you've been earning, enough for at least a month or two. And that you've stayed in contact with several of your former clients. And that you got some good samples of your work for your portfolio when you had a chance—you're going to need them.

Even though clients come and go, try to keep three regular companies, catalogs, or agencies that regularly book you, and fill in with the others that hire you for a one-time job now and then, and you won't find your-self an unemployed self-employed stylist.

## STYLISTS ON STAFF

Most photo stylists work as freelancers. There are some exceptions, how-ever. Fashion editors for magazines are generally on staff, developing and styling their own feature "stories," those gorgeous and inspiring pages of models in the latest fashions.

Some photo studios are large enough operations to employ a full-time stylist. The studios may be a part of a large retailer that is constantly producing advertising flyers and other promotions. They may be connected with a large printing company that seeks to produce all its digital files in-house.

The main requirement for companies to hire stylists is steady workflow. If they find they need freelance stylists consistently throughout the year, it's probably more economical to have someone on staff who will be there for all the shoot days and help organize the schedule.

### A Look at the Life of a Staff Stylist

One such stylist is Pam Tocco. She works for a catalog company in Florida that produces three catalog titles. One of them sells assorted items such as women's clothing, clever gadgets, and gifts. The second is a bedding catalog featuring well-styled bed linens in beautiful room sets. The third catalog, which rarely uses stylists, sells cigars. Pam worked freelance for the cataloger for a year before deciding to give up her independent career for the security of a job.

Here's the career path that Pam took on her way to styling. First, she got a college degree in graphic design. Though she'd had just one class in basic photography, she found a job as a photographer for an arts-and-crafts supply company. It was her lucky break. She learned on the job about lighting and using a 4 × 5 large-format camera. She did her own styling for the shots.

### Learning Experiences

Her next job was for the Home Shopping Network. There she was a set stylist for on-air programs, another case of the surprising amount of work that goes on behind the scenes. Her main responsibility was coor-dinating the products that other stylists were to set up. She worked rotating shifts with different crews, and used the time to meet people and expand her technical knowledge. As time went on, Pam was promoted to styling specialty sets, and worked with the set shop to design and build the room environments.

Meanwhile, she wisely kept working freelance for other styling and graphic clients, and maintained her own graphic-design company. Eventually she accepted a position as a marketing director for a specialty company that builds timber bridges for golf courses. She describes the job this way, "Marketing wasn't my favorite work. There was a ton of responsibility for accounts, but I learned about sales. Mostly, I learned I didn't ever want an office job again. Styling was my thing."

Pam is an example of someone who learns from every experience and incorporates her background into each new opportunity. She turned to freelance styling, working on a month-long project in Miami Beach with responsibility for all the props used for an advertising campaign. Working out of a van, she soon learned she should have had a box truck so she could have all the props on hand at every location in case shots were changed. She learned about courier services for moving props quickly from the hotel to the location. Every challenge was a chance to learn.

Another project was working on a movie set. She was responsible for wardrobe for one hundred "extras" dressed in 1970s clothes for a carnival scene. Pam is the kind of person who can point out "the only place in town where you can rent a real police uniform."

## Time for Stability

The catalog company had been her client for a year when a position opened up there. The former staff stylist (who had earlier learned styling by working with her photographer husband) was promoted to studio manager. Pam already knew she liked her co-workers there, and was attracted to the benefits. And she recalled, "I was at a point in my life when I wanted some stability. I knew I would be able to enjoy my life at home without worrying about my career."

An attractive aspect of the job, too, was the opportunity to shoot personal projects with the staff photographers whenever there was free time. When former clients called she told them she was working full-time and referred the work to other stylists.

## Does it Get Boring?

Alternating between two catalogs, Pam enjoys the variety of styling projects and meeting the other stylists who work there freelance. I met her myself when I worked in the studio.

She's responsible for the vast collection of props that the catalogs keep on hand, at least the smaller props. There are two full-time set builders, and a studio assistant who documents and pulls the furniture used for propping the shots. Pam is familiar with every item on countless shelves—small pictures, books, dishes, soap, candles, vases, and feathers. She can find a straw beach bag, holly branch, or a cream-colored envelope at a moment's notice. It's like playing house.

Other employees process and keep track of the actual merchandise. It's sorted into boxes for each two-page spread of the catalog before each shoot.

## Income Adjustment

Pam's income was a bit higher in the year before she joined the company. But when you figure in the benefits, like health insurance and paid vacations, she comes out ahead. Also, Pam is paid hourly, not salaried, so when she occasionally has to work late she is compensated for it. And if there are slow times she can decide to take more time off.

## Choices and Change

Since there aren't very many staff positions for stylists, the choice Pam Tocco made isn't always an option. And in terms of security, she says, "A job is not something you can count on forever, any more than you can count on keeping clients forever." In the catalog industry there is always change and turnover. Catalog companies, ad agencies, and retail chains are purchased by other companies, or go out of business.

As a freelancer, it can affect you when art directors that you have a good relationship with move on to new jobs. Suddenly your favorite client is gone, and the new art director has a favorite photographer and stylist who find they suddenly have more work. Remember the "Three Client Rule."

# Other Roles a Stylist Plays

**N CHAPTER 1, I TOLD YOU ALL ABOUT MYSELF, MY TRIALS** and tribulations, and my winding career path. You can see you don't need to be a perky twenty-one year old with a clear definition of who you are and what your goals are, funded by Mom and Dad (though it wouldn't hurt!), until you get your styling business established. Now I can tell you what attributes you *do* need.

- Enthusiasm
- Responsibility
- Hard work
- Common sense
- Courtesy
- Creativity
- Versatility

## THE IMPORTANCE OF BEING VERSATILE

Since photo shoots are complex and clients are budget-conscious, it is to your advantage to be able to fill more than one role. The definition of "stylist" can be very broad and vary from client to client. Though the primary goal is to control the appearance of the items in a photograph, a stylist can be expected to perform diverse functions. Many of these merge into "production" of the photo shoot. You may scout locations, get permits, cast talent, book models, arrange travel, rent an RV, buy snacks, and build props.

## PRODUCTION

The producer, or production manager, is the person in charge of the logistics of a location shoot. My background as an art director of fashion photography prepared me for this role and taught me about the many details that need to be in order on a photo shoot.

You may not be comfortable doing production and prefer to stick to styling. You may pick up these skills gradually, by being observant. Or you may never need to assume this role—sometimes there will be a production manager; sometimes the art director will handle the production. More often, you'll share a few of these duties.

And sometimes you will be asked to be responsible. If so, you will be hired for more days of work before the shoot, known as "preproduction."

The production manager may also serve as a local resource for an out-of-town crew. Equipment rentals, photo labs, delivery services, Internet cafes, and good coffee are among the crew's local needs. I developed a welcome sheet for out-of-town clients that was much appreciated, and brought it to each person the first day of production. It lists local radio stations, restaurants, free-time activities, and of course, my contact information and Web site.

### The Key is Organization

Any of the responsibilities in the following pages may fall under the definition of production. Organization is the key—there are countless details to keep track of and none of them can be overlooked. I keep a job envelope for all but the simplest of projects. Inside are a notepad, all papers and forms related to the job, and an envelope for receipts. I never am without it during the time the project is going on. (In chapter 12, I'll give you more details about the job envelope.)

## LOCATION SCOUTING AND PERMITS

Location scouting is not my favorite aspect of production. It's not so bad finding a park, a charming sidewalk, or other public space. I'm not personally fond of knocking on doors and asking homeowners if they'd be interested in having their homes used for a photo shoot. But there was one period of a few months when nearly all my projects were location scouting.

I was glad I could do it, or I'd have had little work. Other times I've had a cluster of wardrobe shopping or prop building. Versatility pays off.

## Finding Residential Locations

Scouting locations requires conversation. You explain what's involved in having a photo shoot, and what it pays, how courteous and unobtrusive a photo crew is compared to a film crew; you flatter the homeowner and build a relationship of trust. You take some digital shots of the house. And after all that, your client may decide not to use the location. If you like to talk to people, spend time with them, and see their homes, you might be a very good location scout.

View the interior and exterior areas of the house and photograph them from various angles. Large rooms, high ceilings, and neutral wall colors are important factors for photography. Note parking and areas that would be good for the crew to set up equipment. Find a place for steaming and for models to dress.

The photographs and other details of locations you visit can be kept in a notebook or three-ring binder for future clients to browse. Alternatively, you could have a Web site showing your locations. To respect the home-owners' privacy it would be a good idea to issue a password to clients, and not publish names or addresses of the homes.

When shooting in a private home, the client will pay the homeowner a location fee directly. The fees vary widely in different areas, generally ranging from $500 to $3,000. The homeowner, if experienced, may ask you to provide liability insurance—see the sidebar on the next page for more about this insurance. There may be valuable items or delicate floors to be aware of. Some homeowners want the crew to remove shoes, or you can buy a batch of large white "crew" socks to put on over shoes. A roll of protective paper can be purchased at a home-supply store and taped down to protect carpets from wear and dirt.

## Film Commissions and Permits

Most areas where you will shoot will have a film commission. Film commissions are economic development programs and, consequently, they market their region (city, county, state) to the film and television industries. Very rarely do they acknowledge the commercial still photography industry specifically.

San Diego's film commission has one person who works exclusively with photography shoots. Still-photography director Lynn Reizer-Heftmann knows immediately who a production manager needs to call and which areas are difficult or easy to shoot in.

## General Liability Insurance

**What:** An insurance policy naming the property owner or city as "additionally insured."

**When:** Almost always required when shooting in public places and buildings. May be requested by private homeowners.

**Why:** This insurance provides coverage in case anyone is injured during the photo shoot, if there is damage to the location, or an accident occurs when a motorist is paying more attention to the filming than to driving.

**How:** Can be written pretty quickly and faxed or e-mailed to the requestor, followed up by mailing original policy. Production manager should also have a copy on hand.

**How much:** Up to a $4 million policy; sometimes other specifics are required such as automobile coverage and workman's compensation. Liability insurance generally costs the same for an entire year as it does for a short term. Clients such as catalog companies will usually provide the certificate through their insurance carriers. For smaller clients the photographer may provide it. Alternatively, hiring a production company and having them do the permitting is usually the most cost-effective way to fulfill the requirement.

The film commission can provide you with a great deal of information about what permits are required and what government agency controls permits for various locations. For example, some beaches may require a permit through the state or the county. A park may be part of the city or may require permission from a state or federal park ranger. A good relationship with the local film commission makes navigating this process much easier. It's important that you get to know your local film commission before a production project comes along. They may print a production guide that lists local crewmembers at no charge. Many clients request these guides in the early stages of their research. You will most likely find some work because of your listing, and you can learn who your peers are.

The permit application will include information about the client, the number in the crew, the number of vehicles, and a description of the project. It's best—though it rarely fits into the schedule—to allow plenty of time before the shoot for this process.

Occasionally film commissions will contact you following a production to ascertain the economic impact of the shoot. They will want to know number of days worked, number of local crewmembers hired, and an estimate of the amount of money spent in the area. This information is later used by the commission to obtain funding.

## Shooting on Streets and Highways

One location-scouting project I particularly enjoyed was for a British stock-photography company. For a project involving cars and people, the company wanted to shoot at beaches and in the desert. Looking for these locations was fun. However, permits for the locations also involved police and highway patrol. The photos would be taken on streets and highways; and even when traffic wouldn't be stopped or, as in the case of the desert, there was very little traffic, an officer had to be present. I had to arrange for payment for the officers' time and provide them with detailed information about where the crew was meeting and the exact shoot locations—down to the mile markers.

I also booked the models (having e-mailed the models' cards to England), rented vehicles (different cars for different days, and a van for the photographer), hired a photo assistant, found an economical hotel, drove the art director and photographer to preview the locations, and made maps—but I didn't do any styling! As I say, each project is unique.

## Location Preview Days

When a crew travels to a location for a shoot, a day or two should be scheduled to look at locations. A local location scout may have already been hired. The photographer, especially, needs to look at potential backgrounds. The art director, and sometimes the stylist, will accompany the photographer. (These roles were described in chapter 2; the art director either is the client or represents the client and is responsible for the look of the photographs.) Often the stylist will stay behind to steam merchandise or shop for props.

During the location preview, the shoot schedule is refined based on backgrounds, the light at different times of day, distance, convenience, and availability. For instance, a restaurant may only be available for use as a location when it is not busy, before eleven in the morning or between two and four in the afternoon.

## Production RVs

A motor home that has been adapted for use by a photo crew is a production RV. The only change may be that the bed has been removed for extra space in the back room. Unlike in the movie industry, it isn't necessary to have full dressing rooms on set. We need transportation to and from locations for the crew and models, a bathroom, an area for prepping wardrobe, and a place for models to change clothes.

An RV works perfectly for these purposes, and comes with a driver who functions as another member of the crew—drivers are usually helpful. In addition to making morning coffee, the driver can absorb the stress of driving after a long day on location.

Ask your clients if they need a production RV to make location projects easier. You can find a production company that will have one by looking in film commission production guides. If there aren't any production services available, you may need to rent an RV and find a crewmember to drive it.

## CASTING TALENT

Casting is the process of selecting the people in photographs. It can be as simple as viewing the cards of models to select the best look and size, or it may involve meeting talent in person. The talent might be professional models, actors, or "real people." This last type of casting is also known as "street casting," finding the talent among nonprofessional people.

### Street Casting

I was once hired by Nike to cast real runners for a catalog. Nike's feeling was that models who say they run may not be as serious about running as genuine athletes. I posted fliers at running-shoe stores and at a park where race information is often displayed. The fliers briefly described the project, rate, shooting dates, as well as the casting date, time, and what to wear. I called running clubs and asked for Web site postings and word-of-mouth communication. A well-known client is easy—people are eager to participate.

The casting took place in a two-hour period in a familiar park where local people frequently run. I provided extra shoes, socks, and shorts in case some runners didn't arrive as requested—in their own running shoes and shorts—or showed up spontaneously. Casting sheets were provided on clipboards with pens. (See the sample casting sheet on page 57. You can use this to make copies or create your own form.) I took Polaroid photos of each person, both close-up and full-length, and taped them to the completed sheets. This helped match the sheet with the video clip later. The runners then proceeded to a video camera where my assistant asked them to "slate" and to describe their running regimen. "Slating" simply means saying your name and model agency, if applicable, at the beginning of a video casting. The slate helped to identify the runners and match them with their casting sheets. It also gave the talent a chance to show some personality. As runners are often enthusiastic about their sport, some of the runners had to be interrupted and gently reminded that they were here for pictures, not sound bites. They were then asked to run about twenty feet away from the camera, make a small turn, and sprint at full speed toward the camera.

# CASTING SHEET*

**Place Polaroid here**

Today's date: _____________

Name: _____________________________________ Age: _________

Phone: Cell: ( ) ________________ Other: ( ) ________________

Email address: ___________________________________________

Agent (if applicable): _________________ Phone: ( ) _________

Measurements:

Height: _______ Weight: _______ Chest: _______ Waist: _______

Hips (Women): ______ Dress size: ______ Suit size: ______ Shoe: ______

When are you available? __________________________________

Any dates unavailable? ___________________________________

Acting experience: _______________________________________

Hobbies, interests: ______________________________________

Sports: ________________________________________________

*Casting Sheet courtesy of Cox Productions

After collecting their casting sheets, I thanked the runners for coming. I let them know the client makes the decision about who is best for the catalog and that they would be contacted only if they were "selected" (a more diplomatic word than "chosen").

At a more recent casting, for a teenage clothing and accessories catalog, I mistakenly told the first few teens that we would "let them know." As soon as the phrase was out of my mouth I knew I would not be able to identify who I'd said that to—and that they might tell their friends we'd call them either way. Over the course of two days of casting, eighty enthusiastic kids arrived.

My client had requested "real people" because, she said, they are more open and genuine than models, but I suspect it had something to do with cost. I contacted a few high-school drama teachers and acting coaches with a description of the catalog and the casting, reassuring them that I was a legitimate production manager and providing information about my Web site. I suggested that parents were welcome to accompany the kids. The teachers explained to them that the selection had nothing to do with the kids or their appearance, but with what the client was looking for. The instructors, the people who helped me with the casting, and I were all very sensitive about how the casting process could affect the kids' self-esteem.

Back to my promise to let them know: I notified the kids who were selected and started to call the ones who weren't. Upon hearing that I was calling, their voices were so hopeful that after the first few I couldn't bear it and gave up and took it as a lesson learned.

## Casting Models and Actors

Most castings are held for professional talent, which is easier than walking less-experienced people through the process. If your project is expected to portray "lifestyle," a realistic family, or an unusual character, your best bet may be an agency that represents actors. They will have plenty of people on the roster representing all types and ages. Model agencies have a narrower range of standards for the people they represent. Height, weight, age, and appearance are among the factors limiting their talent, though model agencies may also represent children, petites, plus sizes, and pregnant women.

Casting does not necessarily mean previewing the talent in person. You may be requested to simply contact model agencies and ask them to provide "comp cards" to you for selection. These are models' promo cards with photos, sizes, and agency information. They may be mailed to you or viewed online.

Or you may need to see the models in person, especially if there are clothes or shoes to fit. One recent client of mine is a high-quality shoe company that distributes shoes through retail stores and catalogs. The shoe samples are size six for women and nine for men. Most professional models have much larger feet, so the agencies really had to explore their rosters to find models small enough to fit these shoes, and then the talent had to represent typical customers, in case their faces weren't cropped out.

I previewed the talent for the shoe catalog through model-agency Web sites or by e-mail. Most agencies protect the privacy of their models by requiring that clients register and have a password to see models' information, such last names and sizes. I forwarded the best choices to my clients, who narrowed the list down to their favorites. Since the photo shoot was planned for another city, I worked with agencies there. We couldn't have the talent "go-see" to try on the shoe samples until arriving—and that was the day before the shoot!

It was like a Cinderella story as the models squeezed their slightly-larger-than-stated feet into the shoes. Since I didn't know the sizes of the eventual talent, it was particularly challenging to shop for the wardrobe, especially men's pants, which are so visible in photos cropped from the knee down. I picked clothing for the most part that was larger and fitted it to the models with large safety pins.

When casting talent from agencies, you will call the agent with the time and location for the casting. The agent informs the talent. You should also provide any special details such as what to wear and a cellphone number, probably yours, in case of emergencies or lost talent.

## BOOKING TALENT

Booking is the process of notifying the agency who has been selected for the shoot and arranging the specifics. This is far easier than with non-professional individuals, as the agent serves as a layer between you and the talent, making it more efficient (and less painful). At this time, you may find out that someone is not available after all. This generally happens right after you have created and perfected a shot schedule, which must then be rearranged.

### Call Sheets

Assuming that all your talent is available, and the agents let you know they have spoken to and confirmed it with them, your next step is to provide the job information or the "call sheet." Review the hourly rate and number of hours that you discussed earlier with the agent. Then you can tell or e-mail (a safer bet) the information to each agent you are working with. When the talent arrives at the shoot, greet them and introduce yourself and the crew, so that they feel at ease.

## MAKEUP

While the makeup artist is a key member of the crew, there are occasions when the stylist may be asked to do the makeup. In smaller markets (everywhere but New York and Los Angeles), there is more expectation that the stylist can perform both functions. Tighter budgets are one reason. In addition, the projects may be less "editorial" (magazine pictorials) and more commercial.

### Information for the Call Sheet

- Client and project name
- List of models from that agency
- Shoot date
- Call time (time the talent is expected to arrive)
- Location
- Directions (and a map if necessary)
- Crew contact names and cell-phone numbers
- What to bring (see wardrobe list in chapter 14)
- Arrive makeup-ready or clean face/no makeup (tells talent whether there will be a makeup artist on the shoot)

Even as an art director, I was not skilled at recognizing whether a model's foundation was a good tone or if lipstick was too dark. Makeup artists have experience with how makeup appears in photographs. Says San Diego–based makeup artist Claire Young, "Skin tone needs to be evened out, blemishes covered, shiny places matted down. It's a lot harder than it sounds, because you need the model to look flawless, but you don't want it to look obvious that she has makeup on."

For lifestyle shots, as opposed to fashion or beauty (when a makeup artist is nearly always present), the model is often asked to arrive "makeup-ready." I am quite willing to maintain a model's makeup, applying powder when the face starts to shine. That's basic knowledge, and sufficient for booking a simple lifestyle job. If you are trained as a makeup artist, you may be able to fulfill both functions on fashion shoots, but you'll be awfully busy and should consider adjusting your rate accordingly.

### Professional Responsibility

The unfortunate thing is that you may bump someone out of a job because you are doing the makeup in addition to styling. Conversely, makeup artists are sometimes asked to style wardrobe; this may eliminate the need to hire you. We must encourage our clients to respect our professionalism; don't be too willing to do everything. We can be reasonable and say no. Taking on too many responsibilities usually means not doing any of them well. It may be a slow process—educating our clients while still getting their jobs—but the quality of our work will be worth it.

A makeup artist has an extensive kit with countless tones of foundation, eye makeup, lip color, and brushes. As a photo stylist, your kit might contain a few makeup items. (I'll list some of them in chapter 5.) You'll decide how much you want to invest in this facet of your styling career.

## MEALS AND SNACKS

Another production role that a stylist may fill is making sure everyone at the shoot is fed and hydrated. Providing snacks may be part of your daily role on location. Use a cooler and make a morning stop for ice, refilling anything that is getting low. Many clients will not think about this necessary aspect of a shoot and will appreciate your suggesting it.

Another popular part of the day is a "Starbucks run." There is usually a nearby coffee spot and if a crewmember can be spared, the response is always favorable, especially in the slump after lunch. The expense for snacks should be established as part of the client's or photographer's budget.

### Popular Snacks for Crews and Models

- Water, water, water

- Soda and diet soda

- Gatorade if in a hot climate

- Altoids (a photo-shoot basic, especially after coffee)

- For morning: Cereal bars, muffins, bananas, grapes, juice, and if possible, coffee (with cups, cream, and sugar)

- For afternoon: Candy, especially red licorice (sure to create excitement!), small crackers, string cheese, and fruit. For a real treat try chips and salsa, or unbuttered popcorn. Be sure to bring hand sanitizer or moist towelettes to clean messy hands.

- Avoid: Oreo cookies, spinach, and poppy seeds (imagine why!); colored juice and caffeinated soda for children

Snacks should be easy to eat (think about models who have on makeup), and not leave grease or residue on the crew's hands. Most makeup artists bring straws for models to use; you can add some to your kit too.

## Snacks and Lunch in the Studio

Generally when you are working in a studio, you won't have to worry about feeding the crew. The studio manager, assistant, or photographer will make sure everyone is fed. It's a matter of hospitality. Most studios are equipped with a kitchen, which is often used for food styling. Coffee and pastries are usually arrayed on the counter in the morning, and the refrigerator is stocked with water and soda.

One of the finest traditions of photo shoots, in my opinion, is lunch. The meal is nearly always provided. Exceptions are in-house photo studios run by corporations or catalogs. While working in an environment where there are full-time employees, you are often expected to take a lunch break, as they do. If you aren't sure what to expect, bring lunch or lunch money on the first day.

In a photographer's studio, the photo assistant may order takeout food from a nearby restaurant and pick it up or have it delivered. The cost is written into the photographer's estimate for the project. The pleasure of this meal is balanced by the fact that you will most likely take a very short lunch break. Don't plan on doing any lunchtime errands when you're on a shoot. Just wash your hands and get back to work.

Lunch on location is anything from a catered meal to a group lunch in a restaurant. The production manager usually makes this decision. This expense is part of the budget; still, be sure to thank the person who pays for the meal. A catered lunch is a pleasant experience. There are some caterers that specialize in photography productions. When they cater for films or video it's known as "craft services." I almost learned the hard way that on location for video or film, nobody goes to the craft-services table at lunchtime before the director. I wanted to eat while I had a chance before steaming sheets for the next scenario, but a co-worker pulled me aside as I was on my way. Morning snacks are fair game at any time, however.

No matter how brief, crew lunches are relaxing and a good time to get to know each other and build rapport.

# SHOPPING FOR PROPS AND ACCESSORIES

"A person who shops for props" is the description of a stylist that I'd heard many years before becoming one. Most people who are attracted to this field are people who love to shop. It's pretty exciting to think you can get paid for it!

## Shopping Addiction

I am not a "shopaholic," someone who has an addiction to buying things. This compulsion, while temporarily satisfying, has been known to cause some serious problems in people's lives, as much as we make light of it. I tend to consider carefully before spending my own money on clothes or household items. But spending someone else's money and getting paid for doing it is a fun way to make a living.

Though I don't look first at the price tag when prop shopping, I think I am very careful with my clients' money. They want me to be. They're already spending a good bit on the crew, models, travel, and other expenses. If you do have a problem with shopping addiction, it's a good idea to keep your receipts for styling separate from any personal items you may pick up.

## Generic Props

You are using props to enhance the photograph, not to draw attention to them. Catalog companies, in particular, want the props used in the shots to help sell their products. Sometimes they get phone calls from customers who want to buy the props. They would prefer the customers don't even notice them. It's good to try to use props from the cataloger's merchandise whenever possible. If a catalog sells bags, belts, or jewelry, these items should be used as accessories throughout the catalog.

You want to avoid any easily recognizable brands—props should be "generic," suggesting a plain wine bottle, for instance, rather than distracting the customer with an identifiable label. You can create more timeless photos this way, too. Props that are fashionable or trendy would make the photo appear dated. If electronic equipment is shown, make sure it's the latest technology available, since these products change quickly. Magazines can be rolled so that only a portion of the cover shows. Calendars can have the year marked out. Careful use of props can make the photo real and, at the same time, simple.

Even if you're not working as a food stylist, edible props may come into play. A bowl of fruit, a lime slice on the edge of a glass, or a bucket filled with ice and chilled beer bottles may all enhance your shot. It's fun to shop for the perfect pear, a bottle of the finest champagne, or some other gourmet item that you might not typically allow yourself to buy. You're actually looking at the food as a perfect object, rather than being

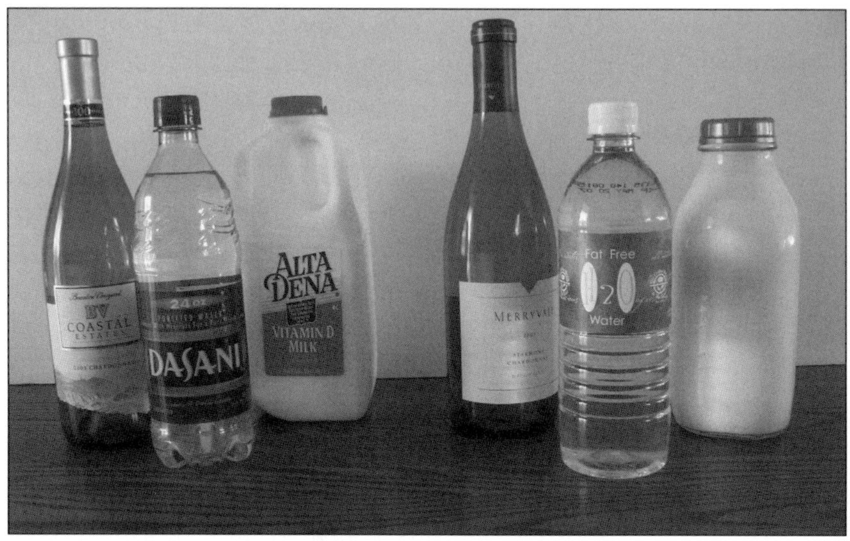


At left are obvious brand-name food props. The items at right are generic and less distracting. © Susan Linnet Cox

practical. (The Basic Kit List in chapter 13 lists a few items for styling these food props.)

Pay attention to details that make the photo "real." For example, construction and factory workers appear more realistic with hard hats or safety goggles. On that note, don't forget that it's important to be aware of appropriate safety devices. A model posing with a skateboard and bicycle should have a helmet and other protective gear, even if the model is only holding them. This is required for riders in some states.

## Seasonal Items

The print-production industry works two to six months ahead of the seasons. Two or three months usually elapse from the time a catalog is designed and the photographs taken until it's printed and distributed. Magazines stories are photographed two months or more before the issue is available. Publications are presenting the styles of the upcoming season, so overall, you are going to be styling the opposite season throughout the year. This can make finding seasonal props a challenge. Searching for sandals or a beach ball during January in Minneapolis is nearly impossible. In warmer climates it's a little easier, but still a challenge. Keep your eyes open for sources so you'll know where to begin. And don't forget, there's always the Internet.

## Prop Rentals

Not all props are purchased. While most items on your list can be found at various retail stores, you may need a special item like a Victorian sofa or a large area rug. When you find the sofa at an antique store, the storeowner might be interested in renting it to you. A carpet store may be willing to rent the rug to you. This is actually fairly common, with a standardized rate of about ten percent of the retail price per day, with your credit card number on file in case the item isn't returned or is damaged. Generally, the arrangement can be negotiated for longer, and owners are pretty flexible.

It's not a bad situation for storeowners—they make some income from the merchandise and still get to sell it later, and your credit card deposit is on file. One glitch might be if the storeowner wants to keep the store stocked for a busy shopping day. You'll need to arrange transportation and take very good care of the item while it's in your possession.

## A Treasure Hunt

Searching for props can be like a treasure hunt. Sometimes what seems like the simplest thing to find becomes impossible. One spring I needed to find a basic red cooler chest. We've all seen a million of them. That year, though, all the coolers were blue. I went to store after store and found nothing but blue coolers. I told my client I'd be glad to spray paint the chest red, but we agreed that blue would work.

My first project as a studio manager was to find a "kiddie car" for an ad-agency promotion. A man in a suit and tie would be flying down a set of stairs in front of an office building in a 1950s-style, child-size toy car. I started out with the yellow pages, calling antique dealers. None of them had one but each suggested someone else to call. It seemed like the chain of phone calls would never end, but at last I found the ultimate collector of children's pedal cars, and he was very generous about renting a pink kiddie Cadillac for our shoot. Never give up—the prop you are searching for is just around the corner. If not, there's always another solution—making props.

## Making Props

Your creative skills can come into play when a prop is impossible to find. This is when it gets fun. The finished prop just needs to last long enough to get through the shoot, and most important, look like the real thing. For one outdoor-products catalog, I constructed a willow branch that was used countless times. I found a sturdy, curved branch about six feet long at a florist supply store, and silk willow leaves, which I attached using a glue gun. The branch was used for an evening shot of some colored party lights; it was suspended over a lighted swimming pool so that a pleasing background could enhance the lights. The branch has since been used as an out-of-focus foreground element and also to decorate the area outside a large window.

## "UNSHOPPING," THE ART OF RETURNS

One important thing to remember when shopping for props is to always get twice as many of an item as you need. Having options makes you a better stylist and often the alternative ends up being the favorite choice. However, buying twice as much as you need will inevitably lead to one of your most difficult duties as a stylist: returning props and wardrobe to the store where you purchased them. You'll get used to it, but it is never easy.

Your clients' budgets should allow for a certain amount of props, but they generally will not expect to own all the props after the shoot, especially items they are not likely to use again. That's where returns fit in. I call it "unshopping" when you undo the prop shopping you did at the beginning of the project.

It is an accepted practice within the photo industry that props, and even wardrobe, are purchased for use on a shoot and then returned to the store. Some stylists have a policy of only returning items that aren't worn; if it's been worn, it's not a return. This is fair and should be clarified with the client at the beginning of the project. It could be difficult when the shoot is a test shoot or the budget is very small. The garments could be given to the models, kept by the client or stylist, or donated.

When I did a styling job for Buick I found out that GM's policy is to donate all props used on their photo shoots. This is a good and honorable way to handle the moral question of returns. I'm surprised more clients don't follow it.

Most stores, particularly the national chains, do have a generous returns policy—returns within thirty days with a receipt, if items are not worn or damaged, price tags attached, credit on a credit or debit card. Before you do prop shopping be sure to check out the store's policy about returns. You will want to avoid stores that give only store credit.

I used to love shopping at small local stores, to support local commerce, until I realized how convenient and predictable national chain stores are. They are everywhere you go and you know what you'll find.

## Sales Commissions

Some upscale department stores also gladly accept returns as a customer service. This seems like a great source for expensive dresses and men's suits. But when I realized that the salespeople are paid commissions on items sold and then have those commissions taken out of their paychecks following returns, I didn't feel as good about it. How hard it must be to be thrilled with your extra income and then receive less in the next pay period.

Department store outlets offer a comparable selection but at a discount, and generally don't use the commission system.

## Tagging

Not graffiti, but simple devices for replacing store tags on clothing, "taggers" are available at store fixture suppliers. These are the same suppliers where you buy steamers, rolling racks, mannequins, and tissue paper. A tagger is a gun-like tool for re-inserting price tags that were removed from the garment. The trick is keeping the tags in order, so the right one is attached to the right garment. I have had moment or two of panic when I was returning a cotton tank top to which I'd attached a $40 price tag, whereas the silk blouse was marked $12.

It's best, of course, to keep the tags attached as long as possible; if the item isn't used at all you don't have the difficult decision about returning it. You can use sticky notes or envelopes to keep track of the tags. Be sure to bring these supplies to the shoot, along with a pen for noting which tag goes with which garment.

If you purchase designer sheets or other packaged linens and use them on a bed, you might want to return them, as long as they are clean. It looks like you'll never be able to fit them back in the original packaging. Save the package and the cardboard, having noted the original presentation. If you have an extra package on hand—from the multiple options you've provided—you have something for comparison. Believe it or not, the sheets will fit back in and look just like when you bought them.

## Your Mental Story

You will notice that other people are returning purchases. It goes on all the time. Rarely does the cashier ask you the dreaded question, "What is your reason for returning this product?" But I find that it makes me feel more authentic if I have a story in my head when doing returns: "These didn't look so good when I tried them on at home"; "The color wasn't right"; "My daughter is picky"; "My brother bought all his own house-wares at the same time that I was buying these for him!" Poor me, now I have to return them!

I read one suggestion by a stylist on a blog suggesting that you consider yourself a "personal shopper." And it's valid—you are purchasing items and taking them to someone who will decide whether they're appropriate. That can be a good mental cover story.

## Twenty Percent Loss Formula

You can figure on about a 20 percent rate of items that will be damaged, kept by the client, given to the models, or kept by you. This figure can effectively be part of your budget estimate. Also, if for one of these reasons you keep one or two items from each large purchase it will ease the discomfort of returns. When you calculate it into the budget you may enjoy the occasional scarf, sunglasses, slightly worn shoes, or even a giant pile of lemons, as long as they were props requested or needed for the shoot and are not returnable.

The pile of lemons brings us to shopping at grocery stores and garden centers for props. You can usually expect these to be nonreturnable purchases. You and the crew often get to bring home garden plants and extra food props. Evenings of celebrating the wealth of props bought for their beauty will follow.

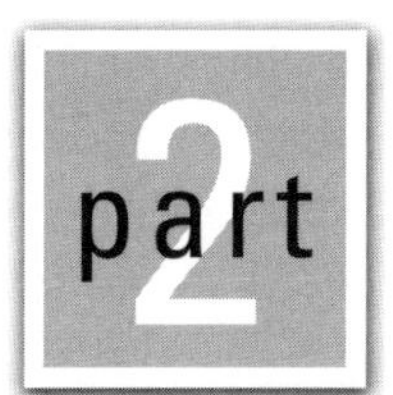

# Photo Styling Specifics

chapter **5**

# Fashion Styling

**I** **MIGHT AS WELL TELL YOU ONE THING ABOUT ME RIGHT** now. I am not really into fashion. I'm not possessed by the wardrobe fantasies of a fashion student, or the desire to design outrageous garments. I don't shop for designer labels, though I do know who most of the designers are. My favorite color to wear is heather grey and I also wear a lot of khaki, white, and black. (I understand some fashion designers wear only black.)

What I do love is the construction of clothing, and I appreciate the characteristics of fabric. I learned to sew when I was quite young. In those days, girls took home economics in junior high and every year thereafter. Half the year we learned cooking and the other half sewing. Girls did not have the option of woodworking, drafting, metal shop, and automotive repair. If I had, my life might have been different—I think I would have really liked those classes. But I spent my happiest school days in home economics, sewing on a Singer machine, and learning about casings, darts, facings, collars, and set-in sleeves.

So, I love clothes, but I am not passionate about fashion. That love is the number one requirement to be a fashion stylist.

71

## EDITORIAL FASHION STYLING

Fashion styling is a very wide area. Drawing on a fascination with fashion and clothes, stylists are attracted to fashion photography. Whether they are working with merchandise available for sale or pulling together new combinations, these stylists must have a love for fashion and creating new looks. In an ideal situation you can live in that world—and many do. Others find that there is not enough styling work available exclusively in fashion and also do other types of styling.

The people involved in fashion styling were described in chapter 1. To review briefly, a magazine fashion editor researches the coming styles and trends to create fashion stories. Fashion stylists may work with advertisers, either featuring the garments or creating a mood. The bulk of freelance fashion styling is less glamorous work for catalogs, creating a look the customer will want to buy.

The biggest difference between catalogs and magazines is that catalogs are selling specific merchandise and magazines are promoting a style that their readers are interested in. The fashion editor draws the reader in. Readers must be engaged enough to buy magazines, which are largely financed by advertising;

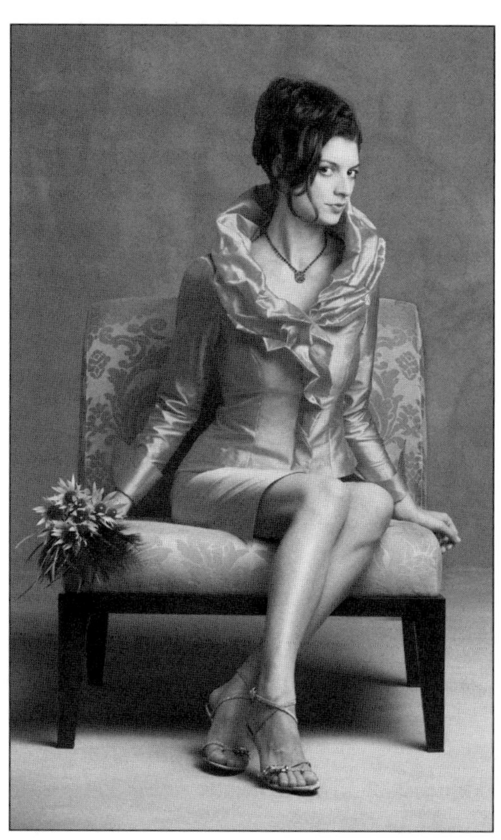

Classic fashion styling of apparel and props. *Photographer:* Tim Mantoani. *Art director:* Cindy Cochran. *Styling:* Susan Linnet Cox. *Hair and makeup:* Claire Young. © Tim Mantoani

subscriptions and cover prices provide only a small part of a magazine's income. Catalog income results from the items sold in the catalog. The stylist should be aware of these subtle differences.

In the magazine world, a fashion editor is the stylist—and much more. Staff fashion editors and their assistants do most of the styling themselves, along with following the fashion industry.

Styling fashion stories in magazines seems to be freer and more creative than most areas of styling. There is not usually an art director looking over your shoulder—the editor independently creates and directs the project. The editor/stylist works exhaustively on the project, researching fashion trends, creating story concepts, finding resources, hiring photographers, producing the shoots, and styling the fashion. These are the steps the editor takes in developing a fashion story.

## Steps to Fashion Editorials

1. Attend semiannual fashion shows. Look for upcoming shapes, colors, and texture. Sort out the fads from trends.

2. Follow up with visits to showrooms to see collections in person. There, editors can have a close look at garments, see how they feel, find out how they are made, and get prices and availability of samples for their shoots.

3. Keep notebooks and sketchbooks to track items for more than one shoot at a time. This recording may also be done on a laptop computer.

4. Request sample clothes for a shoot, working with public-relations representatives to procure them.

5. Design and produce photo shoots on location or in studio. Really the most intensive part of the process, the shoot is only one part of the editor's job.

6. Take notes during the shoot of every garment and accessory worn in each shot, for writing captions, the description of items, prices, and sources that appear on the fashion pages (or at the back of the magazine). Notes help later when matching items with copy; it may be hard to remember every detail. Makeup and hair products may also be included in captions. Check name spelling for photographers, stylists, and makeup artists for listings.

7. Return garments right after the shoot to the representatives. Careful labeling and organizing helps, and the reps appreciate having samples back in good order.

## Viewing the Runway Shows

Editorial fashion stylists get ideas by constant exposure to the fashion world. The ultimate part of keeping on top of the latest trends is viewing the major fashion shows. Semiannual shows in Milan, Paris, London, and New York, when new lines are presented, are the biggest source of inspiration.

The major shows occur in approximately February and March for autumn/winter collections, and September and October for the spring/summer collections. In addition, there are haute-couture shows in January and July. Menswear collections are presented in January and August to September of each year.

## Editing the Fashions

Editing the collections to suit one's own ideas is the next step of a creative mind. The personal touch of combining elements from collections or mixing them together makes the stylist's approach unique. After the shows, the editor has the opportunity to visit showrooms and see the fashions up close. This step refines the impressions from the runway shows. Since the editor may be planning up to six months of stories at this phase, the garments are sorted into themes or stories.

## Sourcing Fashion

Publicity for fashion lines is assigned to either a staff or an independent public-relations representative. These representatives are the main contact for obtaining samples for fashion stories. Early in the season, there may be only one sample of a garment and the bigger fashion magazines with good relationships seem to have first choice.

Extra options are usually pulled for stories; some items may not fit the model or work well once they are on set. If the sample has to be borrowed for more than a few days for travel to a location, the sample should be included in the story. Returning samples quickly after the shoot and in good order is important. Keeping a good record is essential.

The search may not take the fashion editor far from the office. Samples are continually sent to magazines by PR reps. I accompanied my daughter, Elizabeth, to *Teen* magazine for one of her first bookings. She was to appear in a monthly one-page feature of a girl explaining what clothes she likes and why. We went into the magazine's stuffed sample room where Elizabeth chose several pieces to wear at the shoot (she didn't get to keep them). The editor asked her some questions about her background and the garment choices. We anxiously awaited the issue and were crushed to see a shot of her jumping up; her head was cropped off the top of the page. But that was the editor's call for an effective presentation.

Designer Nanette Lepore was an acquaintance of mine years before she started her successful fashion line. I understand her husband does her public relations and obviously has been very effective at sending out samples to magazines. I always spot one of her fashions or accessories in the features of new items floating on the pages in major magazines.

## Prop and Location Concepts

The fashion editor works with advertising and other editorial departments in developing fashion stories. Accessories or home editors may collaborate on feature stories.

A prop stylist may be hired to work in conjunction with the fashion editor. A fashion story may be enhanced by creative styling of outside props. Inspirations result from pulling in elements for props, such as feathers, furniture, or any "out there" ideas.

Locations can provide a big part of the fashion story, too. Unusual architecture, hotel rooms, gardens, cities, Airstream trailers, and beaches all can provide a major part of the theme.

You see these fashion stories in *Vogue, Elle,* or *Vanity Fair.* Here's an obscure European hotel room, somewhat dated looking, with the model sprawling on the bed in a gown. On the floor next to the bed is a French telephone. The funky wires extend to an outlet. The flaws in the room add intrigue to the story.

My own family's Victorian home in Pittsburgh, which was in ill repair, had possibilities. It would have been an inspiring, bizarre location for a fashion story had I been able to bring myself to produce it. But it was a little too "close to home" for me. An objective stylist/editor could have created a fashion story including a model in front of peeling wallpaper. A shot looking up at a model might have included this background: a vine that had climbed through a cracked window and created an oval on the bay window ceiling. A fashion editor is alert to these possibilities.

## Magazine Job Descriptions

Job titles for magazine fashion positions are different from the commercial styling world. Though many duties are the same, the language of the editorial realm is quite distinct.

The magazine's **senior editor**, or **editor-in-chief**, is responsible for all aspects of producing the magazine, including editorial features and advertising. Editors for each department such as current events, arts, health, beauty, and fashion make presentations of their concepts to the magazine's editor. During the issue's production, layouts and images are presented to the editor for approval.

A **fashion editor** edits next season's fashions into fashion stories. In essence, the role is that of a full-time stylist with inside knowledge of fashion and extra production duties. The stories are created with the readership, or "market," of the magazine in mind. There may be six to fifty pages of fashion, depending on the magazine's focus. At larger magazines, a fashion director may supervise the fashion editor.

The fashion editor position is often filled by the young and fresh, aspiring for a life in fashion. While many fashion editors are well-known figures who have spent a lifetime in the career, the average length of time on the job is about ten years. Long hours, travel, and the demands of a family can result in career shifts to related fields such as public relations or fashion consulting.

The stylist, whether fashion editor or freelance, is usually given credit in a story. "**Contributing editor**" indicates a freelance stylist. Minor projects and those at smaller magazines are more likely to be given to freelance stylists. Sometimes an entire story will be subbed out to an independent stylist, including the production work.

On occasion a magazine may accept a fashion story created "on spec." A stylist and photographer would collaborate on a concept, hire models, pull the fashion, have a layout designed, and produce a finished story that is presented as a complete package to a magazine for purchase. An ambitious but exciting project.

Unlike **art directors** for photography, the art director at a magazine develops the look and style of the magazine, rather than supervising photo shoots. A fashion editor works with the art director of the magazine to lay out a fashion story, considering the number of pages, color themes, and other visual elements. Then it is presented to the magazine's senior editor for approval, before and after photography.

**Hair and makeup artists** are nearly always freelance roles. They may work with a salon or a cosmetics line or be represented by an agency. A credit generally appears in the article, sometimes along the gutter side of the page.

## FASHION ADVERTISING

Stylists for fashion advertising are those already involved in the editorial fashion world. How they create looks is the most significant attribute. Laura Beckwith, a booking agent at Art House Management in New York, says stylists are hired based on a strong book, reputation, and organization, but more than anything, on their own distinctive style.

They may also work as contributing stylists to magazines and are often former fashion editors. One recognized stylist in the field of fashion advertising was formerly an editor for a major fashion magazine; she also works as a creative director for a fashion line. With extensive contacts in the fashion photography community, the stylist may even be responsible for booking the photographer for these ads.

Stylists of this caliber in the New York fashion world are almost always represented by an agency. With a busy schedule, lots of travel (often international), and multiple projects to organize they need the help of an agency to coordinate, negotiate, and promote.

There is also the more mundane world of advertising for less glamorous fashion brands. These jobs are more accessible to the stylist who is not based in New York and repped by an agency. One job I did preproduction for was the clothing company Hang Ten; another stylist was styling on the shoot day. The ad was placed in *Seventeen* and other teen magazines. Shot in one day at two different locations (scouting them was my role, along with hiring the RV), the ads showed a group of girls and boys playing football in Hang Ten clothing and running through a sand dune at the beach in swimwear. That way the company was able to produce their summer and fall ads efficiently with the same models and crew.

## CATALOG FASHION STYLING

This is the bread and butter of fashion styling for those not in the magazine world. In spite of economic fluctuations, the catalog industry is enormous and growing, with both print and Web sales. And apparel is the largest segment. Producing catalogs—including photography, design, paper, printing, and mailing—is expensive. Catalog items have been carefully selected to appeal to the target market, and the financial aspects are highly controlled. The catalog company is looking for photographic teams to create great selling images.

### Catalog Terminology

It helps for a stylist to understand the language used on catalog shoots. Some of it pertains to merchandising and some to graphic design and printing. The terms provide information on how a product or a photograph is presented in the catalog. This is a sampling of the language; you will hear other terms at shoots or meetings and grow to understand, especially if you ask questions.

**Star** and **Inset.** The star or feature is the largest presentation in a catalog spread. Most likely the largest sales dollars are expected for that product.

You'll spend more time and effort on a great photograph of that product. Conversely, an inset is a small image of a garment placed near a larger photo, a back view, or an alternate color. It may be a close-up view showing just one detail of the garment.

**Colorways.** This merchandising term is usually used in the plural, since it refers to the assortment of colors in which a product is available. One color is featured on the model or the top of a stack of folded items, but the others need to be shown clearly. Sometimes the color shown on-figure is more attractive in photography but expected to sell less than another color. In that case the second color is likely to be featured prominently in the stack.

**Reshoot.** The dreaded term reshoot means a photograph needs to be taken again at a later time for one reason or another. It may be a technical flaw in the photography, in which case the photographer might pick up the expense of a new shoot. This is rare, however, with digital photography (no more fears about not having film in the camera).

The garment may be an incorrect sample or may have been changed after the shoot. Or the shot may not be quite powerful enough. Buyers generally review the shots with the art director to make the final selections; they may not be thrilled with some shots and are more likely to classify them as reshoots if there is already another shoot scheduled for late samples or other reasons. It's not the end of the world and may result in another day's booking for the stylist.

**Color Corrections** and **Post.** You may hear someone say, "That's OK, I can fix it in post," meaning postproduction. With digital images, the photographer, art director, or a retoucher can do a lot to improve a shot in the computer. Light switches and telephone wires can be erased much more easily than in the days of film. Color shifts can be corrected this way also. Previously, photographs were scanned by a professional service prior to printing (known as Scitex). But it was time-consuming and expensive to make color adjustments and revisions. Now such changes can be accomplished in Photoshop before a digital file is presented to the client.

## Working with Merchandisers

As you've seen, merchandisers are important to the catalog companies. In addition to buying, they are involved in everything from determining portions of pages for their products to editing the images. Most likely there will be a preproduction meeting where buyers present the products to the photo crew and discuss presentations. As the stylist, this is your opportunity to find out as much as you can and thus avoid misinterpretations. Ask questions—it's often hard to understand someone's visual concept.

A sample manager will probably be on staff at the catalog company making sure the needed photo samples are ready for the shoot. There is often only one sample for each garment, and it may have a hole cut in the back or the word "sample" written across the back, due to import regulations. Often sample sizes are much larger than the models' sizes, and that's where you come in on location. Dresses are usually a medium or size eight and women's shoes are size nine. Fortunately, most models seem to have size nine feet while their dress sizes are four or six.

And remember, whenever possible, accessorize with items for sale in the catalog. If this isn't an option, use generic items that won't distract from the products.

## THE FASHION SHOOT

Each photo shoot is a unique experience, making your styling career ever new. There are, however, some typical aspects of a fashion shoot. Your day on location will start before daylight, as there's a lot of preparation to do before the first photograph is taken. Meeting the crew and traveling to the location, unloading the garments, prepping and putting them in order, are your early tasks. The model spends a good deal of time with the makeup and hair stylist. Since they may have started the hair and makeup early at the hotel, the model can travel to the location in rollers, where final touchups are done. Meanwhile, you get the wardrobe ready and discuss the first shots with the art director and photographer. There is often a slow start the first morning, before the crew develops a rhythm of working together.

### Dressing the Model

When the model is made up and in wardrobe, she will proceed to the set or location in front of the camera. At this point she doesn't have to be perfect. There is time to refine clothing fit and accessories after she's in place, while the photographer and assistant are perfecting the lighting and looking at the shot as a whole. Wait till after the first preview to go in and start "tweaking." When you step back and look at the shot, you'll see what's important.

One person should be designated to communicate with the model. There should not be multiple voices calling commands at the same time to a model far from the camera. Suggestions should be quietly funneled to the art director or fashion editor, who determines the priority and then, if it's determined a change should be made, communicates with the photographer. Sometimes things work themselves out; a model will shift into a new pose and the sleeve that looks wrong will suddenly fix itself.

## Preview Shots

At the beginning of each photograph, there is a process of building. Lighting the shot, positioning the model, creating the background of the set, perfecting the clothing, accessorizing, and other refinements gradually build the perfect image. During this process the photographer, art director, and stylist are looking at, analyzing, and improving details. In chapter 2, I described the Polaroid process in detail, the etiquette, and the order of the crewmembers making their contributions. It works the same whether the shot is traditional film or digital: there is a preview before the real shooting actually begins.

When you, the photographer, and art director are looking at a Polaroid preview shot or an image on the monitor, elements that you may have overlooked will become obvious. As you concentrate less on the model and clothing, other aspects of the image, such as the background, will emerge.

In a preview, be alert for any distracting juxtapositions in the background. Horizontal lines shouldn't cross behind the model's head, neck, hips, or any point that catches the viewer's eye or makes the body look heavy. Watch for vertical items too, such as a palm tree coming out of the model's head. (See the preview shot on page 253.)

Often the background will be out of focus. Fashion photographers often use a telephoto lens so that the model and clothing are sharp and other elements are blurry. This helps the eye sort out what is important. Backgrounds may be just blurred areas of color. See how well they enhance the product.

Other fashion photography techniques incorporate sharp detail throughout. Look carefully to be sure every background item is perfect. Sometimes you'll find yourself picking up cigarette butts from a sidewalk. You don't want to see a flaw when the photograph is printed.

## Looking at the Model

Beyond the clothing, look at the model's position while the shoot is going on. He or she should be standing in the most flattering position for both the body and the clothing. There may be some direction based on the layout and position on the page. Generally the model won't face off the edge of the page. Check that your clips aren't showing if the model turns to the side.

Watch out for missing limbs. An arm that is tucked behind the model can have a disturbingly truncated look. Usually women's fashions look more flattering when there is a space between the waist and the arm. Look for an angle that will help the body seem narrower. A hand in a pocket should not be placed too deeply; about the length of the fingers is enough, more a suggestion of a hand in a pocket.

See how the model's legs and feet look. Minor shifts can drastically affect—or improve—the shot. When a model is sitting there are particular challenges. There may be an extra lump of fabric at the front. Creases that pants and skirts make at the groin and pulling at the hips require increased attention on the stylist's part. Models know how to tuck and release fabric under their legs. It's always a good idea to warn the model about what you're about to do in this part of the body.

The photographer, particularly an experienced fashion photographer, is going to be seeing the same things as you. You may notice something at the same moment the photographer asks the model to change her position. If so, you are on the same wavelength and on your way to creating a great fashion photograph.

## A Long Day

A fashion shoot might consist of anywhere from five to twenty shots per day, with one or several models working. Obviously you will be busy, even if you have an assistant. There are many garments and accessories to keep track of while you move back and forth between the dressing area and the shot. Your presence is often needed in both places at the same time. Lunch is a welcome break and the sun is usually too high and bright for shooting then.

In the afternoon, it all starts again with the makeup artist refreshing the models' faces and hair; there is pressure to finish the shot list. You can expect to work hard physically and be mentally organized, without any down time. But you will be creating something beautiful.

## TECHNIQUES AND HOW-TOS

As with all types of styling, there are no absolute rules. Creative problem solving applies to almost every styling situation. The following tips and suggestions will help your days run more smoothly.

## Production Cycles

Catalog photography is usually produced in the opposite season; winter and holiday catalogs are shot in summer; summer catalogs are shot in the middle of winter. Magazines are shot about three months ahead of the issue. On location, these cycles can make for a pretty uncomfortable model.

Experienced models will often bring a warm jacket to a shoot so they can stay warm between shots. If you're comfortably dressed, it helps sometimes to take off your own coat and put it around the model's shoulders. When I've done this I can see how much they appreciate my pre-heated, toasty jacket. It also reminds me how cold the models feel.

You have probably heard stories about models freezing in swimwear on California beaches in the winter. Even worse is when they're asked to splash in the water. Sometimes a homeowner will turn on a heated pool when shots require talent being in the water. It's expensive and they may reasonably expect compensation for the cost.

While the Pacific Northwest is often cool and rainy, July is usually a hot, sunny month. That is when we would shoot locally for Norm Thompson's winter catalogs. The fashions were cashmere sport coats, wool sweaters, and heavy jackets. Clearly, the models were roasting and the makeup artist was busy applying powder. Be aware of how the models feel, carefully holding warm clothes—or ice cubes!—for when the camera isn't rolling.

## Ironing and Steaming

Many delicate designer fabrics respond better to ironing than to steaming. The imported silks shown earlier on page 72 could not handle the moisture of steam and had to be ironed by an assistant. As with all fabrics, test a small hidden area before steaming. Ironing delicate fabrics should be done on the wrong side of the fabric, at least until you know how it will respond. You can also protect fabrics by using a pressing cloth or a thin cotton dishtowel. Using a "ham," a small rounded cushion for ironing, helps with tricky curved areas.

(Instructions for steaming garments were provided in chapter 3, along with a guide for putting up a rolling rack.)

## "Going In!"

This is the cry of warning by stylists who want to enter the area in front of the camera. Ideally you will quietly let the photographer or art director know first, but sometimes something catches your eye that you want to change before another frame is shot.

An experienced model shouldn't lean down and look at what you are doing; this changes the drape of fabric that you are trying to adjust. I find I need to ask newer models frequently to stay as they are and not move.

Going in inevitably results in the occasional stylist butt shot. Try to keep a sense of humor and hope a fashion photographer doesn't get inspired to publish a book of them.

## Fitting Clothing

In catalog styling, where most sample garments are medium-sized and the models are size four, there is a lot of tweaking to do. What goes on behind the model to make them fit is shown below. Some stylists use safety pins or straight pins, whereas others use various clips and clothespins.

You want the clothes to look comfortable, not too tight, and flattering to the typical body. In addition to checking the width of the clothing at the waist, chest, and hips, take a good look at the waist length, shoulders, neckline, and sleeves. Fabric in these areas should never look pulled; leave a little slack.

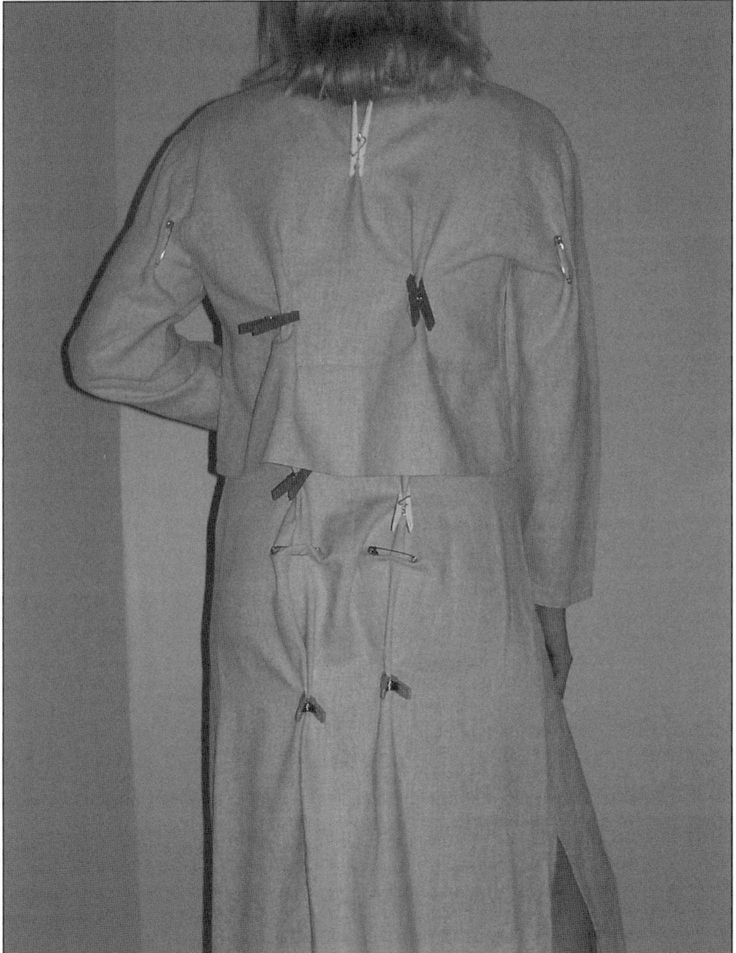

Clipping an oversized outfit, rear view. Notice safety pins used for tightening sleeves and raising skirt to avoid return. Plastic clothespins and small clips are used for narrowing jacket and skirt. © Susan Linnet Cox

Earlier in my styling career, I had a batch of wood, spring-style clothespins in my kit. I learned the hard way that they are not good for styling. In this case, I was working on an advertising shoot for which the models brought some of their own garments. When I adjusted the back of a model's silk dress, my clothespin made a tiny pull in the fabric.

I was able to smooth the fibers and I thought it was satisfactorily repaired, but after a month the photographer had not yet paid my invoice. At this point he let me know that the model had come to him with a complaint about her dress. After awkward negotiations, I deducted the value of her expensive dress from my invoice. Now I use only smooth plastic clothespins for adjusting garments.

## Return

An uneven hemline, longer at the back than the front, is known as return. Frequently at shoots, a stylist exclaims, "I see return!" Skirts, like shorts and slacks, are constructed with more length in the back, to accommodate the human rear end. How much length is visible depends on the fit of the garment and the height of the camera. Returns can usually be resolved by shortening the back of the skirt, as shown in the photograph on page 83. The two safety pins near the top of the skirt lift it just enough.

## INTERNATIONAL TRAVEL

Travel to international locations requires more preparation than domestic travel. The team for an editorial shoot may be drawn from the local talent in a major fashion center, such as Milan or Paris. But when travel is to a more obscure location, the team is usually assembled at home. This is almost always the case for a catalog shoot, for which there are preplanning meetings and product previews.

Customs regulations vary for different countries, and it's crucial to have the right documents in place beforehand. A local production manager in a foreign country can be a great help with these procedures. When merchandise is being shipped, regulations can be quite complicated, because importing—and the possibility of your selling the items—is a big concern for customs officials everywhere. A list including every item is required; the same items have to be identified upon return.

A carnet is a document that insures the officials that merchandise samples and photographic equipment won't be sold in their country without taxes being paid. Issued through the United States Council for International Business, the carnet requires up to a week for processing and a deposit of partial value of the items. The site *www.shoots.com* provides more information about the process.

When I directed a photo shoot on a cruise ship in the Caribbean, I had some interesting experiences. It might sound glamorous but the cruise line that hosted us was a very basic Russian cruise line. Our ship, the Gruziya, had been a Soviet military vessel made over into a cruise ship after the fall of Communism. Our photo crew traveled for free and was able to shoot travel wear on the ship and in three ports. The cruise included a good bit of culture shock when we would find ourselves in the ship's Russian culture.

Along with other cultural adventures, I had the responsibility of meeting with the local port officials of Honduras, Belize, and Mexico when we arrived in ports there. The local port officials boarded in shirt sleeves, carrying brief cases and looking very much what you would expect the government officials to look like— somewhat intimidating. I, along with Yuri, the purser of the ship, met with them. They reviewed our paperwork, which included lists of all the items we would take on shore, from garments and accessories to camera equipment and lists of crewmembers, their passports, and our schedule for the day. Once cleared, we met with a local guide who took us to nearby sites, which naturally had not been pre-scouted. In Honduras, we traveled in an old VW van that was started with a screwdriver held to the battery. But the chance to see back roads of Honduras, women washing clothes in a river, and people carrying goats and chickens down the road was worth all of it.

For a travel-magazine shoot in Mexico, I was hired to do wardrobe shopping for a couple, two models who were to be shown in an article about a charming and historic city there. They would also be shot for the cover. My role was not to go on the shoot, unfortunately, because a makeup artist had already been booked and would maintain the wardrobe too. My assignment was to purchase the couple's wardrobe items and accessories (purse, hats, scarves, jewelry, and shoes), remove all the tags, pack them in a suitcase and deliver them to the photographer's studio the afternoon before the trip. They wanted to avoid customs declarations on the items since it was a nominal assortment of garments and a casual touristy photo shoot. Looking at my packed suitcase, I thought it did look exactly like a suitcase that would be packed for such a holiday trip and would therefore be unnecessary to declare. People who travel frequently to different countries eventually get a good sense about when and where they could get away with this kind of thing. Don't attempt this if it makes you uneasy or if you think it will add an unnecessary stress to your trip.

Different systems of electricity have to be taken into consideration for steaming, ironing, and hair dryers. You may need to purchase adaptors for such equipment.

## GETTING STARTED IN THE WORLD OF FASHION

Any exposure to the world of fashion contributes to your understanding of this career. College fashion study is an excellent start. This coursework provides a background in fashion design, marketing, clothing construction, fabric, and textiles. Some programs offer occasional courses in styling.

Workshops such as those I offer provide a background on the business of styling and an opportunity for hands-on practice with a model and with off-figure clothing.

Take basic photography classes if you can and expose yourself to photo shoots at any opportunity. Observe and learn the language of photography. Even looking at magazine stories is a way of educating yourself. Look at all the elements of the photo in addition to the fashion. As you have more exposure to photography and observe everything that goes on, you'll see aspects of photos that you didn't notice before.

### Interning and Learning

Interning with magazines, model agencies, ad agencies, fashion public relations, or any business related to fashion will provide valuable knowledge about this career. Fashion interns are sometimes included in the editorial listings of magazines. In this position you might do much of the less interesting detail work, but the occasional opportunity to attend a shoot would be invaluable.

Students in fashion or graphic design programs may be required to complete an internship. Instructors and guidance departments can be a great help with arranging them. If you're not a student, you'll have to make your own arrangements. You may be paid for your time or you can contribute your time for free, providing a benefit to the company taking you on.

An internship with a catalog can teach about the inside workings of photo shoot preparations. A student at FIDM in San Diego interned with Road Runner Sports catalog. There she coordinated the samples used for shoots, made copies of merchandise lists, and sometimes went to the shoots. She was gradually given more responsibilities and ended up with a position as a buyer there.

Another fashion student who had set her sights on London's culture had the courage to walk into Burberry's offices on her own. Through the course of a conversation with an executive there she was offered an internship that lasted three months. Then she was offered a position heading the visual department.

It's not usually so easy. Remember, all your life experience contributes to your ability as a stylist. Jobs help too. Working in a retail fashion store provides insight into the customer and how people shop for clothing, as well as knowledge of the workings of retail sales. Assisting catalog or store merchandisers, while not always glamorous, gives you an understanding of the numbers and other critical factors involved in buying decisions.

## Working on Runway Shows

A great deal of behind-the-scenes experience can be gained by volunteering to assist with fashion shows. The shows could be a student production, a benefit, or a commercial production. Organization of shows is overwhelmingly complex, and any chance you can get to see what goes on can help with runway and styling projects alike.

Fashion students at Mesa College in San Diego present an annual fashion show, "The Golden Scissors Awards." They do everything themselves, from designing the fashions, developing a theme, writing the script, promoting it, styling, and modeling. I volunteer to assist with this show for the thrill of seeing their work and enthusiasm.

Fashion shows are often presented as a fundraising event by nonprofit organizations. They may feature historical or designer fashions, or hand-sewn clothing. Sponsors of these events are always glad to have you volunteer as a "dresser," and you'll get to be involved first-hand. Separating and steaming the clothes for each model, dressing the models, getting them quickly in and out of their outfits, helping them with buttons, buckles, and bows are some show day tasks. You might find out about these opportunities in advance through a fashion-school career office, and any assistance behind the scenes should be welcomed.

Work with photography students or contacts in the industry to create fashion concepts and make them come to life together. You will learn from these projects and develop your personal portfolio. This creative habit should continue throughout your styling career. The next section will provide you with inspirations and information about testing.

## Creative Ideas for Testing

You are already a creative person if you're interested in fashion. You can stay current by being observant and keeping an eye on trends. By arranging test photo shoots throughout your career—with photographers, makeup artists, and models—you will continue to challenge yourself and enjoy these creative collaborations.

Test shoots are an opportunity to develop your own creativity, build a team, and create beautiful work for your portfolio. The results make a more attractive presentation than most catalog pages. If you include test shots in your portfolio, along with the editorial work and the catalog covers you've collaborated on, you can give clients a better picture of the full range of your styling abilities.

Allow for failures. Not all tests produce great portfolio pieces. But tests that don't work as planned teach you about shoots and styling—and at least the less-than-perfect project wasn't done for a client.

These shoots don't need to involve sourcing designer fashions. The reps wouldn't be very interested in lending you items for a project that won't be printed in media. Improvise from your own collection, borrow from friends, or find a start-up designer who will trade use of fashions for photos. Models' own clothing mixed with a few new pieces can provide an inspired look.

A color theme, geographical influence, or historical context can pull the shoot together as much as the fashions themselves. I recently participated in a group project inspired by a classic car. The photographer, Nick Nacca, had set up his studio for automotive photography and had access to a pale yellow 1969 Buick Electra. He, makeup artist Claire Young, and I developed an authentically historical fashion shoot based on the era of the car. Claire purchased the Afro wigs and I found most of the fashions at thrift stores. While our two models hadn't been around in 1969, they enjoyed recreating the era.

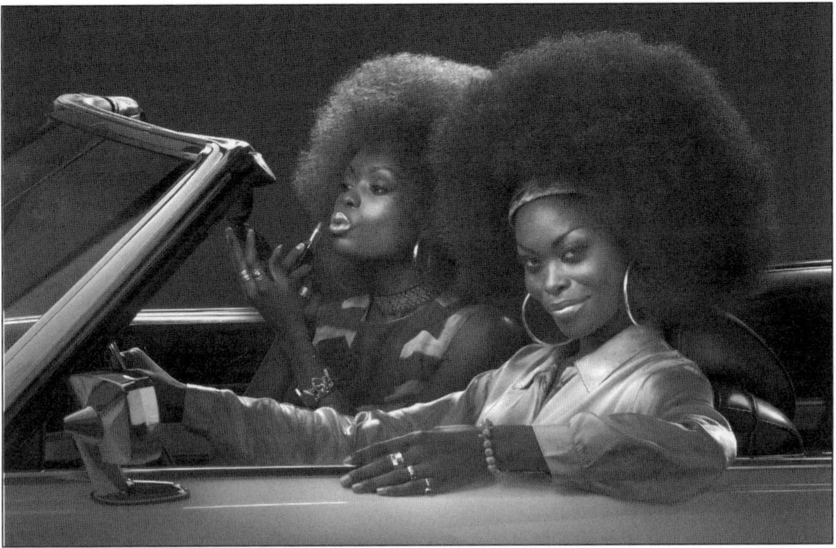

Back to 1969. *Photographer:* Nick Nacca. *Styling:* Susan Linnet Cox. *Hair and makeup:* Claire Young. © Nick Nacca

## Trend Watching

Looking at trends and directions is an ongoing process, as fashion is ever changing. In addition to your own observations, be awake and aware when viewing all media from magazines to music videos. Notice what's current and get ideas for new combinations.

Research into trends is a significant industry. One example is Pantone's color research. Pantone is a company that provides color standards and technology for consistent communication of color for many industries, including fabric standards for fashion. The company is well known for its annual color predictions, developed by studying social trends and other influences. The Web site *www.pantone.com* provides more background.

As the world becomes more unified in style terms, inspirations are everywhere. Keep sketchbooks and take notes when you travel. Visiting museums can be inspiring too. Contemporary art, classical paintings, photography exhibits, and even anthropology will offer ideas to the creative person.

An understanding of styles, fashion history, and geographical influences is critical to your performance as a fashion editor or stylist. "Traveling and seeing the world allows you to become grounded with reality, all the while experiencing fashion from those who have not the slightest idea that they inspire us all," says New York fashion stylist Albert Mendonça.

## RELATED CAREERS IN FASHION

Along with editing and styling, there are many other careers in fashion. Working with designers, researching fabrics, marketing the fashions, and representing lines are some of the countless less visible aspects of fashion. Styling designers' runway shows and dressing celebrities are among the more high-profile careers.

### Runway Shows

Runway fashion shows are presented by department stores, designer lines, and also as community benefits. With the complexity of runway shows and their importance to the world of fashion, there is a variety of work to do. Organization is probably the most important task in producing a runway show.

Before the show there are time-consuming tasks such as writing the script, choosing music, designing the stage, booking models and makeup artists, and planning the outfits. During the show, the stylist is literally behind the scenes. You can only imagine what it's like out front. But you don't have time to think, what with supervising the details of each ensemble and sending the models out on time.

My former intern Paula Tabalipa found a job for Saks Fifth Avenue as a fashion director. Her responsibilities were both presenting runway shows and creating store displays. Now she works freelance to manage Saks's fashion shows. For a single show she handled everything from pulling thousands of dollars worth of merchandise, the choreography (how and where the models walk), runway lighting, hiring a DJ, and selecting the music. This in addition to dressing thirty-two teenaged models in three changes each. She found volunteers from fashion schools to assist her on show day.

### Visual Merchandising and Styling Celebrities

Even without responsibility for runway shows, visual merchandising in retail stores is a significant fashion-related career. Many chain stores have uniform standards for presentations, merchandise, and props, but there is always creativity involved. Window and in-store presentations incorporate a combination of dressing mannequins; folding, stacking, and hanging apparel; and decorating with props—very much like styling. Upscale stores hire creative designers like Paula to create eye-catching and inventive window designs, especially for the competitive holiday season. Their concepts are inspired by merchandise, props, and themes.

As in much of styling, celebrity styling is a job that many just fall into. Being at the right place at the right time, with the right kind of style, can open a door.

Wardrobe stylist Veronica Guzman tells this story: "One celebrity stylist I met in Los Angeles told me she was friends with a man that happened to manage a singer. He was in a bind and needed a stylist for his client's shoot at the last minute. He always liked her personal style so he asked her if she would be able to help him out. From that one job she ended up styling everything for them, including photo shoots, movies, and tours."

This field can range from sourcing fashions for events to styling photo shoots to advising on everyday dressing.

## SPECIALTY KIT LIST

This list includes some specific items you will need for styling apparel in addition to the basic kit list described in chapter 13.

| ITEM | DESCRIPTION, USE |
|---|---|
| *For Wardrobe Styling* | |
| ❑ Clothespins, plastic | For adjusting clothing; be sure not to use wood |
| ❑ Safety pins, assorted sizes | For more precise adjustments |
| ❑ Clamps | For heavy-duty adjustments, like belts |
| ❑ Generic double-sided tape | For emergency hems; find a sturdy brand |
| ❑ Stitch Witchery | Iron-on hem-repair tape |
| ❑ Simple jewelry | A selection of stud or tiny hoop earrings, simple bracelets |
| ❑ Scarf | Over model's head, protects makeup during wardrobe changes |
| ❑ Nail polish remover | Disposable packets, in case models come with colored polish |
| ❑ Nude seamless bra, underwear | In case model doesn't bring her own (wash between shoots) |
| ❑ Push up enhancers | Lifts inserted into bra for creating cleavage in models |
| ❑ Topstick | Double-sided tape for keeping strapless garments in place |
| ❑ Pantyhose | Several neutral colors |

❑ Shoehorn — For putting on tight shoes

❑ Men's T-shirt — Layer under shirts; white

❑ Anti-static spray — In case of clinging clothes

❑ Sunscreen — For crew, doubles as moisturizer for models' elbows or knees

❑ Umbrella — To keep models and photographer cool and out of sun

*For Prepping Fine Garments*

❑ Iron, ironing board — Use your own clean steam iron

❑ Ham — Rounded cushion for ironing curved areas

❑ Steamer — Use on fabrics that can withstand moisture

❑ Rolling rack — For organizing prepped garments

❑ Plastic swivel hangers — Hanging garments carefully; also skirt/pant hangers

*For Makeup or Touch-ups*

❑ Foundation powder — MAC Studio Fix used wet or dry; several common skin tones

❑ Lipstick and liner — Three or four basic colors

❑ Makeup sponges — Absorbing shine or applying foundation

❑ Q-tips — Touching up makeup mistakes

❑ Makeup remover — For goofs or for models to clean up after the shoot

❑ Nail file — Touch up unmanicured nails, cuticles

❑ Tissues — Small pocket pack

❑ Hairbrush — For changing hairstyles (clean between shoots)

❑ Hairspray — For smoothing and taming hair

❑ Hair gel — For styling men's hair, or short styles

❑ Ponytail holders — Assorted neutral colors

❑ Bobby pins — Brown and decorative styles

❑ Dental floss — For models' teeth

❑ Straws, bendable — Protect models' lipstick when drinking

❑ Mirror — Small compact style for models to use

❑ Children's barrettes — Plus other decorations for children's hair

Be *sure* you also have the following items from the basic kit:

| ITEM | DESCRIPTION, USE |
| --- | --- |
| ❑ Scissors, small and sharp | For clipping threads and removing labels; use only on fabric |
| ❑ Scissors, bigger | For cutting everything but fabric |
| ❑ Spray bottle of water | Spray wrinkles out of clothing on location |
| ❑ Wrinkle release product | Water works as well, but this product may be better |
| ❑ Lint roller and refills | For removing lint from fabric |
| ❑ Sewing kit | For mending; pick up kits at hotels |

## Styling Supply Sites

Browse these Web sites to find unique and specific items for fashion styling. Here are a few: *http://wardrobesupplies.com*, for Topstick and many other wardrobe supplies; *www.camerareadycosmetics.com*, for professional makeup palettes.

Fashion is the exciting world that many people imagine when they think about styling. While this area provides a great deal of the styling projects available, it is only one part of what styling is. Stylists frequently combine fashion with other specialties, depending on the projects available in their geographic areas. A knowledge of on-figure fashion styling, combined with off-figure and prop styling, can greatly expand your opportunities.

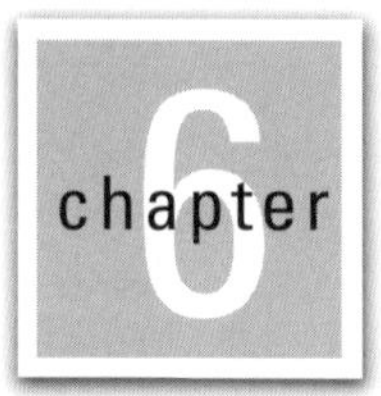



# Wardrobe Styling

**T**HE DIFFERENCE BETWEEN WARDROBE STYLING AND FASHION styling is subtle and confusing. As we saw in the previous chapter, fashion styling is done for magazine features about the latest fashion trends, or for selling clothing in a catalog. Wardrobe styling is not "about the clothes." The photo is focused on something else; the clothes are essentially props.

## LIFESTYLE PHOTOGRAPHY

A lifestyle shot depicts real-life situations and people for an advertisement or for stock photography. A scenario that tells a story is being created. Or the talent may be there to enhance a lifestyle concept for a specific company or brand. For lifestyle photography, the stylist is dressing the talent in generic items so as not to distract from the implied activity. In addition to acquiring the right clothing items and dressing the talent, the stylist may be asked to style product items, provide related props, and decorate the entire set. In advertising photography, the talent may be interacting with a product such as a cleaning product, car, or food. The wardrobe is generic so as not to distract from the featured product.

The same principles apply to both television and print wardrobe choices. Look at what people in TV commercials are wearing. It's fairly predictable.

You often see the usual crew neck sweater over a collared shirt in a small plaid on men. For a detergent ad, you see a housewife wearing a denim shirt with rolled sleeves over a tank top and khaki Capri pants. In ads featuring a group of people, you see each person dressed in different colors, or all of the people dressed in shades of the same color. You begin to notice all the details you are meant not to notice. You'll also see the same type of wardrobe styling in print ads.

## Stock Photography

You may be familiar with stock photography and not even know it. Stock is defined as images that have not been shot for a specific client, but rather are sold to clients for a licensing fee. Photographers may create specific shoots on spec for a stock agency, or may select outtakes or extras from their commercial or editorial projects. These photographs are available to be licensed again and again because the copyright almost always belongs to the photographer. Sometimes an agreement is made with a client to own the rights to the image. The photographer negotiates this at the beginning of a job.

Stock photos are used in cases when it's not practical to assign a photographer and set up a shoot. For either a flat fee (royalty-free) or a fee based upon usage and exclusiveness (rights-managed), the client uses an existing image. Popular stock photos depict families, couples, business people, and other everyday scenarios, as well as photos that do not include people. The images must be model-released if people are recognizable (especially when faces are shown), whether they are professional talent or the photographer's friends and family.

You might have the occasional opportunity to style the people in a stock shoot. The principles of generic wardrobe styling are similar to those used in commercial projects depicting lifestyle.

## EDITORIAL WARDROBE STYLING

In the last chapter we looked at fashion features in magazines, where fashion editors pull clothes from designers' collections and then assemble inspiring photo spreads showing models in the latest or upcoming fashions. However, fashion magazines use images of models for editorial features, like health and fitness. Many other types of magazines on the market do this as well. These images of people usually provide lifestyle accompaniments to editorial stories.

One editorial shoot for which I did wardrobe styling was for a specialty women's magazine, *All Woman*. The feature was a food story—a couple

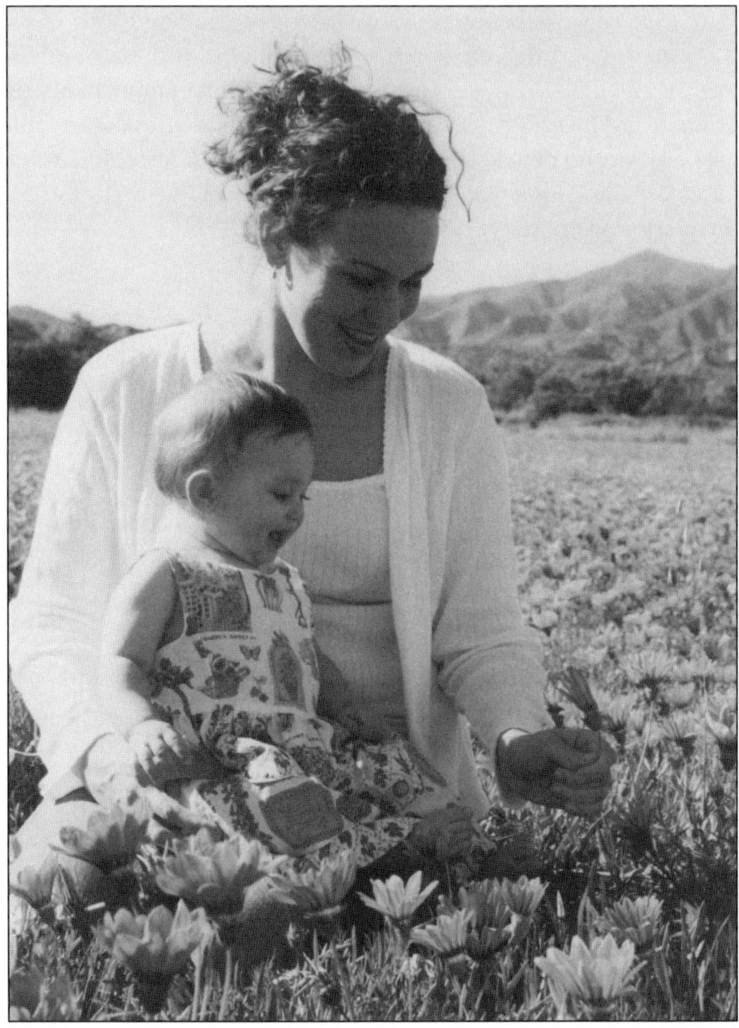

Generic wardrobe choices enhance a stock photograph. *Photographer:* Jenessa Nye. Courtesy of Mistral Images. © Jenessa Nye

entertaining friends at a backyard barbecue. The magazine hired a food stylist and a prop stylist to handle the food presentations, and I was responsible for wardrobe. The homeowners had invited their daughter's family and several neighbors to participate. They were given a list of suggested clothing to bring with them.

The magazine had also sourced wardrobe from Lands' End and L.L. Bean catalogs. Huge boxes arrived at the location filled with khaki pants, chambray shirts, and casual knits. My intern and I quickly sorted them by size and category, so that when the guests came I could make decisions about their own wardrobe and fill in with pieces from the collections. Each person's wardrobe had to be approved by the art director before the guests could get dressed. The director was being pulled in many directions at the same time, so this was a hectic and frantic time. The makeup artist had to borrow the guests for makeup before they got dressed; this gave us just enough time to steam the clothing.

At last they were all dressed in complementary hues and generic styles. That was when the homeowner became self-conscious about her wardrobe, and we started over with her. The shoot became pleasurable once the guests were dressed and needed only occasional adjustments to look good. After the shoot we sorted clothes, repacked the boxes, and looked forward to seeing the images in print a few months later.

For another editorial project, I was contacted by *Self* magazine to style soccer players for a feature about the WUSA women's professional soccer league. I had been following the creation of the league, so I was happy to have a chance to style the key players. Athletic companies were sponsoring most of the players, and it was critical to dress them in only those labels. Again, the magazine editors had put in requests for the garments. This time they were shipped to my home, and I brought them to the field where we were shooting.

Although the final images were small and the clothing could barely be seen, I enjoyed the project. It's a shame for women's sports that the league has been disbanded.

## FILM AND VIDEO

The world of wardrobe styling for television and film is another large area of opportunity. The focus of my own career has been on print photography—there's plenty of work there—so when my intern, Veronica Guzman, had the opportunity to work on a Los Angeles film production, I pumped her for information.

She described her duties as a wardrobe assistant, working mostly in the production trailer prepping the clothing in the familiar way, and documenting the actors' wardrobe for continuity. She photographed them in costume with a Polaroid camera, labeled the images, and posted them in the trailer.

This is just a small hint of the complexities of styling for film. It is a separate field, with its own workshops and classes. Here is a bit more information Veronica shared about her early wardrobe projects:

*In television or film, when you're shopping for wardrobe you have to keep in mind that you will be needing "doubles" or in some cases "triples." For example, say the principal actor was in a fight scene. You would need one outfit for the actor, another outfit for the lighting stand-in, and a third outfit for the stunt double. If you were in a situation where you only had "doubles," you would put your stand-in in an outfit that resembled the one of your principal actor. Even if the movie didn't have a stunt double, you would still need at least a "double" in case something happened to your principal actor's clothing.*

Wardrobe specialist Pippi Robben agrees that multiple wardrobe items are necessary for work in film and video. She even thinks in terms of four of each item, which can necessitate shopping for pretty generic items. Some may have to go to the laundry at the end of the shoot day, some actors may take garments home, and still others mysteriously disappear. Even jewelry items should have duplicates. If the wardrobe stylist spends time away from the production searching for a matching necklace, that's not productive use of time and it costs more in the long run.

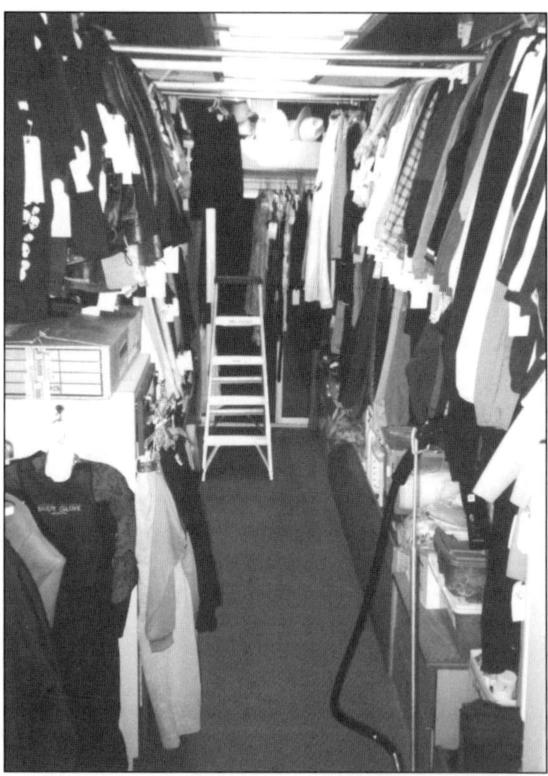

Inside a wardrobe trailer at a video production. © Veronica Guzman

Fitting is not as crucial in print photography as it is in film. If a garment does not fit a model you can place clips where they won't be seen. Veronica says, "In film, you can't hide clips because the actors are moving around. The clothing has to fit them correctly so that they can concentrate on their lines and not be distracted by thoughts of losing a skirt in a gust of wind."

## ACQUIRING WARDROBE AND ACCESSORIES

As a photography wardrobe stylist, a major part of your responsibility is to bring plenty of clothing options to the shoot. Early in the project, you should create a list of items needed for the talent. You may have some items on hand but need to purchase others.

The wardrobe choices will have to be approved by the art director and the photographer. They often defer to your expert opinion but they have the last word. The photographer will know what items work best on camera and may already have a vision of the shot. If possible, spend a few early moments at the shoot reviewing wardrobe options and suggest combinations that you think are the best. Especially tricky is combining the garments that different people will wear in the same image. Tops and bottoms that contrast and complement each other, color variety, and related styles must be selected from what is available. Sometimes it's hard to nab the art director at the crucial moment since there are other things going on at the same time.

### Shopping

This is really one of the most gratifying aspects of photo styling. Sometimes it hits you: you can't believe this is your job! But it's hard work when the easiest item on your list can't be found. You have to be focused, fast, and tireless. (Chapter 4 includes useful information on shopping for clothing items.)

To save time and ease the visual stimulation of walking into a store, I carry a list of the exact items I'm searching for. I look for color and category. "Sweater, ivory; men's denim shirt; dress slacks, charcoal," I chant to myself. In the outlet and discount stores—I seem to spend a lot of time there—I'm more likely to walk along the racks scanning for color, category, and fabric. In these stores, merchandise is sometimes hung on the wrong rack, or marked with the wrong size.

This shopping trip is going to be on your own credit card unless you negotiate money up front for wardrobe shopping. It's a good idea to at least arrange an estimated amount for expenses in advance, especially with new clients. You can make a deposit in your business account and know that you will be able to pay the credit-card bill when it comes. You'll apply the credit balance to your invoice when you have completed returns. Since there will be multiple choices for each person, much of the clothing will not be worn and can be returned after the shoot. Though many items will probably be returned, you are covered in case they are all kept or some unforeseen circumstance occurs. It's tricky to estimate how much the shopping will cost but with experience and prior projects to refer to, it will become more automatic.

While you'll be bringing selections to the shoot, you can also present model agents with requests for clothing the models could bring. I have found that models respond well to these requests and bring lots of good items from their own closets. These wardrobe items will definitely need to be prepped, because they're going to arrive stuffed in a suitcase or piled on wire hangers. Color guidelines should be presented for the talent. Generally the best choices are in bright or pastel solids. White and black clothing do not photograph well, especially when worn together. These colors also contrast too much with other elements in the scene. Large prints are usually not good, but on occasion they might work as an accent. While small stripes or prints can be effective, it's safer to go with solid colors.

At the time of the September 11 tragedy, I was involved in an intense wardrobe project, styling the participants in "Chairdancing," a series of exercise videos for people who have limited ability to exercise. The creator of the program was fond of bright colors like purple and pink, and the style was unintentionally developing a retro, 1970s exercise look. I found myself looking for slouch socks, headbands, and colorful shoelaces. I had developed a color theme for each of the three videos—jewel tones for one, bright warm colors for another, and softer colors for the yoga video. It became a mathematical problem, charting out the wardrobe items and then converting the chart into a shopping list with items, colors, and many sizes.

Especially challenging was the need to view the three groups of people from various camera angles, to make sure that there weren't participants wearing matching colors from each diagonal view. This caused endless revisions to my list.

My shopping skills became extremely focused at this time and the list was specific. I was looking for a bright blue plus-size T-shirt, orange extra-large men's tank shirt, magenta stretch Capri pants, yellow ponytail holder. I walked into stores and saw, like radar, only those colors.

What surprised me most about this project during the sad, dark days of September 11, was that I started to really enjoy this search for colors. I hung them on the rolling rack at my house and looked at the bright color combinations. I think that wardrobe styling project really helped me get through that time.

## Renting Costumes

Styling an ad shoot for WD-40, I had to do the following: cast an actor to play a "regular guy," find a mechanic's jumpsuit, and acquire an array of auto parts on loan from three garages. These had to be labeled and returned after the shoot. I found a source, Western Costume in Los Angeles, to rent the jumpsuit. Catering primarily to the world of movies, it also rents to professional photo stylists.

What a wonderland of costumes! There were three levels of racks stretching up to the ceiling of a warehouse. There were endless rows of choir robes, medieval dresses, military uniforms. Striped prison uniforms were hung outside on a fence after being spattered with mud. I saw a huge room of hats, and another of shoes. Needless to say, I had several choices of mechanic's jumpsuits.

Naturally, there are costume warehouses in Los Angeles, but what about in other cities? Movies are filmed everywhere now. Local theaters may rent their costumes to you. In addition, rental costume shops or uniform companies are available in most areas. You can look in the phone book or online for resources.

## Making and Sewing the Wardrobe

If you have experience with clothing construction, you may have an opportunity to use it in wardrobe styling. Unique garments might be requested—I once sewed a *Cirque de Soleil*–type clown outfit for a pharmaceutical executive who made a dramatic appearance at a conference on a scooter. Another time I constructed some Santa Claus pants out of a red velvet thrift-store dress for a pair of legs coming out of a chimney. I constructed the legs with just enough room at the top to fit into a real fireplace, and sewed Santa's bag of gifts. I also had to find a fresh cut Christmas tree in August and decorate the set!

Other sewing projects may include altering a found garment to make it work, changing buttons, or shortening a hem. If you don't sew, you may need to hire a seamstress on occasion.

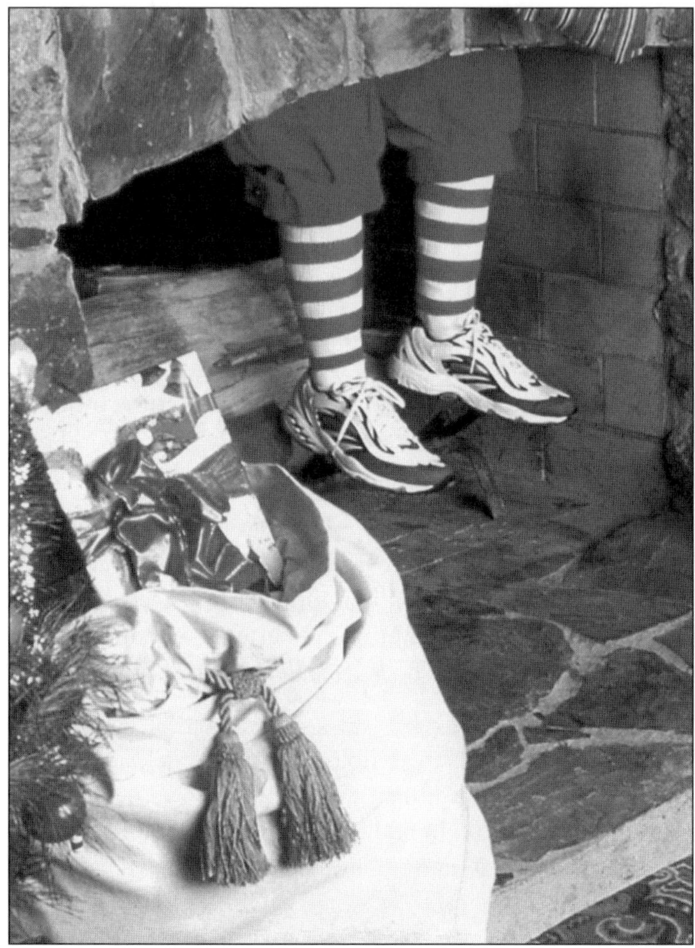

Propping for a holiday cover. *Photographer:* Tim Mantoani; *Prop construction, wardrobe, and styling:* Susan Linnet Cox. © Tim Mantoani

## Generic Wardrobe List

The suggestions below will help you plan the most basic wardrobe selections:

*Generic Items for Women, Men, and Children:*

- Jeans
- Khaki slacks, shorts, Capris, skirts
- Polo shirts, short and long sleeved
- Pullover and cardigan sweaters
- Collared shirts and blouses in light stripes or small plaids
- Generic white sneakers

*Women:*

- Dressy sundresses
- Strappy sandals
- Natural stockings

*Men:*

- Dark suits
- Dark dress shoes
- White T-shirts

*Accessories and Props:*

- Generic jewelry items (small earrings, studs, and little loops; simple necklaces; wedding bands)
- Watches (don't need to be working)
- Purses
- Sunglasses
- Hats (straw hats, baseball caps)
- Scarves
- Props for people to carry (shopping bags, cut flowers, French baguette)

## DRESSING THE MODELS

There will be some intense and dramatic moments when models are made up and needed on set. You may need to keep track of labels, hangers, and hang tags in the pandemonium. Then suddenly they are dressed and walk in front of the camera and you can take a breath before you go in to make adjustments.

When you style wardrobe for any of the scenarios described above, you are striving for neatness. Let the photographer have a look at the dressed talent before you step in. You'll have a chance to clip and pin garments while the shot is being set up and the lighting is improved.

There will be times when the talent you are working with are not professional models. Perhaps "real people" are cast for the shoot because the client prefers a variety of looks that model agencies may not have. When an older, overweight, or unique-looking person is needed, the results will be better from agencies representing actors rather than models. Actors have experience with dressing and being in front of the camera, though they're less accustomed to having their clothes pinched and adjusted.

Novice talent will be quite unfamiliar with the whole process. They will all need a briefing about the basics of dressing, like carefully putting the clothes over their heads, and not tucking in shirts or putting on their own shoes. They're likely to immediately fold their arms, wrinkling the front of shirts and the sleeves. They'll want to sit down, causing folds in skirts or pants. Lots of gentle reminders will help them stay camera-ready.

## Working with Professionals

Most models are very nice, intelligent people with full and interesting lives. During the time you spend together, you'll get to know them well. When they arrive at the shoot, greet each of them and introduce yourself: you are the main contact for the talent. (Read chapter 14 on working together from the model's viewpoint.)

Models who are helpful and considerate are natural favorites. When they bring the clothing back to you on hangers and right-side-out, your job is easier. In turn, they will appreciate your kindness and compassion. Modeling is actually hard work: holding awkward poses or standing up for a long time without moving are harder tasks than you'd imagine. On set, as you make adjustments, you'll be working very closely with the models; try to give them a word of warning before touching them, especially when reaching up under a skirt, or clipping a thread on a man's fly.

# ROLE OF AN ASSISTANT

With complex projects involving dressing a large number of people, having an assistant can be easily justified. The assistant can help organize wardrobe items, steam them, and get the talent into clothes at the right time. Assisting is an excellent way to learn about styling and provides an opportunity to be at a photo shoot soaking up information. However, it is hard work and your focus at the shoot is to support the stylist you're assisting.

Arrive at the shoot early and help the stylist carry wardrobe and props. After greeting the photographer, plug in the steamer so it's warmed up and ready. Always ask the photographer's assistant which electrical outlet is best to use. There will most likely be a lot of prep work to do. Later you may be asked to go out for coffee or last-minute props, which you'll do happily. Your primary duty is to make the stylist look good, whatever it takes. Be attentive and ready to step in to do what the stylist requests. You're probably going to be busy behind the scenes while the stylist watches the shot. Don't expect to sit down all day.

Other ways to show your professionalism are by not handing out your card or becoming overly friendly with any of the crew. You must not express your thoughts about the shots or make suggestions to the model on set. (I have to keep my opinions to myself sometimes, even at this point in my career.)

Samples from the projects you assist on will be primarily for your own reference, looking back on the shoot. If you ever do include them in your portfolio, you must be very clear that you were the assistant on the shoot and not the stylist.

If you perform well as an assistant stylist and have the opportunity to work with that stylist again, you can build a beneficial relationship, receive the stylist's guidance, and gradually build your own kit and career.

Having stumbled into her role as a wardrobe assistant in film and video happily but unexpectedly, Veronica Guzman has the following advice for assistants in this area:

> *In my experience, it pays to be inquisitive. If you're really interested in something, show it by asking the right questions. Don't think that just because you get in the door and you keep saying you're enjoying the experience, you will be called on for another job in the future. If you show that you want to learn and are willing to put in the hard work, then they will want to help you in the industry. When I worked on my first television show as a production assistant, I asked a lot of questions, and it was obvious that the line of work intrigued me. On the last day of shooting, the costume supervisor told me she could see that I "wanted it" and that she would help me if I was serious about pursuing this career. She said she would keep me in mind for future jobs. About a month later, she called me to work as her assistant.*

## KITS FOR WARDROBE SHOOTS

Kits for wardrobe shoots are pretty much the same whether you are styling with fashions or generic wardrobe. Have envelopes handy for saving hangtags cut from garments. Be sure to have a scarf to cover the models' heads when they dress, as they may not be experienced with protecting their makeup. (See the previous chapter, Fashion Styling, for special kit items.)

If you are doing wardrobe instead of fashion styling, you are even more likely to be asked to do minimal makeup. Often, without the focus on beauty, a makeup artist won't be budgeted into the project. The talent will be asked to come to the shoot "hair and makeup ready." Providing they do it well, your job will be doing touch-ups and controlling shiny faces and stray hair.

You can see that wardrobe styling can take various forms—from neutral, almost unnoticeable clothes to historical or unique characterizations. All of it is fun and challenging, especially when combined with other types of styling, as it usually is. You will never be bored.

# Styling Off-Figure

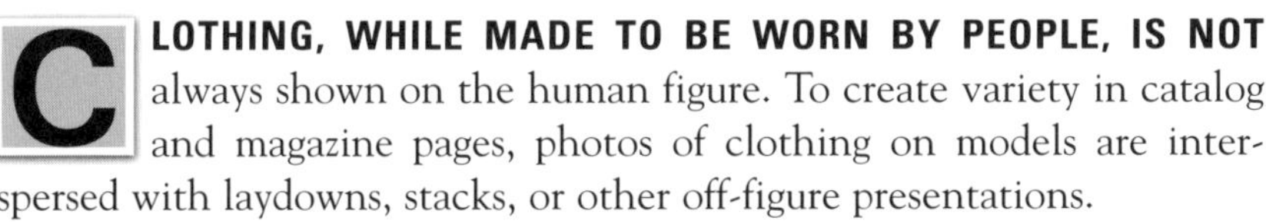

**C**LOTHING, WHILE MADE TO BE WORN BY PEOPLE, IS NOT always shown on the human figure. To create variety in catalog and magazine pages, photos of clothing on models are interspersed with laydowns, stacks, or other off-figure presentations.

In this chapter, we will focus on garments and leave the occasional throw, tablecloth, or carefully rippled napkin for other styling chapters, like product styling and room sets.

## WHY USE OFF-FIGURE STYLING?

While we tend to associate fashion with models, much of it is photographed off the figure. Off-figure photos show color choices, fabric, and features, while the model shots create lifestyle and mood, and show how the clothes fit. Some features of garments may be shown better when off-figure. Button plackets, cuffs, pockets, and side slits can be positioned, brought to the front, or lifted. This is done in a precise and exacting way that wouldn't work on a model. Features can be specially lighted for emphasis in studio shots; a light or reflector can be directed inside the smallest fold.

Catalogs that sell apparel usually mix the presentations. Combined presentations make the catalogs effective and more interesting. Eye flow is important to catalog design, because the reader is visually encouraged to keep looking at the page, stop at interesting features, and then turn the page for more.

By the time the shoot is booked and the stylist hired, the catalog has already been roughly designed. There are probably sketches in place for the off-figure clothing. The art director may or may not know exactly how these outlined garments will be set up in the studio.

Looking at fashion magazines, you may have noticed off-figure features. These styled items are used for comparing designer fashions with more affordable options, mix-and-match travel wardrobes, lingerie, swimsuits, accessorizing, or a sampling of new products. The clothes and accessories aren't always shown in scale; a bracelet may be as large as a blouse. But they are all styled using off-figure techniques.

## Fabric Textures

When we shop in a store, we touch the fabric of clothes to make buying decisions. Notice, the next time you browse in a department store, how often you reach out and touch the clothing on racks. Something that feels particularly soft or textured can make you stop for a closer look. Fabric stores are a particularly sensual experience; many times I have walked along the rows feeling every bolt of fabric on display.

This is a disadvantage for catalogs. Their only opportunity to give customers the fabric experience is through photographs. The more touchable the clothing looks, the better. The customer wants to know how it feels to wear this item, how it hangs on the body, and what it will be like when washed.

Studio photographers are experienced with the challenges of lighting garments to enhance the texture. At the same time, they are working for continuity in lighting various items. The light source should be similar throughout the catalog, with a strong light coming from one side and a softer light coming from the other side to fill in some of the deeper folds while still preserving a three-dimensional effect. As you're styling the garment, the photographer and assistant are refining the lighting. Your styling will show them some areas that need emphasis, and thus the shot evolves.

## Showing Colors

In addition to creating a tactile experience for the customer, catalogs need to show all the color choices, known as "colorways" by merchandisers. While the model looks lovely in the blue sweater, the customer may prefer the black or red sweater for herself. Merchandisers have studied the color preferences of customers and have ordered quantities of the fashions based on those preferences. The color expected to sell the best is generally the "star" or feature. This may be the one shown on figure or at the top of the stack. The on-figure color is rarely featured again in the stack. Other colors may appear in relative importance, or this may be an aesthetic decision for the stylist. Be sure to clarify these priorities before styling a stack.

When merchandisers elect to feature a black garment, photographers are often frustrated. The difficulty of showing detail in dark fabric is further complicated by printing. Usually dark colors run together a bit even in the best quality printing. And each type of fabric absorbs light differently. A black satin blouse, with its reflective shine, will need completely different lighting than a black knit top which seems to soak up light. Another unpopular choice is placing black and white next to each other. Since their lighting requirements are so different, it is almost impossible for a photographer to capture detail when they're side by side. A better plan is to place a transitional color between them.

Sometimes the photographer will shoot different exposures of the same grouping and then blend the images in the computer.

## CLOTHING CONSTRUCTION

Although a sewing background is not a requirement for styling, it can be helpful to understand how clothing is constructed. You would know that stitched seams can pucker slightly or hemming can stretch a knit. Most fashion students have studied the basic features of clothing construction and will know how they affect the garment. This can help in styling.

A set-in sleeve is shaped like the human shoulder and upper arm, and has a limited range of motion. A raglan sleeve has a seam going diagonally from the underarm to the neckline and a less defined shoulder. A third style, the dolman sleeve, has ample fabric under the arm, like a wing, which could make it challenging to show the fabric and could be unattractive. Shoulder seams generally are placed a bit in front of the shoulder ridge.

Pants are constructed with more room in the rear than in the front. The pattern is designed to be wider and longer in the back; the place where the crotch and inner leg seams meet is actually more toward the front, resulting in more back fabric. When you're styling pants, you need to tuck away and conceal this extra fabric to see two separate legs. And the back of the waistband is higher than the front. This must be evened out so you don't see a large expanse inside the pants.

Just as with styling on figure, the clothing needs to be prepped and organized. Concentrate on steaming or ironing the portion that will be shown, and get rid of side creases so the item can be shown full and rounded. Stage the merchandise for the shots that follow so you can stay ahead.

## SETTING UP THE PHOTOGRAPH

Techniques used for shooting off-figure styling vary depending on how they are set up in the studio or location.

For stacks or single folded items, the tabletop is easiest for the whole crew to work on. The camera is generally directed downward at the scene from about three-quarters of a right angle starting from eye-level.

When a full outfit is being shown, the photographer may need distance to fit it into the camera's field of view. A head-to-toe presentation might work as a floor setup if the camera can be looking straight down from many feet above it. This actually can be achieved in a studio with a ladder or an upper loft-style level. Products may be styled on a low table or a background surface. Awkward to work on, such a surface does provide a flat area that will fit in the camera's view. This setup may be used to shoot down on an array of folded items and other laydowns, or a lifelike human figure.

### Avoid the Flattening Effect

Gravity is the deciding factor in many off-figure presentations and something you will constantly be aware of. When garments are placed flat and shot from above, they need to be filled and shaped to avoid gravity's flattening effect. As you hang garments on a wall, gravity is an advantage, but you'll need to use techniques to counteract it when bending an arm or lifting a skirt hem.

For the most part, with all types of off-figure styling, you can let the garment and fabric direct you. Before you try to control it, see where it wants to go and what it wants to do. Let the clothing take the lead and work with it. Sometimes the gentlest lift or tug can create the most natural effect. And there are times when you realize you're overworking it. Start over instead of struggling.

### Shooting Products on Location

Off-figure clothing may be shot out of doors for a more interesting background. As with shooting models on location, challenges consist of wind and changing light.

Be sure to have all your supplies with you. If a stack is placed on a bench or on steps, you need to be able to clean them first. For a hanging presentation there are questions: what to hang the item from (perhaps a tree branch or C-stand), and how to attach the monofilament, which helps keep the clothing in place, to the ground. To make visual sense, the clothes should probably be on a hanger—it helps explain why they are there in a natural setting. And the background naturally is a critical element in positioning the shot.

## STACKS

The designers of the J.Crew catalog are masters at utilizing stacks. When I think of the catalog, a stack of men's dress shirts or women's wool sweaters comes to mind. They are so big they fill the page. There's white space around the presentation and almost no copy describing the merchandise. Why use words when the button placket or neckline is so large you can see every thread?

The natural look of such a stack fools the public. It looks like someone came and plopped them there for the photographer, implying how nice they'll look in your closet. Of course, the stylist was very exacting in creating the stack, placing thicker stuffing in the bottom items so they maintain the same thickness when the top ones weigh them down. The sides are neat; there is no sleeve hanging out unless it's the top one with a sleeve casually brought up to show the cuff. There's a gentle ripple on some items, and the shadows help show the fabric.

But even when a stack is not a star with its own page, it may be needed to show color options. Perhaps it's partly concealed on one side by the fashion photo. It may be placed in an environment to create a story about the merchandise, on a chair or table. Some favorite shots of mine were styled for Road Runner Sports, using a locker-room setup in a studio. We had a wall of lockers and shot some stacks in the front of open lockers and on a bench that was built from a wood shelf.

### Techniques for Stacks

When styling a stack of shirts or sweaters, begin by laying each one face down with a sheet of batting cut to the width of a folded shirt. Fold the sides inward and then make another fold in half (see illustration on page 112). Each shirt in the stack should have the same dimensions. If the shirts are heavy, add more thickness in the lower ones to compensate for the weight of the stack. The top shirt may have a sleeve coming out, as shown in the illustration.

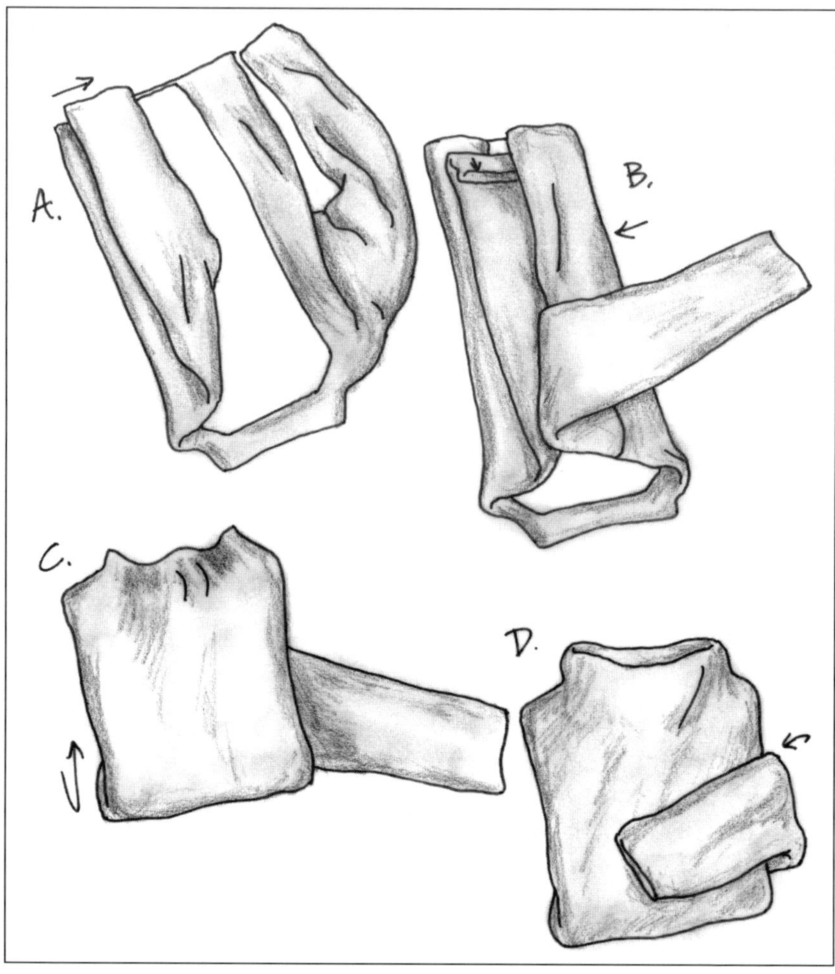

Folding a sweater (the same technique is used for items in stacks without sleeves showing): (A) Lay garment face down, place batting the width of the stack, and fold sides in. (B) Fold under extra sleeve length. If a sleeve will show on top, leave it out. (C) Fold top half of garment back. (D) Raise back of neckline and fill opening with some batting. Position sleeve over garment, tuck in wide edges, and soften with some batting. © Susan Linnet Cox

Your stack may be neat and straight or casually staggered, but the top item will most likely need to be filled and lifted a little at the back so the neckline doesn't settle backward. You might use cardboard or another handy material to lift it. Some studios have bricks covered with white tape for this purpose. Look at the stack from the camera view, checking for rough edges, and clean those up. It will take more precision than you might expect to get the outlines perfect.

The basics of styling a stack of shirts can be used for styling other items. A stack of shorts might include some items turned so the waistband shows. Demonstrate as many details as possible while still presenting an attractive stack.

## HANGERS

A row of clothing items on hangers can make a nice catalog presentation to break up the routine of fashion and stacks. It's appropriate for tailored clothing and blazers. Propping with the right hangers is critical; they can be traditional wood, something modern, or even everyday wire hangers for a funky look. I've used some of the antique wooden hangers I collect for these presentations.

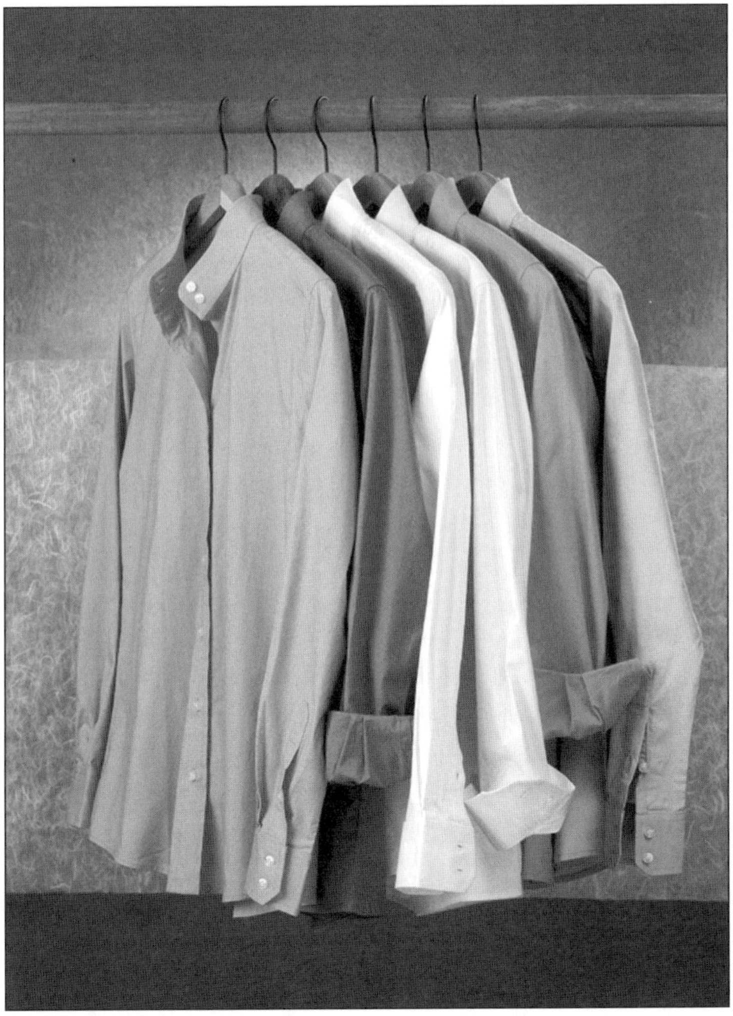

Blouses styled on hangers. **Photographer:** Mike Smith. **Styling:** Susan Linnet Cox. **Client:** Mary's Tack and Feed. © Smith Studios

The shot on the previous page I styled for an equestrian catalog. It includes six colors of riding blouses while showing the crisp fabric, collars, and cuff styling. Tissue was rolled around my own arm to shape the sleeves, monofilament was used to position some of the hems, and the hangers were carefully held in place with tape at the back of the rod. The photo took about an hour to style.

Another presentation consists of a clothesline and clothespins, usually incorporating a sunny day, bright blue sky, and the illusion of a nice breeze. Monofilament can be attached to the bottom corners of garments with a bit of tape or by feeding it through a tiny hole, and then taped to a weight out of frame to create the breeze—if you're lucky enough to be styling on a still day or in the studio.

All the styled shots appear simpler than they are to create. Every detail is crucial, from propping to the drape of the fabric to backgrounds.

## LAYDOWNS

My first actual styling job was a wholesale catalog for Adidas. It was a week's worth of laydowns portraying the full line of athletic clothing for that season, including running jackets, pants, sweats, shorts, running bras, and T-shirts. The second week, there were insets of athletic models wearing some of the clothes. At that point I'd directed countless fashion shoots but hadn't often visited the photo studios for the off-figure shoots.

Wholesale catalogs, which present a manufacturer's line to buyers for stores, are often nicer printed pieces than retail catalogs, with heavier paper, better printing, and less copy.

Since I was figuring it out as I went along, I was fortunate that my instincts were right about the techniques and materials. I brought lots of tissue paper, fiber fill, and batting to the shoot. The clothes were laid on a flat board two feet off the floor, with the photographer on a ladder. Uncomfortably squeezing between lights and reflectors, I managed to fill the garments and create realistic, athletic, but imaginary bodies inside them. This shoot was done on traditional film, years before digital was common; and any speck on the merchandise would have involved costly retouching, so a good part of the styling included keeping the set dust-free. Tiny rolls of masking tape and bits of putty helped me with that task.

### Techniques for Laydowns

A laydown without dimensionality is going to look especially flat on film. And the shape of the clothes usually looks very unattractive if they are

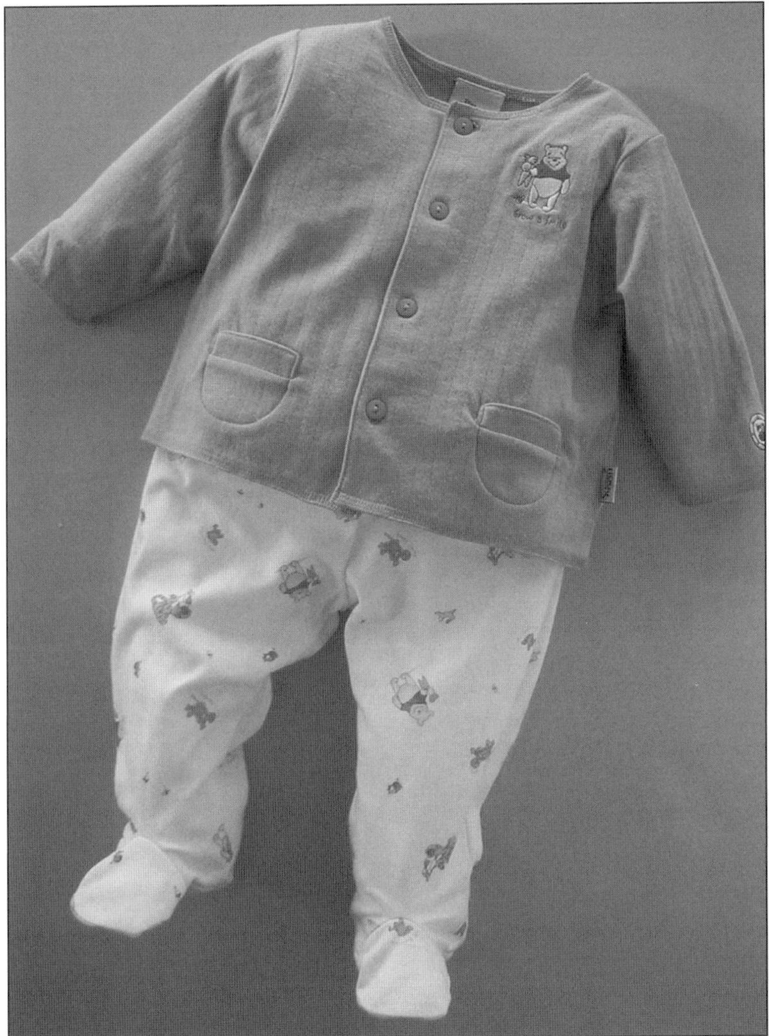

Laydown styling of baby outfit. *Photography and styling:* Susan Linnet Cox. © Susan Linnet Cox

lying flat. Adjustments include tucking extra fabric from the back of pants, evening out the waistband, narrowing the torso for both men and women, and placing sleeves in a natural way. The stylist creates the impression, to some degree, of a human form inside the clothing.

A problem created by gravity is flattening, as when lightweight fabrics like T-shirts seem to be sucked down onto the surface and really need to be built up. Also, the fabric may be translucent. A piece of white felt or fabric cut to the shape of the item can alleviate the show-through and allow you to place some batting or tissue inside for shape.

A wad of batting to soften the edge of the shoulders is a good start. Filling in sleeves with tissue paper or batting can create a soft shape and make the arms less wide. For women, create the illusion of breasts and a waistline. Some gentle folds in one direction make the garment much more appealing and give the photographer some dimension to light, just as you do with stacks or wall styling.

I wanted to add some infant clothing to my portfolio recently, and shopped for a cute outfit to style as a laydown. Since I wanted only an online portfolio piece, I decided to shoot it myself outdoors on a piece of blue poster board. When I started stuffing this shot I realized there was a fine line between creating a lifelike pose and a lifeless one. I think one key element in this illusion is making sure it does not look *too* real. For example, filling the booties could cause confusion. I held back from having the legs up and kicking and left the chest area and arms a little flat so the outfit would look more like merchandise.

## MANNEQUINS

Occasionally a mannequin is used for off-figure clothing. At first, dressing full-length mannequins is like a puzzle. For a stylist with retail display experience, this will be a snap. For the rest of us, decisions have to be made about how to get clothes on a stiff body. The arms twist off and need to be rotated back into place after a blouse is put on. The rod that is inserted to hold the mannequin up can get in the way of putting pants on. But at least it patiently stands still.

I styled a shoot for Univibe, a skater-style men's shirt manufacturer that revived the odd styles of the 1950s. The shirts were shown on male torso mannequins, much easier to dress than the full-length ones. Without arms or a head, the torso stands on an adjustable base. The shirts needed to be pinned, clamped, pulled, and adjusted, just as with on-figure styling, to create a good look. Filling the body and sleeves with rolled tissue paper helped with what I was trying to achieve, which was a human aspect.

## WALL STYLING

"Wall styling" is the creation of a lifelike presentation of clothing, often an entire outfit, styled against a vertical surface. With or without a hanger included, the fashions suggest living human figures. (Unable to find any specific description for this style, I came up with this term.)

Looking through catalogs, you'll notice evolving trends in styling. In the late 1990s, a few catalogs started shooting all their fashions off-figure.

There were no models. The idea was that models were distracting and the customers might not relate to them. Soon other catalogs mixed off-figure fashions with models or lifestyle shots, and gradually imitated the leaders by doing away with on-figure fashions altogether. Some used scenic shots as backgrounds and others set up the off-figure shots on location. No matter how it's shown, the off-figure clothing suggests a human body in a way that lets the customer imagine herself or himself in the clothing.

Though the trend has swung back toward models, off-figure shots styled vertically are still used frequently in catalogs, but it's not a specialty that all stylists feel comfortable with.

This type of styling gives you an opportunity to display more features than on a model. Side slits, pockets, linings, layers, and tricky button plackets can get lost when the garment is being worn. Here I'll show you the techniques to emphasize them. Remember how much your art director will appreciate your pointing out special details, since your goal is to make the art director look good *and* sell products.

## Sculpting the Figure

For most wall-styling jobs, your job is to create lifelike poses. Your client may sell sports clothing, travel wear, or business suits. The client wants you to imply the active person who will wear the clothes. How much activity is shown is the art director's call; the look the company portrays in its photos will set the standard.

I find this part of the process to be like sculpture. You are building a three-dimensional structure with a human form and realistic body language. In this case the implication is not that the clothing has been tossed on a bed or stacked on a closet shelf, but that there is actually an invisible "someone" wearing it.

Using tissue paper, batting, foam, wire, and monofilament—and sometimes, a preconstructed form—you will be bringing the garments to life.

Keep in mind that customers—women and men alike—want to visualize their best physical attributes in the styled fashions. The desirable female form will have defined yet feminine shoulders, rounded breasts at a realistic level, a waist that is narrow but believable, hips that are curved but not wide, and healthy long legs and arms. This is the body that most women want to have, and the one they imagine they will present if they buy these fashions. It's credible but not extreme. Strong squared shoulders, a full chest and neck, flat stomach, and slightly tapered waist define the desirable male figure. Long legs with no hip bulge complete the full-length presentation. Each catalog will have its own standards for the figure based on the customers; they want to attract but not alienate them.

## Human Proportions

It wouldn't hurt to pick up one of those how-to-draw books, the ones about drawing the human figure. You don't have to draw if you don't want to. Just looking at the diagrams will be a good start. If you have taken a

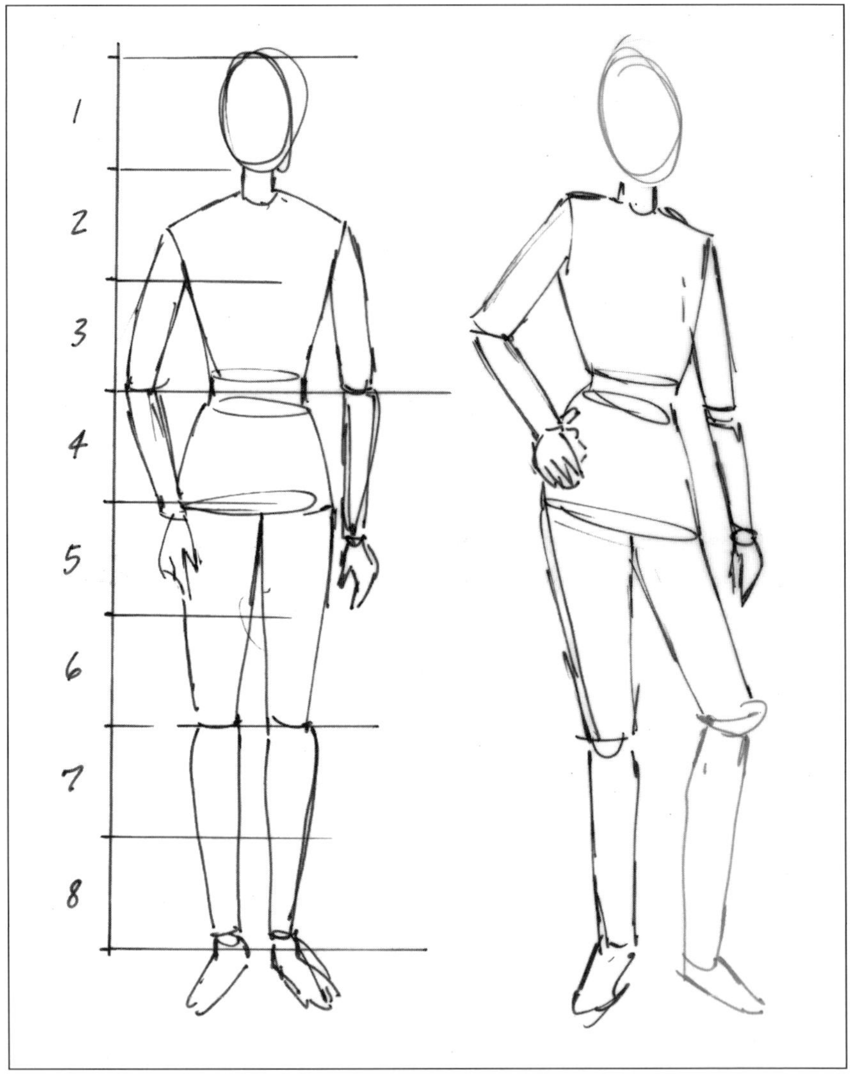

The ideal human figure is eight "heads" tall, important to visualize when doing wall styling. In a *contraposto* pose, the left knee bends as right hip is raised, forming a gentle S shape to the body. © Susan Linnet Cox

life drawing class, you may know exactly where the elbow bends. Notice it is not a curve but an angle—there are bones in there. You will also learn by looking at other people or in the mirror.

Generally the human body is divided into eighths. The top eighth is the head. The hips come about four heads, or halfway down. The elbows bend at a point just above the waist. If the arms are straight down, the fingertips brush the hips just below crotch level. Bend the arm slightly and the hand is raised high enough to slide into the pants pocket. The bent elbow will extend out away from the body or toward the back.

The distance from waist to crotch is about one head, or one eighth of the entire body. The knee is about halfway down the leg. If the knee bends, the hip joint bends too. This lifts the leg. These two joints mostly move front to back, not off to the side. The leg can assume a casual sideways movement but don't let it be too exaggerated, like a marionette. When this leg is bending, the opposite hip is going to rise up a bit. The torso curves in the other direction to compensate, toward the bent leg. An S-shape is formed, a position called *contraposto*. Now the shoulders are affected. They balance by lowering in the direction of the raised hip and straight leg. Study the illustration.

See how all the parts of the body are connected and balanced? The body seems to be in movement. It could be walking, or at least standing and listening to a friend talk. It is friendlier already.

## Techniques for Wall Styling

Depending on the client's preference, the process of styling garments begins with a hanger, a form, or just building the form on the wall surface. Let's start with women's items on a foam board wall.

Position the outfit on the foam board, outlined with pins holding the neckline, shoulders, and waist in place, step back and look. Let it drape and see if the shoulders are even and the proportions look right. If so, start styling. You'll take some foam and shape two shoulders to place inside the garment, pinning them through to the board. Shaping has begun. The breasts can be mounds made of tissue paper covered with batting and tape. These are shown in the wall-styling illustration on page 120. A pin goes straight through the top and into the backboard at the right position. Form the collar in a rounded shape to indicate the neck.

Sleeves are filled with tissue paper rolled around your own arm and placed into the garment sleeve from the top.

Early in the process, before refining too many details, call your art director over for a consultation. How is this looking? Is this the look you had in mind? Look at the monitor if the shoot is digital; if it's digital you can

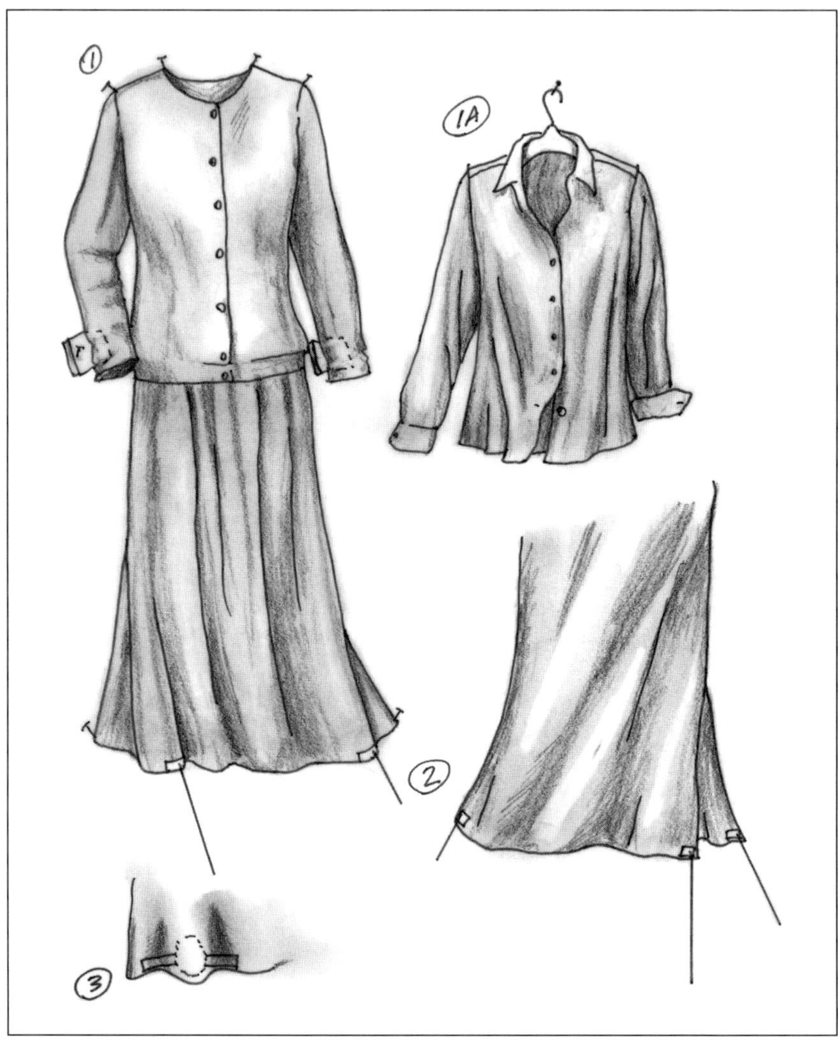

Wall styling: (1) A sweater and skirt styled without a form or hanger, showing blocks of foam positioned behind sleeves. Note T-pins at shoulders. (1A) A blouse styled on a hanger. (2) Skirts styled with monofilament taped to inside of hem and to floor or stand. (3) Rippled tape attached to two folds of skirt with batting under raised portion. © Susan Linnet Cox

check it out yourself *before* calling in the art director. Invariably the outfit will not be satisfactory. You will need to make changes. This is the part where you do not get discouraged or take criticism to heart. Do your best to quickly make requested adjustments and you will find the clothing looking better and better.

Small blocks of two- to four-inch-thick foam rubber can be used behind the figure to move it away from the wall. Shown in back of the sleeves in the illustration, they may also be placed inside the waist to build roundness.

A form can be constructed out of foam board, which has breasts attached and then all is covered with batting. What is challenging is determining a standard for the client's sizes and proportions. If you're using hangers, the form can be taped to the hanger at the shoulder.

The shiny plastic half forms that can be purchased for store displays are too slick to use for the wall techniques; you can't put a pin through them. Something similar can be fashioned out of foam board.

## More Tricks for Wall Styling

There are some special tricks you can use to counteract the effect of gravity and make the clothes do what you want. The button placket of a shirt or blouse looks good with a gentle ripple in it, especially near the collar where it otherwise tends to sink in. Cut a minuscule hole in the fabric near the edge and insert a length of thin wire, feeding it through to the bottom. It can be manipulated to create the curves you want, perhaps lifting the placket out at the bottom. The same procedure can be done along the bottom edge of a hem, to lift and ripple the bottom of a shirt or skirt.

Another technique for lifting a hem is attaching monofilament and taping it to the floor or a C-stand. The line can be attached to the gar-

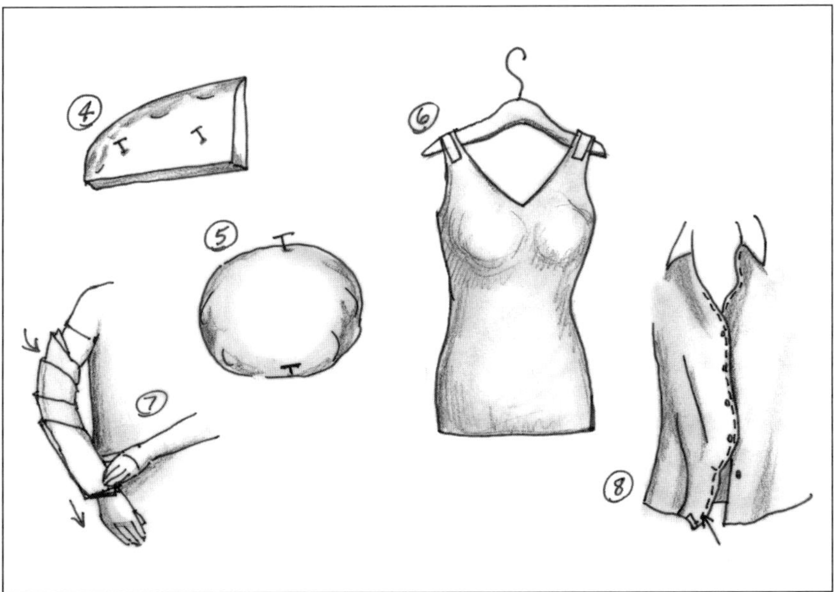

Wall styling details: (4) Foam cut to shoulder shape. (5) Breast made of wadded tissue paper wrapped with batting. (6) A form made of foam board, covered with batting, and taped to a hanger. (7) Wrapping tissue around your own arm for sleeves. (8) Wire (dotted line) inside button placket, held with tape at inside bottom. © Susan Linnet Cox

ment with a small piece of tape inside the hem or poked through the fabric and knotted. A simple trick for shaping a hem, one I usually use on shirts and blouses, is placing a long piece of tape along the bottom edge, leaving some segments free from the tape. The untaped parts can be kept away from the tape by inserting a bit of fiberfill, as the illustration on page 120 shows.

A final trick is shaping lengths of tape into a roll, which can be placed behind the edges of the garment to hold it to the board. Useful for positioning shoulders or other edges, this is a convenient shortcut that can be easily adjusted. When you are working with a background that can't hold a pin, the rolled tape can be a good way to control the garment's outer shape.

One studio I worked in had four movable walls. With a wood framework on wheels and foam board attached to both sides, the walls were very practical for styling catalog shoots. The foam board was used for working with pins to arrange the garments. With moveable walls, the stylist could style the clothing, even starting another shot on the reverse side, and then wheel the wall to the camera.

If large panels of foam board are attached to studio walls, you can be staging the next item on another piece of foam board on a tabletop. Using T-pins, the board can be pinned onto another board that is attached to the studio wall and the styling can be completed vertically. Photographers' assistants generally are responsible for these studio setups.

A background other than white foam board is sometimes preferred. Colored seamless paper, which comes on wide rolls, can be positioned over the foam board. If another background surface, like a wood panel, is specified, the challenges of arranging the clothes in front of it are greater.

## Wall Styling of Single Items

The processes above for styling an entire outfit can be used for simpler shots of single items. A blouse or shirt, skirt, slacks, shorts, or even underwear may all be presented on a vertical surface. This allows the garment to drape and bring itself to life. You can combine that drape with wall styling techniques to create an appealing off-figure shot. Roundness, a couple of gentle folds toward one side, and a gently rippling hem will give life and provide some surfaces for the photographer to light.

## SPECIALTY KIT LIST

As an addition to the basic kit list in chapter 13, this list includes some specific items that will help with off-figure styling.

❑  Foam board

❑  Hangers

❑  Form, provided by you or the client

❑  Blocks of foam rubber

❑  White felt or fabric

❑  Quilting pins, about two inches long and with a large head

❑  Long pins, T-pins or hat pins

❑  Tissue paper, preferably unfolded flat sheets

❑  Fiber fill

❑  Batting

❑  Monofilament

❑  Double-sided carpet tape

❑  Heavy white tape

❑  Wire (florist wire comes in pre-cut lengths)

❑  Wire cutter

❑  Safety glasses

❑  Scissors, sharp and pointed for threads, and others for tape

❑  Degreaser, for cleaning scissors

## A Note about Safety Glasses

Sometimes yellow-headed quilting pins are used for positioning the product into the foam board. They are placed around the edges of the garment and at crucial points on the front. The photographer may request that the heads be cut off for the final shot, to avoid retouching them out later.

The first day I was doing wall styling at The Territory Ahead, a catalog that uses appealing off-figure presentations, the yellow heads cut off of pins were flying everywhere. The studio was filled with the heavy clipping sound of wire cutters followed by the "pling" of the plastic pinheads hitting the floor, the walls, or some remote corner of the studio.

That's the way the other stylists were doing it, so that's the way I did it. Then, one of my pinheads didn't make the pling sound and I realized it was nestled in the inner corner of my eye. I plucked it out with its tiny nub attached and decided I needed safety glasses. I told the art director about the near miss, and she sent the studio assistant straight to Home Depot to get safety glasses for everyone. I was, however, the only one who wore them. I don't know how the others managed not to have their eyes poked out.

## LEARNING OPPORTUNITIES

Styling assistants are not hired as frequently for off-figure styling as they are for wardrobe. Sometimes catalog shoots will incorporate on- and off-figure styling in the same workday, which provides an opportunity to observe both. But you may have to learn these techniques on your own. You might try practicing independently. Look at catalogs and magazines, trying to visualize or even practice the techniques that you've just read about.

# Product Styling



**IN THIS CHAPTER, WE WILL SEE WHAT PRODUCT STYLING IS** all about and explore standards and techniques for working with props and products. This type of styling may be used in magazines, presenting a still life to enhance an article. You may work in conjunction with food stylists contributing the environment for the food. But the bulk of product styling work is done for selling products in catalogs.

Some stylists may specialize in pulling together props for a magazine shot; they are known as prop stylists. They usually don't dress models or other talent. Instead, they excel at arranging products and props in an appealing way. In a food shot, for instance, the food stylist would prepare and present the food, but the prop stylist might gather options for dishes, silverware, vases, flowers, napkins, and a tablecloth. Or sometimes there might be a wardrobe stylist and a separate prop stylist. This was the case in the shoot I described in chapter 7, which portrayed a family hosting a barbecue meal for their friends. Crewmembers included the art director, photographer, food stylist, her assistant, me as wardrobe stylist, my assistant, a makeup artist, and a local prop stylist with an editorial background. The prop stylist's responsibilities included providing tablecloths, flowers, and a vast assortment of serving dishes and tableware.

But this is rare. Most successful photo stylists work in several areas, moving back and forth between clothing and hard goods. In most markets you need to accept the projects that are available, and shoots may involve a combination of styling areas. On most of my projects, I am the only stylist and I am focused on both wardrobe and all the other props. While you may be asked to use skills ranging from wardrobe to hard goods, it is helpful to know specific techniques for styling products and props.

Whatever you usually style, there will sometimes be the spontaneous product-detail shot, inspired by the time and place. A careful look at a room the model is in brings your attention to other details you can improve with styling. The purse the model is holding may be photographed on the table for an inset. You will need to know how to fill it with just enough stuffing, position the strap, and pay attention to the tablecloth. As you know by this point, all types of photo styling overlap.

## A PRODUCT STYLIST'S STORY

Florida-based product stylist Leslie Holland freelances for catalog companies and various other clients. She tells us how she found herself in this career:

> *Coming from a theater production background, I basically learned from "doing." In college I was always the one who wanted to be behind the scenes, going to junkyards, thrift stores, even going through dumpsters to find the perfect prop for our student productions. If I couldn't find it, I'd make it.*
>
> *During one of my final portfolio reviews, my scenic design professor suggested getting into photo styling. I had never heard of it until then. He put me in touch with a stylist friend of his in Atlanta and after picking her brain, I decided to try it.*
>
> *After college I moved to Orlando and started assisting a wedding photographer who put me in contact with a lot of people in the photo community. I met a product stylist who needed help on a shoot and that was my official start.*

When asked about her most challenging and satisfying styling projects, Leslie relates the following stories and what she finds rewarding about styling work with animals:

> *I've had a couple of challenging projects over the years. Working with a full-grown leopard was probably the most interesting. It was slightly medicated, which helped with calming my fear of being attacked. Good thing I like cats. I had to find live butterflies and keep them on a branch during a cosmetics video. Thank goodness they were young and*

*loved sugar water. I found and styled baby chicks for a book cover shot (which was kind of a joke, because they really do what they want). I've also had to work with squirrels, rabbits, and an iguana. Definitely, animals are the most challenging but the most fun.*

*The most satisfying are shoots you're really sweating out—hoping the client likes your choices, hoping you have enough choices—and at the end of a long day having someone say "It looked really good" or "I couldn't have done this without you." It's nice to feel appreciated.*

## PROP IDEAS

After making selections with the art director and photographer, the stylist will arrange the props in the shot. The first rule of propping is that props are used to enhance products when the products are the focus of the shot. However, when a photograph is used to capture the reader's attention or to illustrate a concept, the prop itself may be the primary element. Note that the props can be both hard and soft materials.

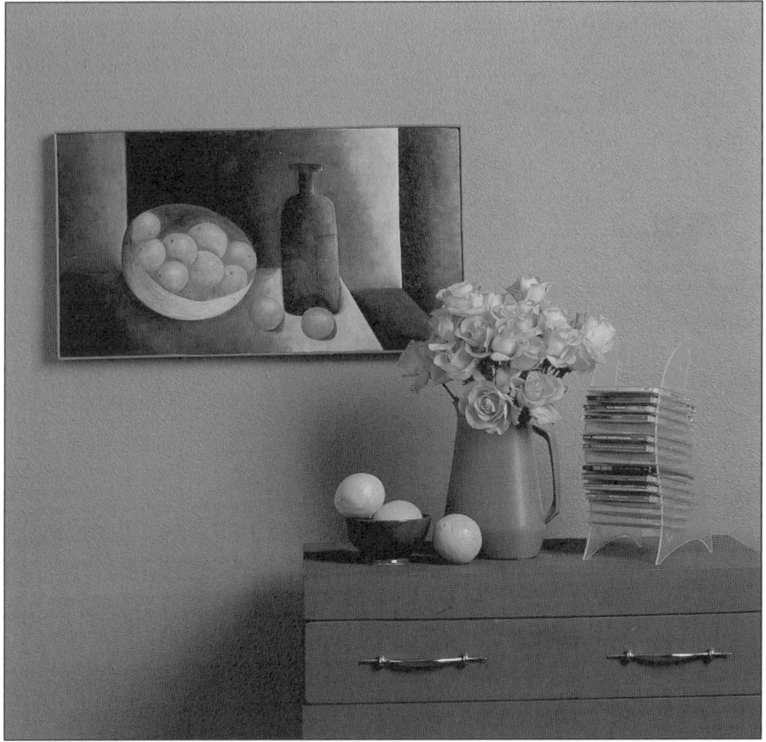

Plastic props on a vintage bureau are enhanced by the painting on the wall. *Styling:* Colleen Heather Rogan. © *Milwaukee Magazine*

## Prop Collections

Magazines such as *Martha Stewart Living* and *Real Simple* keep a bountiful supply of props on hand, as do many in-house catalog studios. For creating images to accompany feature articles and propping new-product stories, these prop collections include everything from furniture to vases.

I was delighted to find my way around the prop collection of a catalog studio I worked in. (The collection was described in the story of a staff stylist in chapter 3.) Nearly every item you might need was there: bars of soap, silverware, candles, vases, beach balls, picture frames, and endless stacks of books in all colors, with dust covers removed. How fun to wander the aisles seeking the perfect props to complete a shot, and finding them right there in the studio!

Many photographers, especially those who shoot a lot of food or other product shots, keep well-stocked prop closets in their studios. Props used for previous shots seem to stay and become part of the studio's resources.

## Propping Suggestions

This is a brief list of ideas for propping shots, meant as an inspiration. Many of these props will also be useful for room sets.

- **Fake ice cubes, ice gel:** Photographers may have these (or see resources on page 154).

- **Food props:** Popcorn, potato chips, pretzels in large bowls; lemons, apples, or tropical fruit piled in a bowl; slices of lemon or lime in drinks.

- **Generic food props:** It's best to *suggest* products. (See the photo of generic products on page 64.) Turn labels partially away from camera, if using brand name products, like a bottle of Perrier water or Corona beer.

- **Water droplets:** Pet conditioning spray or leave-in conditioner; hypodermic and glycerin.

- **Books:** Remove dust jackets of hardcover books, look for color and size, or wrap books in art paper. Collect small and old books to have on hand.

- **Vases:** Flowers; enhance with vines and branches or fill with tropical leaves or tree branches.

- **Pictures in frames:** Use your own snapshots, color copy to size; but use nothing copyrighted or with visible people (you'd need model releases).

- **Driver's license or diploma:** Obscure name and address, partially cover, or show far enough away to be illegible.

- **Keys, money, cellphone:** Needed often for wallets or purses, pull your own from your bag.

## Sourcing Props

Sourcing is the process of finding props that can be lent for use in a photo shoot. It's a benefit for a company's products to be shown in a photo, especially if they are recognizable.

For a branding photo for Marriott Renaissance hotels, the concept included twenty-four chaise lounges lined up poolside in front of a podium to indicate the hotel chain's unique approach to business meetings. Each chaise had a dark red towel and a pair of sunglasses. Acquiring more than two dozen of each prop was a challenge. I contacted the public relations company for Martha Stewart for the towels, but they were unwilling to provide the quantity needed. I purchased them—and returned them after the shoot. Dragon Optical agreed to loan me thirty pairs of matching sunglasses. (A Dragon Optical–sponsored athlete referred me to the sales manager who was kind enough to respond to my request.)

# CATALOG PRODUCT STYLING

Product stylists for catalogs may work in a studio or in various environments on location. Since details of products are being shown, the shot will usually be tightly cropped, rather than showing an expansive environment. A catalog product stylist is, as Leslie says, "visually and physically skilled in creating appealing and artistic tablescapes, to enhance the marketability of the product."

## Generic Propping

Props that are used in catalog styling should enhance the scenario, never distract. To sell a set of bookends, you might select a group of hardcover books in one product-flattering color, with the dust jackets removed and without obvious titles on the spines.

If you're styling a cutting board for serving cheese, you might prop it with some Swiss cheese and a few crackers, a plaid napkin, and a small knife. The crackers could be a recognizable brand, like a Pepperidge Farm assortment or Ritz, or something more generic-looking—they're obviously props. But the cheese knife needs to be neutral and not make the customer want to order it. It should be undecorated and possibly set toward the back of the grouping. If there is a cheese knife offered in the same catalog, of course, that would be a good prop for you to use. The designer could even "line list" it, adding in small type, "Cheese knife sold on page 7."

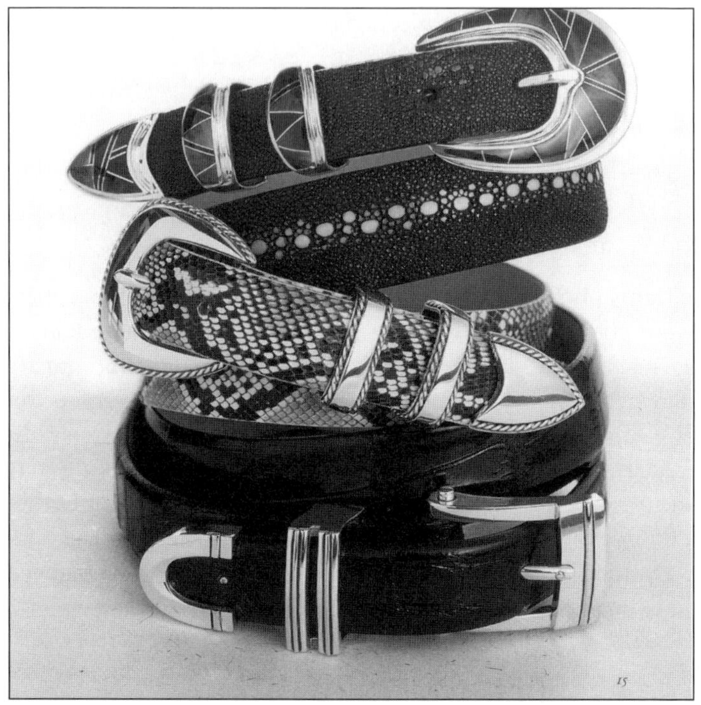

A stack of belts is harder to control than it looks. These were shot on an art paper background. *Photographer:* Tim Mantoani. *Styling:* Susan Linnet Cox. © Tim Mantoani

## Catalog Products

The cheese board in the previous example is typical of many products you will style. The home and food are important to people and products used around the home or with food represent a large section of the products sold through catalogs (they are second to apparel). Products including furniture, decorating accessories, gifts, and kitchen items can provide a great deal of work for the product stylist. (Food styling is discussed in chapter 9 and styling rooms in chapter 10.)

In addition to apparel, catalogs often include footwear, handbags, belts, hats, scarves, and other accessories in their product mix. These accessories can easily be sold to catalog shoppers when presented with coordinating clothing items. They may be shown on the model and also in a separate product shot.

Styling jewelry is a matter of working small and clean, as fingerprints and dust will show in such a close-up shot. The photographer will have particular lighting challenges with trying to control reflections in the shiny jewelry items. You will make small, precise adjustments to positions and allow the photographer to adjust lights accordingly. Chains, earring backs, and other components are precisely positioned to fit into the shot and create an effective composition. Often, the products must be tightly controlled to stay in gravity-defying arrangements.

## A Note About Clocks

Clocks have their own standards for styling. Have you noticed that on analog clocks it is always ten to two, or ten after ten? Most of those who are even aware of it assume that is the most aesthetically pleasing position for the hands of a clock to be in. A British photographer explained the background of the trend to me this way: most traditional clocks had a brand name in the upper center of the clock face. When photographing them, photographers—or perhaps illustrators, if the tradition goes back to before the camera was invented—positioned the hands on either side of the logo or brand name.

When digital and LCD clocks entered the market, the rules changed. A challenge to stylists and photographers involves shooting three digital watches together. If they are actual working watches and not prototypes, they must be set to the same time, but typically (and frustratingly) the minutes on each don't change at the same moment. Almost always, after controlling the lighting to show the display and enhance the rest of the product, and watching the time progress, the photographer layers many exposures together in Photoshop to create a final image. This means much work for one shot of three watches. This is the behind-the-scenes reality of photography.

## EDITORIAL STYLING

Home-related magazines such as *Martha Stewart Living* and *Real Simple* that present many product and propped shots maintain their own photo studios. Therefore, these magazines are more likely than fashion magazines to have staff stylists hired full time to produce beautifully styled images. Many of the products shown may be clothing, so experience with off-figure clothing is an asset for a product stylist.

Styling notes are usually printed in the gutter, the page's inner margin, listing the stylist or prop stylist. The shots are there to enhance an article or to showcase new products.

As I mentioned at the beginning of the chapter, sometimes you will find more than one type of stylist at an editorial shoot. This is often the case with food shots. Nearly every magazine seems to include at least one food story, with menus. Working with food stylists provides an opportunity to find more projects. Get to know local food stylists with whom you work well so that referrals can be shared—both ways. (Chapter 9 presents more information about food styling and related props.)

### Editorial Rates

As with fashion styling, magazines generally pay a lower rate for freelance product styling than commercial clients do. The motivation for working for less is that you will be likely to get some wonderful samples of your work. Photographers usually receive less for their editorial shoots also. Being able to state that you have styled for a national magazine is a plus, and a cover or full-page tear sheet can be an admirable addition to your portfolio.

## MOOD SHOTS AND BRANDING

A styled photograph may be used to create a mood or tell a story, rather than sell a product. An advertising agency is more likely to initiate the concept of this type of image. An example of this is a brochure I worked on for the Florida-based Publix grocery chain. The photo was used inside a brochure sent to soccer-league parents; it included coupons for cleaning

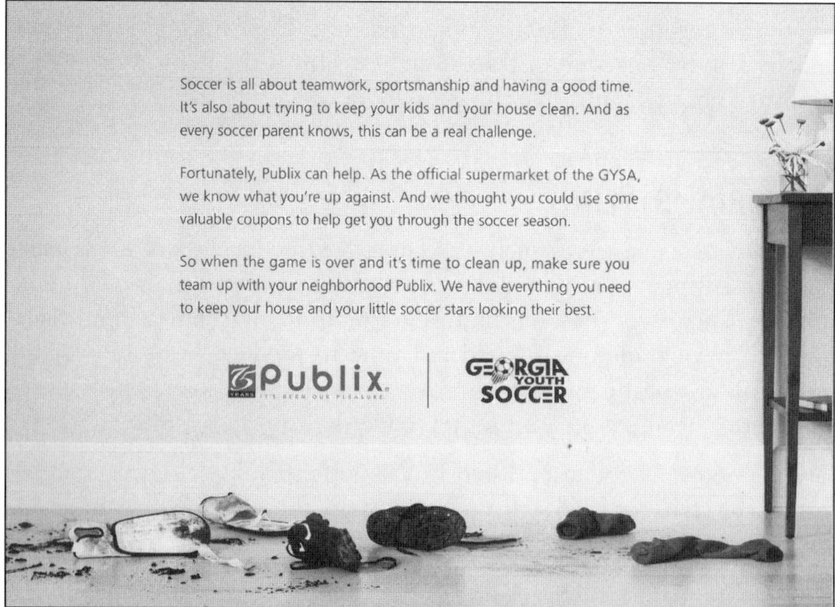


Styling with mud and soccer shoes. *Photographer:* Dave Spataro. *Styling:* Susan Linnet Cox. *Client:* Publix. © Dave Spataro Photography, Inc.

products and a reminder of the grocery's sponsorship of the league. The purpose of the photo is to pull the viewer into a story: you have a small child who plays soccer, has dirty uniforms, and tracks dirt into your home. You don't mind because you love your child and you can simply buy some products to clean everything up.

My role as the stylist included finding children's soccer shoes, which had to be dirty and well worn. I purchased them at used-sporting-goods stores. I also needed shin guards and socks, preferably in green, the chain's color.

The key styling material was mud. It was unique and enjoyable mixing dirt found outdoors with water to get the best consistency, and then dipping the sole of the soccer shoe in the mud to make tracks in the set. I also rubbed mud into the socks and shin guards. Other props included the lamp, book, vase, and flowers on the table. The "hallway" was built by the photographer in his studio, with hardwood flooring and baseboard.

## Branding Concepts

Mood shots are used for selling a brand, a company philosophy, or a service: they may not even include a product. There is a concept being portrayed and your role is to understand and express that concept with your props and styling. Most often, there is an advertising agency producing and art directing these shoots.

There will be a written overview and a well-drawn "storyboard," an illustration of the layout idea, based on resources the art director has viewed for inspiration, or simply on imagination. Some of these layout ideas are realistic, but others are physically challenging for the photographer to reproduce. The layout will usually be sent to you before the shoot so you can develop prop ideas.

## Annual Reports

Public corporations are required to provide an annual report to their shareholders. These are a classic example of corporate branding: the company philosophy is presented along with a financial report of the year's business. These printed pieces are an opportunity for graphic designers to be creative and for photographers to shoot a variety of material, from executives' portraits to mood shots. Annual reports are not a regular source of styling work, but you may be called in by a photographer to develop some of the concepts. The project would be similar to a non-product advertising image.

## SETTING UP THE PHOTOGRAPH

Camera positions for product shots are similar to those used for off-figure shots. The most common view of a tabletop set is a roughly 65-degree angle (three-quarters of a 90-degree angle) looking down from about eye level. The tabletop may be a large board placed on concrete blocks or sawhorses, which allows for variations in height. A larger set may be positioned on the floor and shot from the same "three-quarter" angle or directly from above.

### Tabletop

The boot photograph in chapter 3 (see page 43) is a good example of a tabletop set. The camera is generally looking at the waist-level set from an angle above eye level. And the tabletop will most likely be a comfortable height for styling the shot. Around the set are lights and reflectors for controlling the light and shadows within the shot, so you have limited room to move.

As the shot progresses and the lighting is adjusted, there may be even more small lights, reflectors, and "flags," which are cards used to create small shadows. There will be C-stands in place for suspending products. Always look over your shoulder before you make a move, preventing accidents to both yourself and the equipment.

### Infinity Backgrounds

Often products are shot on a white background, which becomes, in essence, *no* background. The graphic designer may want the item to float on the page. This may be referred to as a "knock-out," "KO," "silo" (for silhouette), or other terms. When the shot is placed on the page, a new shadow usually is added by computer, so you don't need to be too concerned about the area outside the item.

The photographer's tabletop set may consist of a curved white Plexiglas sheet extending above the surface so that the whole shot will have a white background with no visible seam. This is known as a "cove." Many studios have a large built-in cove, with the floor curving into the wall (both usually painted white), for shooting people. The tabletop cove is a similar idea. A cove can be created by unrolling a section of seamless paper, creating a curve where the horizontal table meets the vertical back of the set.

### Surface Options

Decorative art paper, fabric, colored seamless paper, and other background materials can be positioned on the tabletop to create a more interesting shot. These would be used for a "square-finish" or rectangular shot, when a knock-out isn't needed. Pay attention to the dimensions of the layout to see the shape of the image. The catalog or advertiser doesn't want any wasted space around the image so the product can be shown as large as possible and, at the same time, create a pleasing composition. The photographer may create a rectangular frame in front of the monitor (usually by using "croppers," which are two L-shaped pieces of cardboard) to see what the final cropped shot will look like.

Other surfaces like bricks or wood might be used to create an environment that looks like a room or an exterior setting. Remember the finished shot of boots in the cabin room in chapter 3? A small room environment may be built on a tabletop. I particularly enjoy duplicating an outdoor environment in the studio, working with leaves, soil, sand, and other natural materials: maybe it reminds me of sandbox days.

Translucent Plexiglas may be used on the tabletop to allow light to be projected from behind and beneath the product. This technique is dramatic and can be used for products that have translucent qualities themselves. The photographer will also light the object from the front, esthetically balancing the two light sources.

## Set Building

A client may present a layout that includes a specific type of room or some other location for a shoot. While it's always an adventure to go on location, studio shoots are much easier, even though a set must be built. Not only is the studio environment controlled—there are bathrooms, coffeemakers, convenient electricity, and control over lighting and equipment—but it is often difficult to find a location to match the client's layout.

Photographers seem to enjoy these set-building projects immensely, being creative people too. The project may require subbing out construction, hiring set builders, or having a prop fabricated by craftspeople such as welders or carpenters.

For a series of holiday shots, San Diego photographer Michael Smith built a fifteen-foot-long wall in his studio. He painted the wall red and then added a fireplace, chair molding, baseboard, and hardwood flooring. We used it for close-ups of products under a Christmas tree, on the brick fireplace hearth, and for a wide layout of socks. I booked my husband, who has great runner's calves, to sit out-of-frame with a female model resting their sock-covered feet on an ottoman I rented. The scenario to the left of them was a lighted Christmas tree, gifts, stockings on the mantel, and a lively fire in the fireplace. While the models sat very still, Michael lit

Sterno and newspaper behind the fireplace to create the perfect roaring blaze, which was captured during a long exposure. I hoped we wouldn't be affected by fumes in the studio. We weren't, and ended with a great shot—all to sell running socks in a catalog.

On another full-page shoe shoot, a photographer built a large box so we could create a stream environment. We filled the box with soil and rocks, then added vinyl to form the stream bed. Final touches were smaller rocks, water, ferns, and moss (use of my old plant-store experience). Three styles of water-resistant hiking shoes were presented in this natural-looking world. I made ripples in the stream with a stick.

## On Location

If a location shot is specified, you need to be sure to have all your props, supplies, kit needs, and especially the products with you. A whisk broom and window cleaner are especially useful to have on hand to make an outdoor scene presentable in a photograph. Unexpected litter or dust can be quickly cleaned up.

On the plus side, the products can look much more interesting in a realistic location, and the outdoor spots can provide a story line or theme for the studio shots. Finding the perfect set of tiled stairs or tree branch to display a pair of shoes can be lots of fun.

## TECHNIQUES FOR MAKING OBJECTS OBEY

Much of product styling is problem solving and logic. There are plenty of materials and techniques that you will use, but as with other types of styling, there are no absolute rules. Useful materials that a photographer might have in his or her studio include the putty, small wooden blocks, pieces of foam board, mat board, bricks, concrete blocks, metal weights, black permanent markers, and all types of tape. Wrapping a brick with white fabric tape prevents it from sliding on the set and also keeps it clean and smooth.

Photographers can clean up the shot in postproduction—they will let you know how much they are willing to do—but your objective should be to make your shot look as close to perfect as possible.

## Putty

Photographers' putty has been a mainstay of studios forever. But when and where people began using this practical, sticky material, however, is always a bit of a mystery, even within the photo industry. The information is rarely shared. Several years ago, a photographer from India who had lived in South Africa gave me a flat package of light gray putty he bought there. I mentioned this to a stylist I worked with who was a native of South Africa. She seemed disturbed that another stylist knew about the elusive putty. She'll be sorry to see I'm letting the secret out here. The package lasted until recently, since only a pinch is used at a time (Plus, it can be re-used!) I had to find a new batch of putty and didn't know anyone who was traveling to South Africa, so I took a chance on some putty I found in an online search. This putty is sold to consumers for holding objects in place during earthquakes. When it came I was happy to discover it was imported from—you guessed it!—South Africa.

The uses of putty range from holding something in place to lifting an object the tiniest amount. Mostly it's used for controlling where an object is positioned. A little dab can be molded as needed. If the putty leaves a residue on the product or set, it can be cleaned up by touching it with more putty, as it sticks to itself. It's similar to the material used for putting up posters, but more durable.

There is a similar product called clear museum gel. I was excited to find a jar of transparent gel at the Container Store checkout stand and had the opportunity to try it for a jewelry shoot that included see-through watchbands. It did work well for positioning the products with minimal touch-up for the photographer—we were shooting on art paper backgrounds and needed the color and light to show throughout the shots. My only disappointment was that it left a tiny oily mark on the art paper. When online, visit *www.got-putty.com* for earthquake putty (same as photographers' putty) and *www.improvementscatalog.com*, one of many sources for clear museum gel.

## Monofilament

Translucent and nearly invisible, monofilament is the second most useful tool for product styling. A strand can be taped to the back of the product at one end and taped to a C-stand at the other. The tape lets it be more adjustable than tying would. Monofilament, also known as fishing line, is for sale in sports and fishing departments.

This is how you would style a handbag and add the perfect curve to its strap. Start with the bag at a slightly turned view rather than straight on, unless it's required by the art direction. See which portion of the bag has the most important features. Stuff the bag with tissue paper or batting. A towel might work for a large bag or suitcase.

Tape a strand of monofilament to the back of the handle or strap where you need it to be lifted. Lift the other end of the monofilament above the set till you create a good "drape" for the handle. Tape the monofilament strand to a C-stand, which has been moved into place by the photo assistant. The stand can be moved and adjusted as needed. Perhaps you will want to do this to a couple of areas of the strap. A longer strap looks good draped behind the bag and gracefully looped around to the lower front. This arrangement helps the layout stay compact. Keep an eye on the layout and on features of the bag. Floppiness at either end of the strap attachments can be corrected with small pieces of tape or putty.

## Plastic Stands

If you visit a plastics shop, you're likely to find a scrap bin with odd sizes of clear Lucite, Plexiglas, and other scraps. There will be plenty of other shapes and sizes available in the showroom. These can be used to create a variety of levels for positioning items within a shot.

The advantage of using these clear materials is that light can shine through them on to other parts of the set and the blocks are nearly invisible. Having several different stand heights will help you to stagger products in the shot and choose the height you need. Some photo studios will have clear stands on hand. If it seems like a crucial need, be sure to check first.

# STYLING SHOES

Some clothing catalogs have so many shoes in their merchandise selection that art directors assign certain photographers just to shoot footwear. They may become bored with endless parades of shoes, but they do have steady work. Other catalogs sell nothing *but* shoes. Along with fashion footwear, the athletic-shoe market is huge. I love styling shoes, finding variety in combinations of three or four single shoes and showing the requisite features.

Shoe styling involves certain traditional standards. While a series of shoes may be portrayed in profile, most arrangements show all the features important to a customer. These especially include heel height, toe shape, and colors. The arch side of the shoe is not shown; the outer side is considered more attractive. Shoe samples are generally size six for women and size nine for men, considered to be the most attractive for viewing off the foot.

A grouping may include one or two shoes of each color, a side view to show the heel, and a fairly straight-on view of the toe box. If there are distinctive sole treatments, a bottom view is included. Extra colors are generally shown from a variety of flattering angles. See the photograph on

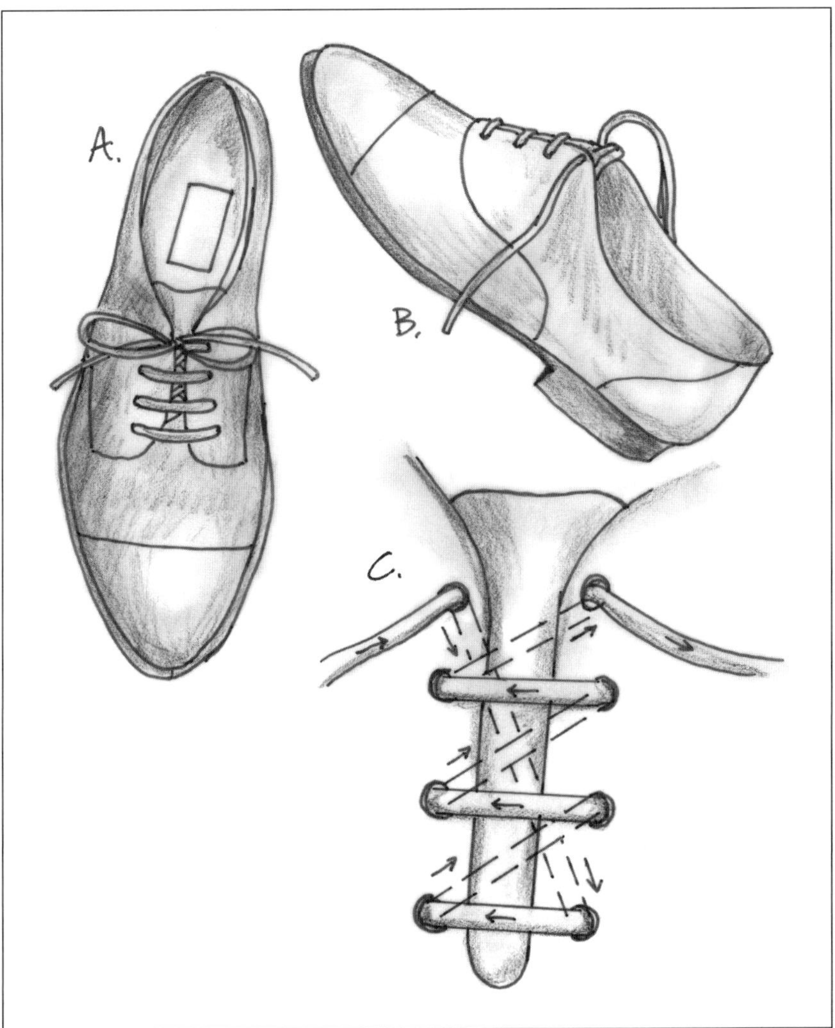


Shoe styling: (A) View of shoe from above showing toe shape and classic lacing. (B) Outer side view shows heel shape and height; laces are undone and draping. (C) Follow the arrows for classic lacing technique. © Susan Linnet Cox

page 43 for an example of grouping. Some shoes may be placed in gravity-defying positions by using Lucite blocks, monofilament, putty, and other tools of the product styling trade.

If the shoes have laces, they are usually shown tied or tucked. See the illustration for some optional presentations of shoelaces for photography.

When I've styled shoes for the Road Runner Sports catalog, different standards applied. Technical features are of prime importance: sole structure, arches, and laces. In this case the arch side is the featured view. The laces may be tied and tucked or shown casually untied. Although untied is rarely the presentation of choice, I enjoy creating a beautiful drape to the untied laces.

If shoes are soft and floppy, plumbing tape, available at builders-supply stores, can be placed inside the shoe. Since it's flexible but stiff you can sculpt the shape you want.

## CREATIVE PROBLEM SOLVING

Your job as a product stylist is finding the right solution for styling each shot, whether it's a stack of belts, an array of shoes, or a vase of flowers. Problem solving and creativity teamed with the materials above will help with each styling challenge. After many years of styling, I still have moments at the beginning of a shoot when I wonder if I know what I'm doing! But I proceed one step at a time until the familiar processes of styling take over.

And, I try to include the tips I collect from others in my "fix-it kit." I learned this valuable hint from a Seattle stylist when I was directing a holiday shot of a model in sleepwear, and I've used it ever since. When I blew out the candle we were using as a prop on the homeowner's antique dresser, the wax splattered all over the top. After I cautiously scraped it off with my thumbnail, the stylist said, "What you do is hold your fore-finger anywhere between your mouth and the candle. When the wind goes around it to blow out the flame, it won't spatter." Try it: it never fails.

## KIT SUGGESTIONS

This list includes some specific items you will need for product styling in addition to the basic kit list in chapter 13. Be sure to have them with you on shoots.

- ❑  Monofilament (fishing line)
- ❑  Putty
- ❑  Lucite blocks in varying heights (buy from plastic companies' scrap bins)
- ❑  Weights (divers weights or other pieces of metal)
- ❑  Plumbing tape (metallic waterproof repair tape, available at builders-supply stores)
- ❑  Jewelry cleaning cloths
- ❑  Clear museum gel

chapter

# Food Styling

**T**HIS IS ONE AREA OF STYLING THAT IS NOT INVISIBLE. EVEN the general public is aware that there are people who style the food portrayed in photos. What people don't know is how much experience and training is required to excel at this career, more than simply being a good cook and knowing a few tricks.

## MEET A FOOD STYLIST

Lisa Golden Schroeder has been a food stylist for over twenty years. Based in Minneapolis-St. Paul, she teaches and publishes *Tweezer Times*, an online trade magazine for food stylists, and also maintains a helpful Web site, *www.foodesigns.com*. She describes the profession this way:

> *The food stylist is responsible for organizing the food—sourcing unusual ingredients, arranging for shopping, preproduction preparation of food, preparing food on the shoot, and the final inviting presentation of the food under camera. Taste is of little concern, but looks are everything. The goal is to create images that appear to be freshly made, coming straight out of the kitchen to your dining table. The ability to do this, despite having handled the food a great deal or having food that must stand for long periods of time on a set, is an art and a science.*

*It's important to have several years of training in food handling, by earning a food or nutrition degree, going to culinary school, or working in a professional kitchen. I put emphasis on good training and experience, because it is very important that a food stylist understand how food works.*

*Problem-solving is a key element of the business, and being able to control what food does is of primary importance. If something is not the right color or consistency, what can be done? Stylists develop an interesting arsenal of equipment to do their jobs—from standard cooking equipment and knives to tweezers, paint brushes, scalpels, artists' palette knives, and cosmetic spritz bottles!*

*A food stylist should have a natural flair for design and presentation. Understanding graphics, color, symmetry, asymmetry, and other elements that are important to an art director and photographer when creating an arresting visual will make you a valuable member of the team. Having the ability to be creative with props—the plates, bowls, utensils, surfaces, and other items to round out the scene—and being prepared with an open mind toward presentation—and lots of ideas— make an even better stylist.*

In addition to being a food stylist, Lisa is a published cookbook author, culinary consultant, and educator. Like me, she is at a point in her career when sharing her knowledge is a mission. As one of the organizers of the "Food on Film" food-styling seminars in Minneapolis, Minnesota, she's an avid supporter of food styling education. She's the chair of the Food Photographers & Stylists special-interest section of the International Association of Culinary Professionals (IACP). Working with other experienced stylists, photographers, and food professionals from all over the world, her site Foodesigns.com is an excellent reference for up-to-date food styling information and networking.

## OVERVIEW OF FOOD STYLING

Photographs of food are everywhere you look—from coupons to Sunday newspapers to almost every magazine you read. Food images are used for cookbooks, magazine features, advertising, television commercials, food packaging, and scenes in feature films.

### Types of Work Available

Projects for clients are surprisingly varied, from restaurant menus to billboards. Some unexpected clients include cruise lines, wine and liquor companies, and barbecue-grill manufacturers.

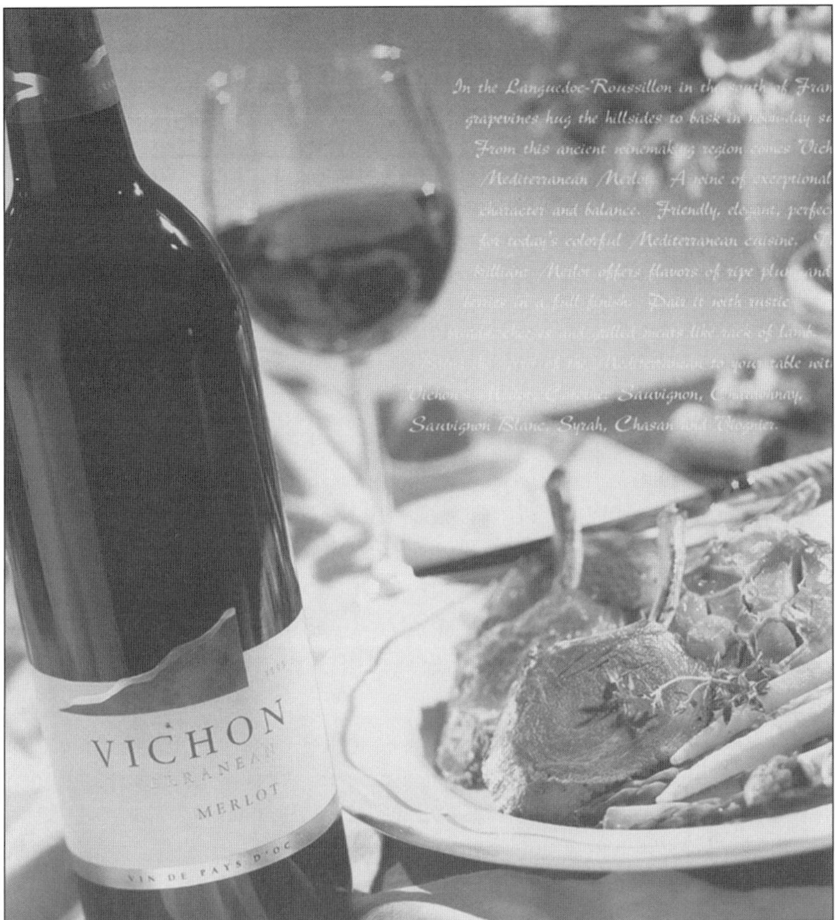

Wine advertisement featuring delectable entrée and props. Notice attractive ad copy reversed out of background. ***Photographer:*** Charles Imstepf. ***Food styling:*** Susan Draudt. © Charles Imstepf

Editorial projects for magazines and cookbooks are plentiful. As with other styling specialties, editorial projects may not pay as well as commercial projects but will provide excellent portfolio pieces.

In all types of styling, catalogs are an abundant source of work throughout the United States. Catalogs market food products such as hot sauce, fruit, or desserts. Other catalogs selling cookware and kitchen products feature styled food shots and even present special recipes. Non-food catalogs use food styling occasionally, propping with food the other products they are marketing.

## A Typical Day

A typical day in the life of a food stylist is as atypical as in any other styling field. With such a variety of projects and clients there is no normal routine. The preparation, planning, and shopping are unique for each job. There may be food preparation the day or evening before the shoot. When you buy, bake, and prepare as much as possible ahead of time, you look more organized and professional.

On the morning of the shoot there may be special items that have been ordered from grocers and must be picked up early. If the budget allows, an assistant will do the shopping or meet the stylist at the store. And there's packing the food items, ice, props, and supplies to take to the shoot.

Then it's on to the studio. Most photography studios, particularly those used for food photography, will have a complete kitchen. While useful for entertaining clients, the kitchen is a necessity for shoots involving food.

The groceries and props are unpacked and organized. The schedule and layouts for the day's work are reviewed with the art director, photographer, and client. The stylist then gets to work, preparing a "stand-in" for the first shot. This is a rough substitute for the actual food, so that the art director can create the desired layout and the photographer has something to light. Once they are satisfied with the look of the shot, the stylist re-creates the food carefully and places it on set for final photography.

For a food-packaging shoot, with its exacting criteria, only a couple of shots are done in a day. The image is presented on a small surface, with lots of type that must, sometimes by law, fit on the package along with the photo. Clients are extremely particular about how the product must look, and these shoots can take a long time. Creativity plays a lesser role in these shoots; technical know-how is what is needed. The crew may spend an entire day on one shot for advertising. The shot volume for catalogs is much higher, as with other styling specialties. Shooting days for cookbooks and magazines also encompass a larger number of shots.

Food projects are usually shot in studios, but occasionally you may need to improvise on location. If you're working at a private home, arrange to use the kitchen. More pre-planning and preparation than usual might be needed.

## Regional Differences

Years ago, food stylists were often advised to live in San Francisco, Los Angeles, Minneapolis, Chicago, or New York—and nowhere else. Now the industry has grown, along with the variety of projects there are to style.

Depending on where you are working, the type of work you do can vary tremendously. In Los Angeles, expectedly, there is more work in film and television commercials. And the editorial rate there is comparable to the commercial rate.

In the Midwest, there are fewer commercials but more advertising and other still photography. Since many food companies are based there, packaging is a significant source of work. Editorial work and cookbooks are less commonplace.

On the East Coast, where there are more publishers, there is more opportunity to work on cookbooks. There is also more competition, so the rates for this editorial work are lower. Dallas, Orlando, and Atlanta are good cities for finding work.

Interestingly, in most areas, a higher rate is charged for work with ice cream because of the difficulties and challenges it presents.

## Staff Positions

There are opportunities for staff employment in the food-styling field. They include working as an in-house stylist for a food company, publisher, printer, or agency studio. There is also work in commercial studios, art direction, and advertising or marketing agencies that focus on food accounts.

## Kit Fees

Fees for materials used, called "kit fees," are rarely charged by food stylists for print projects. Stocking supplies in one's kit is considered a normal part of doing business as a stylist. When special materials are needed for a specific project, they may be incorporated into the production budget. It is more common in television and film to charge a kit fee of about $75; it's considered standard in those industries.

# STYLES OF FOOD PHOTOGRAPHY

For several years I have noticed a certain style in food photography. The shots are tightly cropped, with very selective focus, and they are beautiful. This presentation puts the focus (literally) on the food, making it come alive and appear more appetizing.

This is the current fashion for photos portraying food, but it has not always been the way. Earlier styles included more propping, with other food items shown in the same scene. Looking back at older cookbooks makes this obvious. The crowded, bright, and sharply focused shots of an entire meal are out of place now, but trends may change again in a few years.

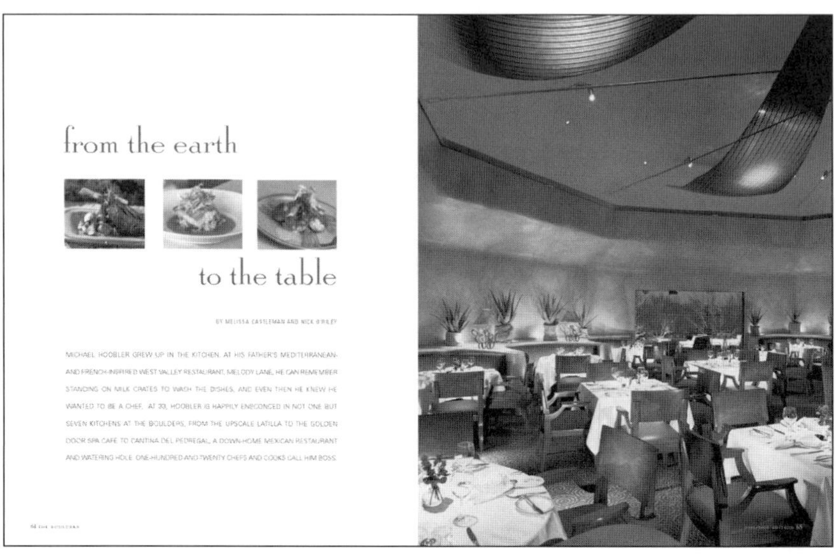


Magazine story about a restaurant features three entrees and architectural photography. *Art director:* Caitlin Beier. Courtesy of *The Boulders*, published by Media That Deelivers, Inc. © Media That Deelivers, Inc.

The most challenging food styling is for packaging photos. Magazine work, compared to packaging, can be looser, more natural, and ultimately more creative. The style is always the choice of the client and is related to the purpose of the photo. The soft-focus dreamy style is not as useful for packaging as it is for magazine presentations.

## Working on Cookbooks

For a food stylist, a cookbook project is an opportunity to collaborate with other creative professionals on an attractive product. This may be considered an editorial project and thus be paid at a lower rate. But the benefits of doing such an editorial project at the lower editorial rate are that the results will be true portfolio pieces and the stylist will have more workdays than is typical, since the project will last longer.

Cookbook shoots are longer, more cohesive projects than most styling jobs. The food stylist works as a team with a photographer and prop stylist to develop a consistent style, schedule the number of shots per day, and determine a budget for the resources.

Los Angeles food-stylist Susan Draudt got her start by writing a cookbook. With a bachelor's degree in food science, she worked in the field as assistant food-service director for a large chain of department stores. Then she wrote *Food Processor Cookery*, which sold 125,000 copies the first year. She enjoyed the process of the photography so much that she became an apprentice to several food stylists. After a year she started taking on clients of her own, and went on to write—and style—four more cookbooks.

## Styling for Film

Food stylists may have opportunities to work with both still photography and film. On a film shoot there are more layers of communication; the stylist may work more closely with the director or art director than the cameraperson. As with all shoots, there should be good team interaction—the food stylist, art director, photographer, prop stylist, and the client all must be in sync with the goals of the shoot.

## Prop Stylists

Frequently prop stylists work closely with food stylists to complete the shot. Although food stylists are often asked to prop the shot, collaboration with a prop stylist can provide a wider array of resources and allow the food stylist to focus attention on the food.

Provided props can includes dishes, utensils, linens, and backgrounds. Essentially, anything called for in the shot beyond the food can be the prop stylist's responsibility. Many photo studios maintain a well-stocked prop closet or employ a studio coordinator who does some shopping.

Details can be very important, especially when working with a recipe; the choice of a measuring container or baking dish can make the shot authentic or throw it off. A food stylist told me about a prop stylist's delight at finding an antique dish that was attractive but too large for the recipe and, furthermore, wasn't ovenproof. Something more believable had to be found quickly. Early and ongoing communication about all the job details is essential.

## Photo Stylists Styling Food

While I am not a professional food stylist, I have worked with food in the course of other styling projects. Most often it has been slicing a lemon to place on the edge of a glass of iced tea or decorating with fruit. But I have styled raw chicken in a faux marinade sauce to demonstrate a unique marinating dish, and I've grilled chicken and vegetables in a grilling basket for a catalog shot. I once applied motor oil to the top crust of a prop cherry pie. The dessert was a prop for a line of cherry-printed plates a catalog was selling. I had heard it suggested somewhere that motor oil painted onto a piecrust would give it a rich, golden look so I tried it. It really worked, and though I am not a professional food stylist, I was proud of that shot.

I was once hired to style packaging for Cermato, a Mexican-influenced clam-and-tomato-juice drink intended to be mixed with beer. The shot involved a salt-rimmed glass of the juice, surrounded by ice cubes (they sure do melt quickly on set!) and clams in shells, a pretty complex project

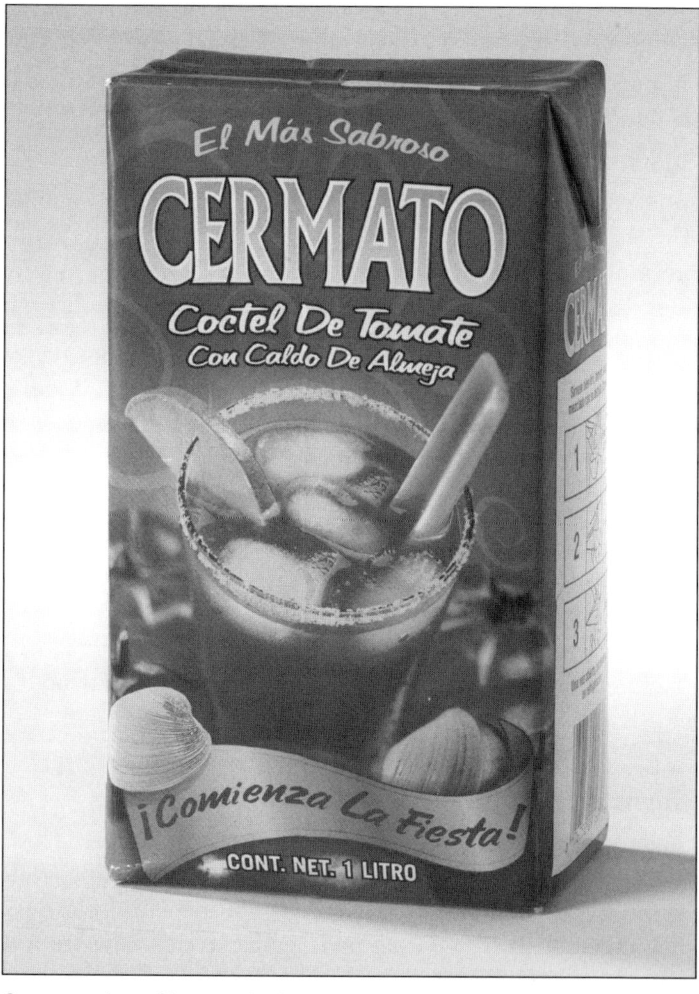


Cermato package. **Photography:** David Harrison. **Styling:** Susan Linnet Cox. Courtesy of Christopher Stickney.

for a non-food stylist. It was fun and a good learning experience for my intern, Veronica, and me; it turned out really well.

The professionals should be called in to do specialized projects, but every stylist, at one time or another, may be asked to work on projects involving food. It's best if you understand the basics enough to feel comfortable, and getting some training from workshops surely wouldn't hurt.

## PROFESSIONAL TRAINING

In the field of food styling, there seem to be more resources available and stylists willing to share them than in any other area of photo styling. Workshops are plentiful, Web sites are informative, and styling supplies are available from specialty suppliers.

While there is no absolute path to getting into the studio, more training is required for food styling than for other styling specialties. The food stylist needs knowledge of how food works, good food-handling skills, understanding of the food industry, and creative vision. Meticulous organization, willingness to experiment, and problem-solving are crucial attributes.

### Education

A food stylist needs solid cooking skills and knowledge of food chemistry. A bachelor of science in food science, nutrition, or home economics is an excellent background for food styling. Alternatively, a bachelor of arts in design or art can provide a foundation, when combined with further exploration into the food field.

Culinary training, either from culinary schools or apprenticeships in restaurants, provides useful, hands-on experience in working with food. In addition to learning what food does, there is exposure to the business side of food through this type of education.

### The Food Business

Time spent in the food industry on the business side could include working in a test kitchen, developing recipes, or consulting with marketing and advertising departments. Work for organizations that promote various food industries, such as the National Dairy Council, can provide a great perspective on the business side.

In addition to having knowledge of food preparation, the food stylist is creative, curious, and organized. While most enter the field through the food profession, many stylists find it another way. With backgrounds in art or advertising, coupled with a love of cooking, they possess a natural sense of design, color, and an understanding of what is visually appealing.

Exposure to the visual aspects of presenting food may come from graphic design for food photography, advertising, supervising shoots as an art director, or even publishing food magazines or cookbooks, as in Susan Draudt's case.

## Experience through Assisting

Regardless of education, most stylists enter the business by assisting other food stylists. The opportunities for learning from an experienced stylist are more plentiful than in other areas of styling. The learning process may take years, until you are prepared to go out on your own.

Food stylists would rather work with an assistant than without.  An assistant is available to run out for items the client comes up with at the last minute. An ideal assistant should have a good knowledge of food preparation, be quick and organized, without any ego in the way, and listen carefully to requests.  While clients often prefer not to pay for an extra person, it saves time and money, freeing the stylist to focus on work under the camera.

Lisa Golden Schroeder states: "Having a good assistant can make or break a day, especially if the client wants to fit a lot into a single day. It can be possible to do much more if there is a competent assistant in the kitchen while the stylist is on the set. I look for assistants that have enough experience to do basic things like shop properly for good produce or baked goods, and understand the way a studio team works, and how they can make the job and day easier for the stylist. I've trained assistants, but also hire others I hear are good from other stylists. I like to work with assistants who have a positive attitude and don't mind working hard."

## Apprenticeships

Many food stylists say they learned the most through an apprenticeship relationship with another stylist. This unpaid mentoring process prepared them for their careers, much the way the photographer/assistant relationship does. When you mature in your career, you can keep this in mind and help other stylists learn the profession.

Contact the best food stylists and food photographers in your area and offer your services, even if you are simply observing or assisting for free.

You can develop ideas for test shoots through this exposure and find photographers willing to work with you so you can gradually build a portfolio. As stated on *www.foodesigns.com,* "the best way to learn all the nuances of the business is by working diligently with someone who knows the ropes." Your helpfulness and willingness to take direction will help you find more assisting opportunities, gradually moving into the profession.

## Networking and Workshops

Talk to food stylists in other parts of the country. Since you won't be competing with them and they are almost always eager to share information, you can ask professional questions. Local food stylists can provide you with a network where you can share techniques, problems, and even referrals for jobs.

If you like to be involved in organizations, you can find groups that include potential clients, such as art directors, corporate home economists, and chefs. These organizations include the International Association of Culinary Professionals (who have a special-interest section for food photographers and stylists), Les Dames D'Escoffier, and other networking groups for advertising professionals.

## Educational Sites

**www.ciaprochef.com**: Culinary Institute of America, presents an annual food styling workshop by Delores Custer

**www.cookingschools.com**: Culinary education, articles, and interviews with professionals

**www.foodonfilm.com**: An educational convention for beginners and professionals

**www.iacp.com**: International Association of Culinary Professionals, an organization of the business-to-business food industry

**www.worldculinaryinstitute.com**: Culinary education and resources

## Networking Sites

**www.foodesigns.com**: Networking site for beginners and professional food stylists

**www.foodphotography.com**: Resources from food stock photographer Iris Richardson

**www.ldei.org**: Les Dames D'Escoffier, an organization celebrating women of achievement in the culinary field

**www.tweezertimes.com**: A subscription online magazine published by Foodesigns.com

Find workshops you can attend to learn what's new and meet other stylists and food professionals. Making a commitment to take classes is very important; you can approach it as an investment in future success.

You may find plenty of Web sites about food styling; those on page 151 are a sample of what's currently available to help you learn about the field.

While there are many routes to food styling, the key to success is having a firm idea of your goals, a willingness to do everything necessary to get good experience, and, perhaps, patience. Being fun to work with, highly competent, eager to learn, and able to anticipate client needs will assure repeat work. Success is entirely up to the individual.

## TECHNIQUES

While stylists use many special techniques, depending on the shoot and the food, the goal is always to present the food in the most appetizing, appealing way possible. Food stylists have a collection of equipment and tools, from basic cooking equipment and good knives to artist brushes and dental picks.

Rumors abound about food-styling tricks, like using glue instead of milk for a bowl of cereal, mashed potatoes instead of ice cream, and blow-torching the outside of raw chickens to make them seem cooked. Lisa Golden Schroeder dispels some of these outdated illusions:

> *There have been so many stories circulated about how the food is faked in photos, but they are generally not true. In past years, there were more instances of using inedible items as stand-ins or added to food. But the trend has been for a more natural approach in the past decade. And most food companies have policies that dictate nothing artificial be used on a shoot—particularly in advertising, where there are laws that govern these issues. There are formulations that simulate certain foods that are very difficult to work with, like ice cream. But the recipe for fake ice cream is edible—it's basically a very thick frosting that can look like ice cream when scooped.*

> *Sometimes foods are cooked down, like maple syrup, so that they become thicker and easier to control. Or in the case of poultry (especially turkeys), the bird may only be cooked in the oven with steam until the flesh is firm but not completely cooked. This is because a fully roasted bird, once cool, will wrinkle and look very unappetizing. By cooking the poultry less, then coloring the skin, the cooled bird looks fresh, like when it first came out of the oven. But again, this method varies. There are many magazines and cookbooks now that completely cook food and shoot it immediately—and it looks natural and delicious.*

## Shopping for Food

Know good food resources, where to get the best produce, and sources for exotic ingredients. Find ethnic markets and explore them. Get to know the growers of produce and herbs at farmers markets. Even when you're not working, scout suppliers for ingredients, equipment, and garnishing ideas.

A good relationship with the produce manager of a natural-foods store is invaluable. Items that are not in stock, like edible flowers or tropical fruit, can be specially ordered with some advance notice. Seafood- and meat-department managers will be very receptive to your requests also. Imagine how special it is to find a customer who appreciates their contributions so much, compared to the routine customers of a grocery store.

Web searches also can yield a wealth of resources, items not readily available in your area, as well as inspirations and style ideas from around the world.

# TOOLS OF THE TRADE

The food stylist's kit is very personal and is developed through a lot of trial, error, and experimentation. You won't need the basic kit described in chapter 13. Your kit will be unique to your trade. Food stylist Susan Draudt can't live without the following items:

- Long bamboo skewers
- Small spray bottle for water
- Scissors
- Very sharp paring and butcher knives
- Straight pins
- Zap-A-Gap brand glue

## Specialty Kit List

The following items comprise a kit available for purchase from Foodesigns.com. The kits come with a couple of bonus items. Whether or not you decide to invest in the whole kit at once, the list can provide you with some suggestions for developing your own kit:

- Surgical-grade stainless steel six-inch tweezers (bent-nose and straight tip)
- Long-handled baby spoon
- Ultra-sharp cuticle scissors
- Wüsthof-Trident paring knife
- Oxo citrus zester

- Mini spritz bottle
- Needle-nose dropper bottle
- Monoject syringes
- Stainless-steel dental picks
- A set of plastic palette knives
- A set of high-quality art brushes
- Pastry brushes (two sizes: half-inch wide and one-inch wide)
- A set of sculpting tools
- Plastic droppers
- Disposable surgical scalpels
- Ruler/protractor
- Permanent marker
- T-pins
- Fun Tack
- Emery boards
- Mini brush for cleaning pastry tips
- Cosmetic swabs (pointed on one end; flat on the other)
- Envelope of whipped cream stabilizer
- Container of instant gel food thickener
- Bottle of adhesive remover for sticky labels on props

## Food Styling Supply Sites

Browse these Web sites for unique and specific items such as torches, realistic molded ice cubes, and other special effects:

- *www.thestylingstore.com:* Assorted professional food styling supplies

- *www.trengovestudios.com:* Food styling special effect supplies, acrylic spills, ice cubes

- *www.foodesigns.com:* Complete food-styling kits available for purchase

Here is some final encouragement from Lisa Golden Schroeder for would-be food stylists. "Like all new ventures, be willing to pay your dues. It might seem like a slow process to get started. But once you have the skills and savvy to do the job, you'll find yourself in a unique business that requires hard work but is also very creative and often fun! Food styling is a competitive business, but if you do good work you'll always be in demand."

# Room Sets and Bedding



**P**RESENTING ROOMS IN HOMES IS A BIG PART OF STYLING. Projects can range from feature stories in decorating magazines to advertisements for refrigerators or windows to catalogs for linens. Titles for professionals who do these projects can vary, but essentially they are doing styling with special expertise in decorating techniques.

Rooms and interiors are styled for video and film, of course, and these set designers have unique skills and techniques. Many stylists work in both still photography and commercials, as do other specialty stylists. For our study of room styling, we will focus on still photography. There is plenty to learn, and the basic skills explored here will carry over to film.

## ARCHITECTURAL PHOTOGRAPHY

Architectural photographers are experts in various areas requiring unique knowledge and specific equipment. Some photograph the interior design of residential spaces; these are the photographers you will usually work with as a stylist. Others may have expertise with exteriors, industrial locations, or commercial spaces.

The stylist must become accustomed to working with an architectural photographer. Lenses, lighting, and camera positions are different from small-scale studio photography; here, an entire room is being recorded.

You need to be able to visualize the space from a ladder or wherever the camera is positioned.

## Who Are the Clients?

There are many home-related clients, because our society continues to appreciate the comfort and security of the home. Magazines geared toward the home contain interior and sometimes exterior shots for feature stories and smaller articles about homes and gardens.

Business-to-business clients such as manufacturers of windows, window coverings, carpets and other floor coverings, kitchen cabinets, bathroom fixtures, countertops, and furniture provide a huge volume of photography work. They produce wholesale distributor catalogs and other marketing materials. They also generate advertising for selling directly to the public.

Retail catalogs sell furniture, home products, bedding, and linens. Some notable catalogs with great styling are IKEA, Crate & Barrel, Restoration Hardware, and Pottery Barn.

Most jobs are generated through the photographer; having a few photographers recommending you for their jobs can keep you sufficiently busy. Find and make contact with architectural photographers in your area, and do the same for magazines, catalogs, and manufacturers. When calling magazines and catalogs, ask for the art director, the photography art director, or the person who books stylists for photo shoots. Manufacturers' marketing departments would be the place to start your contact there. Advertising agencies that represent those clients may provide you with opportunities or at least give you an idea of the type of projects going on. (The self-promotion strategies discussed in chapter 11 are basic to all photo stylists.) Word of mouth is the best form of advertising. Once you have established relationships with architectural photographers or clients who can give referrals, you are on your way.

## A HOME STYLIST'S STORY

Colleen Heather Rogan is a stylist who has been involved in many aspects of the home-styling industry. She has worked for magazines both on staff and as a contributing editor and stylist. She has also styled for various commercial and private clients. After many years in New York City, she moved back to her hometown of Milwaukee, bringing her skills to a new market. She tells us in her own words about her propping techniques and her impressions of different types of styling projects.

*I think the best way to describe what I do is to say that I gather things together, to aesthetically create a mood, character, or context to meet a reader's or client's needs. I do freelance work as the Style and Home Editor of* Milwaukee Magazine, *doing interior editorial styling for the magazine's home features and a monthly "Savvy Home" feature. I also do advertising product styling and personal home styling.*

*Given that I started out as a visual artist, composition and spatial relationships between objects remain paramount to me. I'm a bit of a purist when it comes to maintaining the focus of my styling, and I think it shows in the quality of my work. I approach each room setting, tablescape, vignette detail, or product shot in the same way I would a drawing, painting, or collage. It's hard to explain the exact process of why I choose one particular prop over another or why I place it where I do, because it feels so instinctual with me; it's just what I do.*

*But basically, when I'm about to style a shot or an interior, I familiarize myself with the product or the space I'll be working with before making a "wish list" of the general sort of props I feel I'll need. Having established the "mood" I want to create, I can quickly pick out the props based on whether they'll "feel" as though they "belong" on set.*

## Visual Decisions

*As a visual person, everything I look at seems to resonate with a certain weight, style, or character which either will or won't work for the shoot. My goal is a seamless blend of color, texture, pattern, and surface. While I might not use everything I bring to the shoot, everything I bring will have the potential of aesthetically working together.*

*As I begin to prop or stage a set or interior, I go through a kind of internal editing process, deciding which of the items I've brought will actually be used. Instead of a conscious thought process, this shaping of visual balance feels very internal. I just don't feel completely comfortable until my eye rests easily, with every element contributing to the whole. Like all art, it's a very intuitive process. If I have a personal signature, it's the visual cohesiveness of my styling. Whether establishing something soft and feminine, sleek and sophisticated, cool and urban, warm and homey, or quirky and eccentric, my goal is to always create something where nothing feels out of its own particular place in space.*

*My own styling work has been a natural outgrowth of my fine-arts background, early years spent in a large department-store display department, styling done for New York designer showrooms, and years spent working as a staff editor for a national women's lifestyle magazine. Through it all, I've honed a sharp eye for composition, an astute sense of color, and the ability to pull together the elements needed to create strong visual statements.*

## Editorial Versus Commercial Styling

*I enjoy editorial styling for its creative freedom, even though commercial styling comes with a decidedly bigger paycheck. Though sometimes that higher day rate comes at a cost. For instance, the styling goal of an editorial feature is to visually tell a story or support copy with images; you're working to satisfy the needs of your editor or art director to give visual inspiration, information, or direction to the reader. On an editorial shoot it's usually just me, a photographer, and an assistant or two. Things are styled, film is shot, and that's that.*

*On the other hand, the direct goal in styling an advertising shoot is to, well, sell. To make money. From creative directors to company executives, the primary focus is how well the product looks. And because there's a lot of money riding on the success of a convincing advertising image, there are always tons of people on set—each with a vested interest in every little detail of how the product comes across.*

*For example, it's not unusual to have a creative director along with various advertising or product executives cast votes on whether a pen should be laid facing left or right, ponder which color pie filling is the most complementary to a tablecloth, or question if a stack of towels should move half an inch to the left. Sets are styled, shot, and often digitally sent to others "in charge" for approval. Some stylists can get frustrated with this kind of intense decision-making by committee.*

## Different Markets

*There is a definite difference between styling for a national market and a local market. New York is a styling mecca; the work is intense, sophisticated, and lucrative; plus stylists have plenty of venues to pursue given the amount of television, film, advertising, magazines, retail, and fashion options open to them. California and big cities like Chicago are strong, too. But in other areas of the country, frankly, there isn't as much interesting work. You won't find as many major clients, budgets are often smaller, and in many cases the directives and goals of the shoots aren't as creatively ambitious. Plus, if there's no one to raise the bar by example, the quality of work done can suffer.*

*As a stylist, let's face it, it's easier to get excited by doing an extensive shoot for a national client in a beautiful location with a huge prop budget than it is to figure out how to make mediocre products look good in studio shots for a client with a small budget. Yet in the end, a good stylist's intent should be to make anything and everything look the best it possibly can.*

*Another aspect of smaller markets is, unfortunately, without the challenge of interesting work, good stylists miss the opportunity to get experience and develop their skills to their full potential.*

## Styling Quality

*I believe that if you're presenting something for public consumption— whether it's a table setting or a room shot styled for an ad, a magazine, or a catalog page—just getting it done isn't good enough. Stylists are in the business of inspiration, of bringing ideas to life, of showing what can be done. The importance of their role in a shoot is easily equal to that of the photographer. After all, no matter whether a shot is well photographed and badly styled, or badly photographed and well styled, you end up with a bad photo, don't you?*

*Styling is an art. I'm proud of my ability to do it well. I remain grateful for the opportunities I've been given, for the incredible mentoring I received, and for what I've been able to accomplish. After leaving my hometown as an artist with a discerning eye and some success with dressing windows and pulling together store displays, New York became my graduate school and it was there I really polished my skills as a stylist.*

# HOME MAGAZINES

One of the most fascinating careers I have heard about is that of an editor/stylist I met a few years ago. Her work for a home magazine includes scouting interesting homes in the area, approaching the homeowner about the idea, and presenting the story concept to the magazine. If it is accepted for an issue, the editor/stylist works with a photographer to style and shoot the rooms according to the magazine's approved layout and shot list, and finally, writes the accompanying article. What a nice job to have if you love home decorating and have writing skills. At least that was my initial impression.

On further investigation I found she is a journalist by training. The editor is not on staff and works as an independent contractor, or freelancer, with no benefits provided, or advances for expenses. Most non-journalist field editors don't write articles but do gather extensive facts, sources, floor plans, and "before" photos for use by the assigned writer. Multiple projects are submitted before any are selected for publication, so there is upfront time and money involved. It often feels like a wild goose chase, and that might be frustrating for some. In addition, magazines are particular about selecting applicants and interview extensively for these positions.

While the position is more complex than I initially thought, I still feel it's a fascinating use of skills for the right person.

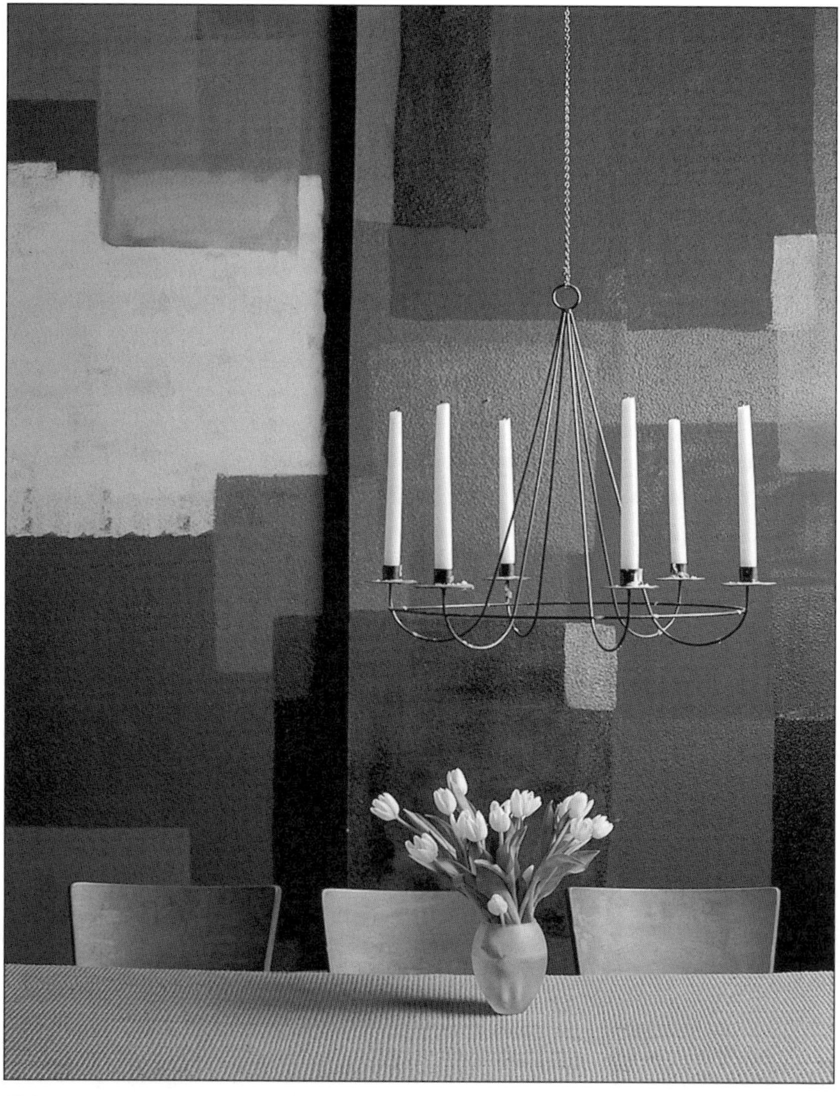

Dining room image features a simple chandelier, a vase of fresh tulips, and custom wall paint. *Styling:* Colleen Heather Rogan. © *Milwaukee Magazine*

## Staff or Freelance Editors

Colleen Heather Rogan, with her editorial background, describes the work this way: "An on-staff editor might style shoots as well as research the bed, bath, furniture, stationery, and gift markets and major industry launches looking for current trends. Some magazines have 'scouts' or regional people who act as a first response to stories and ideas. Their function is to funnel appropriate stories to the magazine for editorial consideration. Some years back, I was paid a monthly fee by a national magazine to find good prospects that fit the magazine's editorial vision. I presented the why, what, and where of the story to them and the magazine would assign someone on staff or freelance to style the stories they were interested in pursuing."

When stylists are hired freelance for editorial projects they may be listed as "contributing stylist" or "contributing editor" in the magazine. Again, no matter how well decorated the home is there are always adjustments that need to be made for photography. Items will be repositioned or omitted, and props will be added.

## PRODUCTION DESIGNER

Jay Bruns is a Minneapolis-based production designer with years of experience in his profession. I first met Jay when he needed an assistant on a month-long photo shoot for Hunter Douglas window coverings. Assisting him was a pleasure, as I had the opportunity to learn about the big picture of styling rooms, renting furniture, accessorizing, and propping for architectural shots.

The photographer, art director, client, and Jay had earlier traveled to San Diego to scout several homes for the series of photos, focusing on the right type of windows and other factors such as high ceilings, open space, and architectural details. The rooms had already been selected when Jay arrived to work with me on a week-long search for the furnishings.

I was the local resource, knowing my way around town, but I found stores I didn't know about before. Each project presents the stylist with such a unique challenge that the work is always new. Together Jay and I visited antique stores, carpet stores, and other sources to find potential items from stores that were willing to rent them to us. I photographed them—after asking permission—and Jay made presentation boards for the art director's approval. We rented a truck, hired a driver and a helper, and bought needed supplies. Daily schedules of locations, styles, and individual furniture and décor had to be refined. Part of my responsibility was coordinating the complex rental and return of furnishings to and from various sources each day.

## Interview with a Production Designer

I was curious about Jay's use of the term "production designer" when defining his profession and asked him how it differs from "stylist." I also wondered how he estimates the amount of time preparing for his projects, and how many assistants are needed.

*The title "production designer" may be different for different people. I use the term to indicate to clients that I have other skills than just photo styling. I'm able to manage an entire production from the ground up, including designing sets, consulting on styles and trends, shopping and dressing the sets, and managing a production crew both on location and at home.*

*Designing sets is fun for me because I get to use all my interior design background: architecture, period details, scale, materials, colors, etc. Then, all of the above has to be designed to be seen through a lens, whether motion or still. Each picture has a product "point of view," and everything—windows, floors, cabinets, and furniture—has to be geared for that product. All aspects of the set are chosen to give the viewer a clear and quick read on the product. Materials and "dressings," or props, need to coordinate with the product, but not take too much attention.*

*Shopping and dressing sets is more the job of stylist. I have many jobs like this too, where the set is already determined, and it becomes my job to do the prop shopping and decorate the set. It can be as simple as adding fresh flowers and moving around a few things that are already there, or more complex, bringing in full rooms of furniture. A great deal of thought goes into what goes where. I can always tell shots that are "propped," meaning the stylist is more of a propper than designer and puts something on a table because it looks bare; the overall result is a propped room, as opposed to one with lifestyle.*

## Prep Time and Wrap

*Every job is different and will have its own particular requirements. Typically I'll ask for two to five days to plan and shop for a job before it's photographed. If there is "design time" involved—designing a set, shopping for set materials, story boards, concepts, and tear sheets—I'd usually ask for another four or five days. Smaller jobs have shorter prep times. I usually do all the shopping, which is useful at the return since I'll know where everything came from.*

*The wrap is usually a one-day task. The assistants do most of the returns. When I can, I like to go along to personally make sure it's all there and in good shape, and to thank the merchants for playing along and letting us use their merchandise. It's also nice to send a short thank-you note to merchants, which is one more level of creating a "comfort zone" with them.*

## Working with Assistants

*Also as a production designer, I always work with at least one assistant and sometimes three or four. I hire hard-working assistants who are geared to solving production issues, leaving me free to concentrate on design and putting rooms together. When we do large shoots involving a lot of furniture, I like to use the "two guys and a truck" method in addition to having my assistant. These workers do all the furniture pick-ups, drive the truck, prep the location, and do returns. It's a great load off my mind to have someone else handle that part of the job. My assistant will also do the out-of-town hiring when we go on location, and many times I'll look for a local stylist to work with to lead me to good resources and help with the shopping.*

## Staying Current

Research for production designers is ongoing and endless. It includes almost everything from visiting places when traveling, such as historical sites, museums, gardens, churches, and new shops; attending classes and seminars; and exploring libraries, books, magazines, movies, and plays.

Jay presents seminars for some of his clients, educating them about trends in home decorating, helping them plan for market positioning and future product launches. This motivates him to keep ahead of trends.

Writing articles, giving talks, and serving as a resource for clients are some ways of establishing yourself as an expert in the home styling field.

## Renting Furnishings

Regardless of the quality of the homeowner's belongings, it may be necessary, for style reasons, to replace them with rented furnishings. If items already in the home can be used, it certainly helps with the budget. Often some combination will be the solution. But keep in mind how things look on film, as Jay mentioned. The camera sees details and flaws while our vision can filter them out.

Flooring (carpet or hardwood) may be placed over existing carpets or other floor surfaces as a temporary solution in room styling. If you're styling an empty room or a studio set, you will start from scratch.

Experience with retail furnishings not only provides knowledge of the industry, but also helps a stylist work with merchants. Contact with wholesale buyers or retail stores early in your career can create a basis for later styling or production design work.

Says Jay, "It's valuable, when shopping for jobs, to speak the language of the merchants and put them at ease when asking to rent their merchandise. You should talk about what the project is, how long you'll need to have the item out of their store, and how well you'll take care of it while you have it."

## STYLING SUGGESTIONS FOR ROOMS

Remember that in styling for rooms and homes you are literally looking at the big picture, unlike the precise, close-up styling you might use in, say, folded garments. Working with an architectural photographer, your awareness of the entire set, your place in the room, and coordinating all the elements you are responsible for are critical parts of your job.

Watch for reflections in mirrors and windows. Photographers will use techniques and materials to minimize these problems. Checking for camera angle and what is visible, be sure *you* don't create a reflection or shadow. Areas outside windows or doors are important. Be prepared to style these areas with bedding plants, potted trees, or patio furniture. The outdoors will generally appear bright, or "blown out," in relation to the lighted interior.

If a photographer is using a dim light indoors, such as a small lamp, candles, or Christmas lights, it will take multiple exposures to allow them to show.

Create the feeling that the resident just walked away, that there is life going on there even when you can't see people. Some props that create this feeling include shoes or slippers on the floor, an open book and glasses, a magazine, a glass of lemonade or iced tea, or a cardigan sweater draped over a chair.

The props used for magazines, catalogs, advertising, and business-to-business promotions are essentially similar. The focus is always on the product or lifestyle, with props used carefully to enhance rather than distract. A food stylist may be booked for food and beverage props, or when there is complex propping in a kitchen or dining room set.

The following lists of props for areas of the home are provided as inspiration and a starting point for your thinking process, not as a complete list.

These props can help create an appealing environment, enhancing larger items such as furniture and area rugs. With many different styles and types of projects you may be working on, your own creative mind will complete the lists.

## Props for Living Areas:
- Flowering orchids in pots
- Flowers in vases
- Tropical leaves in large vases
- Large potted plants like fiddle-leaf fig, ficus benjamina, or palms
- Stand of umbrellas
- Books on shelf or table, hardcover with dust jackets removed
- Stack of large books to serve as end table
- Framed prints, paintings, or mirrors hung or leaning against walls
- Stacks of boxes and baskets
- Flat tray, basket, or dish
- Stack of letters, other mail, car keys
- Lamps
- Candles arranged on platter
- Glass of lemonade or iced tea
- Glass(es) of wine, or martinis
- Plates of hors d'oeuvres
- Bowl of popcorn
- Throw pillows
- Shoes or slippers on floor
- Open book or magazine
- Cardigan sweater draped over chair
- Throws, to add softness and drape

## Props for Bedrooms:
- Flowers in small vases
- Books
- Clock
- Slippers

- Prints or photos on wall
- Small framed photos (Don't use without model releases if people are visible.)
- Glass and/or decanter of water
- Bedside lamps
- Extra blankets or throws

## Props for Kitchens:

- Cookbooks
- Wall clock
- Bulletin board with notes and lists
- Bowls of vegetables or fruit
- Container of cooking utensils
- Coffee cups, maybe next to coffee maker
- Cruet of dish soap
- Dishtowel draped on counter
- Cutting board and knife
- Food being prepared on counter
- Wrapped bouquet of flowers

## Props for Home Offices:

- Laptop computer
- Desktop blotters
- Pens and pencils, loose or in containers
- Notebooks and file folders
- Letters with letter opener
- Racks for supplies
- Collectible paperweights
- Wastebasket
- Office chair
- Desk lamp
- Telephone, either very modern or classic

## Props for Bathrooms:

- Bathrobe
- Slippers

- Glass jars of cotton balls and swabs
- Fancy soaps
- Towels, folded or draped
- Loofah sponges
- Shells, in jars or on shelves

## Props for Exteriors:

- Doormat
- Jute outdoor rug
- Rolled newspaper
- Potted plants, small trees
- Flowering border plants and ferns
- Flip flops, beach ball, or beach towel, for poolside
- Children's toys, bicycles
- Croquet set
- Open book or magazine
- Sunglasses
- Candles
- Tray
- Glass of lemonade or iced tea
- Cardigan sweater draped over chair
- Throws, to add softness and drape

## HOW TO STYLE BEDDING

Quite a few catalogs sell bedding and other linens to consumers. Their goal is to present an attractive environment making readers want to decorate the room where we spend the most time, the bedroom. Seasonal changes and updating color themes result in repeat shoppers.

Over time, styles for all types of presentations change. The current fashion for styling beds is soft and sensual. Look at catalogs and you'll see partially made beds, soft ripples on blankets or bedspreads, and a casual, comforting look. Many beds in catalogs today look recently slept in but still fresh.

Not many years ago the style was tight and precise. The styling had to be perfect and smooth. The days of flawless bed styling are gone; now you need to use fluffs of batting to build the gentle folds. Keep up on design magazines and catalogs as styles continually evolve.

## Sets Built in Studio

Often it is more convenient for catalogers to build rooms in studios than to go to location houses. Even though architectural details would already exist, limitations include smaller spaces, location availability, transporting products and props, and more lighting challenges for the photographer.

Set builders may be full-time or freelance workers who have skills and materials to quickly build temporary walls. They will add details such as window frames, doors, painted walls, sconces, baseboards, flooring, and even bathtubs, sinks, and toilets. When a window is used, there may be large rear-lit film images to create instant exterior views.

The stylist will be responsible for styling the entire room, unless there is an art director on hand who selects furniture for the space, as sometimes happens. Smaller props and details are the stylist's job, in any case.

## Stacks and Swatches

As with clothing catalogs, the merchandise is available in several colors. These need to be shown in very neat or casually irregular stacks. And since this is the catalog shopper's only opportunity to imagine the feel of the fabric, it must be shown clearly and up-close.

Study the section on styling stacks in chapter 7. The same principles apply to stacks of towels, sheets, or blankets. But the linens are more challenging: they are bigger, heavier, and harder to manage. Keeping a very large stack in position can be quite a challenge—use hidden tape, foam board, or other materials to stabilize the stack. A stack may be used to show edge details with some items turned in a different direction. A corner may be flipped over at the top of the stack for the same purpose.

Other presentations are sometimes used. For instance, linens may be fanned out in a radius, rolled, or stacked on top of a made bed. On top of a stack of towels, one may be draped to soften the shape and to show thickness and texture.

## Bedding Techniques

Ironing the linens is the first step in the process of styling a bed. While the top portion that is showing is the most important, the entire sheet should be pressed. Work on a large table that is covered with a blanket; an ironing board is not large enough for most prepping. Steaming just isn't adequate for most sheets, pillowcases, and blankets, though it can be used for towels. Keep a steamer nearby on the set, preheated and ready to use. It will be useful for touch-ups.

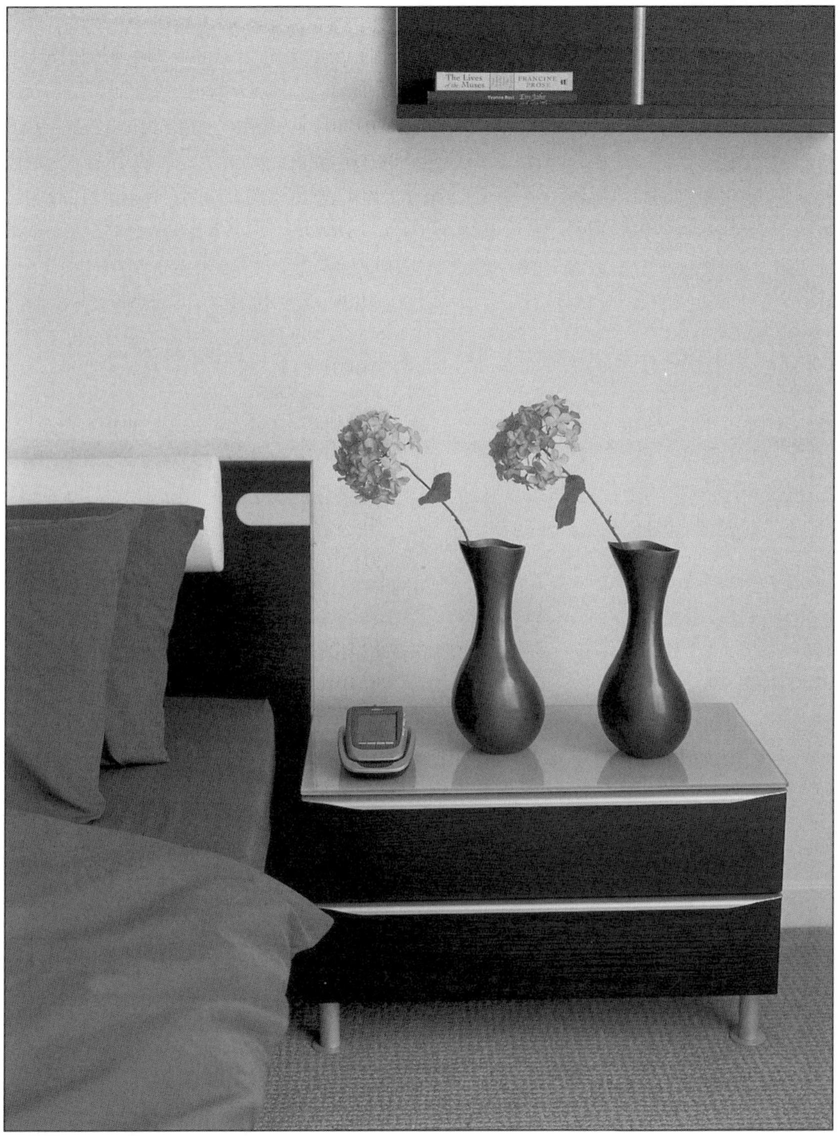

Bedside table with relaxed and comfortable bed styling. Repetition of two vases, two drawers, and two pillows adds interest. *Styling:* Colleen Heather Rogan. © *Milwaukee Magazine*

The bed you are styling may be a real mattress or it may be a fake, made out of lightweight foam carved to a mattress shape. These are much easier to move around a studio. It will probably be placed on "apple crates," or wooden boxes, to the optimum height (but not necessarily level), and have a headboard positioned the same way to make a good presentation.

Cover the mattress with a couple of down comforters folded or tucked to fit the mattress top. The effect will be softer and fluffier, more comforting. The bottom fitted sheet now goes on as usual, but pull it firmly and hold it in place on the far sides with T-pins pushed into the mattress. The top sheet shouldn't be tucked in at the bottom; leaving it loose will allow you to pull it later to the most attractive position without having to take apart the bed. The next layer, the blanket or bedspread, looks better with another layer of down comforter under it. Yes, this is why those beds look so inviting. Pull the top sheet up and over the top of it, adding a soft ripple or two.

Lots of pillows are placed at the head of the bed. Pillows covered by a layer of batting or felt pinned to them are smoother and fill the pillowcases better. Use a complementary assortment of pillowcases approved by the art director to build this end of the bed. By looking at them from the camera view, layer them for the desired effect. Floppy corners can be stiffened by placing a piece of white tape at the back.

The next stage is the top surface of the bed. Based on the style, look, and color of the product, you will have selected some props and accessories for the room to make the bedding look its best in the environment. Will there be a prop placed on the bed? While styling the bed and allowing the photographer to set up lighting, you will be placing other accessories in the room and assessing how well they work.

All this takes time, with a good deal of consultation with the art director and photographer. The project is physically large, the set is far from the camera, and the linens can be heavy. Your bed shots may be interspersed with stacks and other presentations, and you'll likely be working alongside other stylist and photographer teams.

### Related Careers

Creating store displays, though it is not photo styling, requires many of the same skills and techniques. Whether store windows or dressed mannequins, a display is created for the public to view from various perspectives. It is used for store "branding" and to make the products desirable.

Another related area, yet a world apart, is set design for films and television. An imaginary world is created with every detail in place, and it needs to be consistent throughout production and from different viewpoints.

## SPECIALTY KIT LISTS

This is a list of items that are helpful to have in a room stylist's kit, in addition to the basic kit described in chapter 13.

| ITEM | DESCRIPTION, USE |
|---|---|
| *Room Styling* | |
| ❑ Folding table | When you have many props on hand, keeps them in view |
| ❑ Dustpan and brush | For cleaning sidewalks and floors |
| ❑ Broom | For sweeping sidewalks and rooms |
| ❑ Mini vacuum cleaner | Quick vacuum of set; battery powered and rechargeable |
| ❑ Hairbrush | For straightening carpet fringe |
| ❑ Collapsible mop | For quick floor cleanups, reaches to clean windows; compact |
| ❑ Disposable cleaning sheets | For dusting and wiping up or used with mop; both wet and dry |
| ❑ Furniture polish | Even out tones of wood floors, furniture; touch up scratches |
| ❑ Furniture repair markers | In assorted colors, touch up marks and scratches |
| ❑ Cotton rags | For cleanup or polishing |
| ❑ Furniture pads | Adhesive felt disks to protect floors |
| ❑ Paring knife | For slicing prop lemons, etc. |
| ❑ Cutting board | For slicing; find thin type that can be rolled up |
| ❑ Corkscrew | For opening prop wine, beer, or soda bottles |
| ❑ Dishwashing detergent, sponge | For washing dishes prior to use and afterwards |
| ❑ Paper towels | For drying dishes, cleanup, and other uses |
| ❑ Window cleaner | For windows and mirrors; touching up plates and glasses |
| ❑ Torch lighter, matches | For lighting candles or fires |
| ❑ Gardening gloves | Keep hands clean when working with garden plants |
| ❑ Garden shears | For trimming plants, cutting branches |
| ❑ Rake | For clearing lawns of leaves and debris |

*Bedding and Linens*

| | | |
|---|---|---|
| ❏ | Iron and large covered table | For ironing bedding |
| ❏ | Down comforters | To pad mattress |
| ❏ | Rolls of batting and white felt | For wrapping pillows, building stacks |
| ❏ | Fiber fill | To fill and soften beds, building stacks |
| ❏ | Sturdy scissors | To cut batting and tape |
| ❏ | Long T-pins | For positioning sheets into mattress |
| ❏ | Heavy white tape | For stiffening pillowcase corners |
| ❏ | Apple crates | Wooden boxes used by photographers, use for raising furniture |
| ❏ | Foam board | For supporting stacks and pillows |

The home is, more and more, a comforting environment. More money is spent on home furnishings than ever, as people go to movies and restaurants less and less, staying home to watch DVDs. This trend shows no signs of diminishing and there should be plentiful work on home product catalogs in the future.

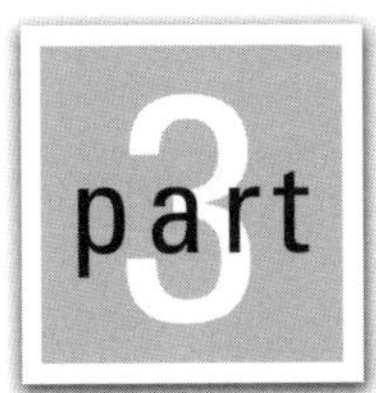



# Business for Photo Stylists

# Marketing Yourself

**T**HE REAL-LIFE STORY OF MAKEUP ARTIST CLAIRE YOUNG has many parallels to a photo styling story. Claire, although creative and educated, didn't know about the "invisible world" of photo shoots. She knew there must a perfect career out there waiting for her, but she wasn't sure what it was. She searched until she found it. She knew the first day she walked into a photo studio that she belonged there.

## A MAKEUP ARTIST'S STORY

The patient and dedicated way Claire went about building her career has lessons for aspiring stylists. Let's see how she did it:

*My makeup career began at Bloomingdale's in Chicago, my hometown. Starting out in retail, as opposed to cosmetology school, presented me with experience being up close and personal with women I didn't know. I was literally "in their faces," touching them and looking at their skin. It may seem strange, but applying makeup to a person's face can actually feel kind of intimate, because it involves touch. It took me a while to get over my resistance to physical contact with strangers; but once I did, I realized that I had a natural capability with makeup application.*

*With a background in fine art and graphic design, I already had experience with color theory and a basic understanding of how colors affect other colors. What I had to learn about makeup application was how color interacts with skin and skin tone. There is a big, big difference between color applied to paper or canvas, and color applied to skin.*

## Looking for Something New

*I stayed in retail for three years until I became restless, bored, and tired of department store sales. It occurred to me that I could sell my own skills instead of selling makeup. I reflected on who would have a need for my particular skill-set. Luckily, the first group that occurred to me was professional photographers.*

*I started out on a fact-finding mission. I knew Chicago was a huge city with a lot of people, but how to track down the particular demographic I was searching for presented me with a substantial challenge. I began by looking in the Yellow Pages! This was back in the late 1980s.*

*Cracking open the phone book, I started making cold calls. Eventually I stumbled upon a photographer, JimVaughan, who took pity on me and invited me to come over and see his studio.*

## Building a Portfolio

*I gratefully accepted his offer and met him at his studio. It was one of those ultra-hip, converted loft spaces in Chicago's meat-packing district. When I walked into his studio, I knew instantly that this was the type of environment I wanted to work in. It was so different from the brightly lit, noisy, chaotic, and sales-driven world of department stores. Jim specialized in actors' headshots, so I started out doing makeup and men's grooming for these photos. Jim would always give me an extra print. I began to create my portfolio, a never-ending process.*

*Gradually I was ready to leave the familiarity of Jim's studio. I met some highly trained, very skilled photographers that I clicked with right away. One photographer enrolled me in doing some experimental shoots, or "testing." At first, I was reluctant to work for free, but as time went on, I began to see the value of testing. Working this way gives the photographer and the makeup artist freedom to play, experiment, and basically do anything and everything.*

## Ready for Prime Time

*Eventually I developed enough confidence to venture into a completely different world: television. I met a makeup artist, Shannon Meder, who referred me to the head of the makeup department at WBBM in Chicago. This woman decided to give me a shot as an assistant and substitute makeup artist based on Shannon's recommendation; so I found myself doing makeup for news anchors and reporters! It was a great experience, and soon I was given responsibility to do makeup for my own show, the early-morning news broadcast.*

*Doing makeup for live news broadcasts proved fun but very challenging. There is absolutely no wiggle room in terms of time. If the broadcast goes live at 5:30 A.M., the anchors must be at their desks at 5:15 to get their microphones hooked up and prepare for the top story of that morning. No excuses are considered acceptable. I always found this aspect of the business nerve-wracking, as opposed to doing makeup for print or a test, where I could take two hours to do the makeup and hair if I wanted to.*

*The early morning show was my domain for a year. During this time my good friend Shannon introduced me to one of the head producers of the Oprah Winfrey Show. The producer had a roster of freelance makeup artists hired on a rotation basis to do makeup for Oprah's guests in the "green room," where special guests waited to go on the air. Eventually I was called in to work on such guests as Maya Angelou and John F. Kennedy, Jr. It was an exciting, fast-paced, and creative environment to work in; I loved it, and working for Oprah Winfrey gave me the credibility I needed when I moved to southern California in 1997.*

## Getting to Know a New Market

*I don't do much TV work any more. Much to my dismay, when I moved to San Diego I discovered that only a few markets like Chicago, Los Angeles, and New York are big enough for a full-time makeup department. The news anchors here do their own makeup; apparently this is the norm for most parts of the country.*

*Now my business occurs in a variety of domains, such as video, print, catalog, editorial, and even weddings. The San Diego market demands flexibility and willingness to take on a variety of tasks, such as wardrobe and prop styling, which is something I never had been asked to do during my time in Chicago.*

*Because the market here is tight and the competition so fierce, I have found that the more willing I am to do everything and anything called for during a shoot—including making coffee or running out to pick up lunch for the crew—the better my chances of being hired again. Being a good sport and a team player are the two essential aspects of this business—even beyond having the best makeup and hairstyling skills. More often than not, what's really called for is a good attitude, a pleasant demeanor, and being someone other people enjoy working with. These attributes have nothing to do with makeup application, hairstyling, or styling, but they are highly valued nevertheless.*

## BUILDING YOUR STYLING BUSINESS

When you're starting out, you'll learn from any role you play in a photo shoot, whether it is assisting a stylist or doing errands. But you want to be a stylist. When you've built up a portfolio, and you're ready to embark on your career, you need to find your first clients.

You can start by looking at the market you're located in and doing some research. Are there catalog companies and magazines based near you? Are there any large retailers that create their own advertising? How many advertising agencies are there? How far will you have to travel to the nearest large city? Do you have a friend you could stay with while you visit possible clients there? Find out who the photographers are in your area and in the nearby city.

### Finding Clients through Photographers

Most often, commercial photographers are your best source of work. Wedding or portrait photographers won't be likely to use a stylist. Commercial photographers shooting for advertising or catalogs are the ones who hire stylists.

Ad agencies, graphic designers, and publications are likely to find the photographer first. Often art directors will contact several photographers for estimates on proposed projects. They may have found one photographer they're anxious to work with but will contact a couple others for comparison. Then the photographer needs to line up a potential stylist and get a quote to incorporate into the estimate. After that, the photographer may not get the project. Don't count on bidding a job as anything more than a possibility. But it might happen and you may work with the same photographer again and again.

So it's good to let photographers know who you are. You can contact photographers, locally and even nationwide, by sending postcards to a mailing list. Introduce yourself to all nearby photographers who do commercial work. Find lists of photographers through local film commissions, and photography organizations such as ASMP (American Society of Media Photographers) and APA (Advertising Photographers of America). Information on these organizations is available on page 197. If you find one or two photographers whom you work very well with, they may be your best source of clients.

## Finding Clients Directly

Other clients, such as catalogs and magazines for example, may contact you directly to work with a photographer they have chosen. Catalog art directors generally hire stylists for fashion shoots themselves, since it's such an important role. Make sure that any local catalog companies or retailers know who you are by contacting the art directors and asking to show them your "book," as your portfolio is known.

Word-of-mouth recommendations are wonderful when they happen; this is where your alliance with photographers comes into play. You might send your postcard to a mailing list of photo buyers or catalog companies. But the most effective, and easiest, marketing method is to let clients find you through your Web site. Remember to include the name of your Website in all listings and promotional materials.

I've been contacted by photo editors from magazines, or their assistants, for styling projects. The key was my Web site and other resources I was listed with (more about these resources follows).

## The Ironies of Styling

I've found, as an amusing irony, that when I have travel plans that can't be changed, I will inevitably get a call from a new client for a great project. When this happens you just have to laugh, get the contact information for the missed client, and hope you get another opportunity.

After you commit to a month-long project, you will surely get a call or two about some interesting one-day styling jobs during the same period. And you'll have to pass them by. When it rains, it pours, especially after a long unsettling drought. This is a good time to mention other stylists you have gotten to know—and they'll refer jobs back to you. You then also become a problem-solver for the caller, who might appreciate it and remember you for the next job. It helps if you have worked with the other stylist and can recommend her based on professional experience. If not, get yourself off the hook by saying that you've heard good things about the stylist.

If your search for styling jobs is really dead in the water, you can always look for a job. Even if you apply for a part-time or seasonal job, it's inevitable that once your application has been submitted and your references checked, some styling work will suddenly appear. If worst comes to worst, and nothing happens, at least you will have a transitional job lined up.

## COLLABORATION AND TESTING

Due to the nature of the catalog business, every page is valuable "real estate." The costs of design, photography, writing copy, merchandising the products, and then printing and mailing mean that there won't be much wasted space. There are a few well-designed catalogs that feature one product on a whole page, but this is the exception, not the rule. You may do a styling project for a catalog, and do a marvelous job. Each individual shot was magnificent, and you can barely wait till the printed catalog arrives. You will probably be disappointed. Your beautiful shot that took so much time will end up about two inches tall—and may even have words printed over it. When you scan the image so you can enlarge and add it to your portfolio, the printing on the back of the page shows through. That is the catalog industry.

But take heart. The way to get around this problem is to participate in testing. It is also known as trade-out or test for prints (TFP). Testing is a group effort in which a crew develops a photography concept, plans the project, and executes it, all to produce images for self-promotion.

### The Creative Value of Testing

Your best and most rewarding work may result from testing. This is also your opportunity for creative expression. You aren't limited by what the client and art director are looking for. You aren't selling a product—you are bringing a concept to life. You may get inspiration from editorial stories in magazines. Perhaps another stylist's portfolio or Web site will give you ideas about what is missing in yours. Your test shoot may be an edgy concept involving fashion, props, and a unique environment. Or it can simply be a "beauty shot" using a beautiful model and classic wardrobe in the studio.

Contact modeling agencies to find new models who need to build their portfolios and are willing to work for images, hence "test for prints." Be clear with the agent that the shoot is a test for self-promotion. When you call the agency later for actual clients, you will already have rapport with a particular agent. The model will need to sign a model-release form at the shoot and will expect some digital files or printed samples for her book.

You may have acquaintances with the look you want, but their lack of camera experience could make the shoot less successful. It might be worth trying for the learning experience or cases when the talent isn't the feature of the shoot.

Use the contacts you make during shoots for your collaborations. Photographers, assistants, models, and makeup artists all should be glad to work with you on tests. It can be an opportunity to work with a new photographer and see how well you work together, sometimes building a lasting professional relationship.

What is difficult is finding a time when everyone is available for a non-paying project. If a job comes up for any of them, they are likely to take it, rather than decline it for a test shoot. In that case a lot of planning is wasted, but the risk is worth it, and the test shoot can always be rescheduled.

Tests are usually done on a shoestring. Since everyone is volunteering in exchange for images, there isn't usually any budget. Sometimes, but not often, an experienced model will be hired to ensure high-quality modeling. Wardrobe is likely to be something from your own collection or items that will be returned, so there isn't much styling expense. And you'll certainly want to find a location that is free.

Actual expenses may be snacks and water, and the photographer's film and printing costs. If the shoot is digital, making image CDs will be a nominal amount. Otherwise, the crewmembers' investment is largely time. It is important to clarify the expenses and how they'll be shared at the beginning of the collaboration.

## Each Test is Unique

In most cases a photographer or stylist will initiate the test, or they may come up with a concept together. Paula Tabaliba, one of my interns, was talking with photographer Jeffrey Brown about an underwater camera he had borrowed. Before returning it, he wanted to use it for a test, so together they developed an idea to shoot clothing in a swimming pool. The photographer had a contact at a public swimming pool and was able to arrange an early-morning shoot.

I helped Paula gather some wardrobe separates and accessories like silk-flower lei and some handbags. One challenge was determining what styling supplies we would need to position the clothing underwater. After some experimentation we used monofilament tied to weights and to long bamboo sticks suspended over the pool, and also used poles for poking and arranging the items. Paula spent a good bit of time diving under the water while I stayed at the edge of the pool, on my belly, reaching out to control floating garments. The photographer, of course, was underwater and communication was limited. Later we all selected some outstanding shots for our portfolios, because we'd each contributed to the project.

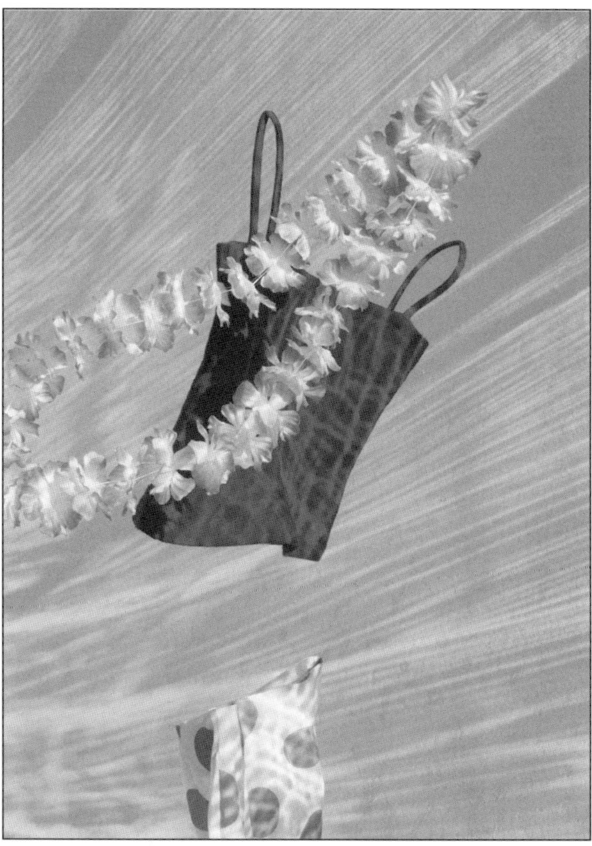

Fuchsia apparel and a lei photographed in a turquoise swimming pool make a unique portfolio addition. *Photographer:* Jeffrey Brown. *Styling:* Susan Linnet Cox and Paula Tabalipa. © Jeffrey Brown

For an earlier test shoot, I was inspired by an old "woody" stationwagon that a friend of a friend owned. Also, my daughter was working on her modeling portfolio. I contacted Greg Bertolini, a photographer who had recently stopped assisting—I knew he was building his book too. It was one of those fortunate tests involving a number of people available on the same Saturday morning. The photographer, a makeup artist, my daughter, a young male model, the car owner, and I met in a beachfront park. The beach restrooms were convenient for changing clothes, and I had brought several surfer-style Hawaiian-print garments.

The makeup artist ended up with a couple of close-up shots of the models' faces. The photographer took photos of the models and also details of the car for his book, and my favorite shot is the one of Elizabeth in the car interior. Finally, we set up a portrait of the car, which was printed as an enlargement for the car owner.

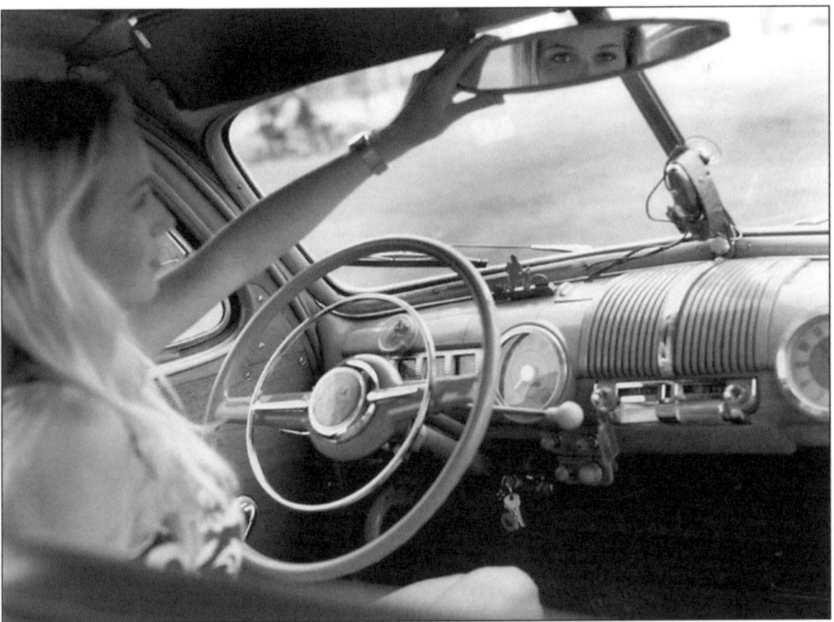

Opportunity to shoot in a classic "woody" stationwagon inspired this image. *Photographer:* Gregory Bertolini. *Styling:* Susan Linnet Cox. *Hair and makeup:* Lilly Widdes. © Gregory Bertolini

Although the benefits—building a portfolio and experience—are obvious for a beginning stylist, you should continue testing throughout your career. It's a habit you can maintain to keep yourself creatively challenged and your portfolio fresh. After the test shoot, make arrangements to view all the images and select your favorites for your portfolio.

## Editing Like an Art Director

This is close to the process art directors go through when editing the photographer's shots. As an art director, I used to edit film by looking at every single frame, narrowing it down to the best six to ten shots, and then making final selections with the merchandise buyers. Knowing how to edit your photographs like an art director will improve an art director's impression of your work. The final choices are ones where everything is nearly perfect. The model's expression and posture, the styling, and visible garment features are the main elements to watch for. When you review the film or digital images from your tests, you'll have a chance to see what you might have done differently and also make the best choices for your portfolio. When a detail was not right in frame after frame, I would be annoyed that I hadn't stopped the process to have the stylist change it.

If you are shooting two or more models, the editing process is more difficult. In addition to the above details, you need to look at the models' body language and how naturally they interact. There is also the matter of where they are looking. It doesn't work if they're looking in opposite directions, but it can work if the guy is looking at the girl, and she is looking down. If the models are caught in a moment when they're looking in the same direction or at the camera, the image is stronger.

## ACQUIRING SAMPLES OF YOUR WORK

Tear sheets, also known as "tears," are actual printed samples of your work. In the ad-agency world it's routine to have extra copies of an advertisement printed on high-quality paper. These are provided to the photographer and also to you, if you ask for one. The tear may also be a page from the actual magazine where the ad was placed. If you have to purchase the magazine yourself to get a tear sheet, cut the page out carefully using an X-Acto knife along the inside margin where the pages are glued or stapled together (known as the "gutter"). This can be placed directly into your portfolio or scanned and printed.

Remember to get the client's contact information during the shoot, so you can follow up and ask for tears. Try to find out when the ad will be in magazines and in which ones, so you can buy them. It's exciting to see your work in a national magazine!

It's not too difficult to get sample catalogs. You can ask the art director to send you some, but most likely new projects will get in the way and cause her to forget. The best tactic is to call the catalog's toll-free number and ask to be put on the mailing list. Do it right after the shoot so you don't forget. The catalog you worked on will probably appear in your mailbox in two or three months.

Although the catalog shots may only be one inch tall, you should still add some printed catalog pages to your portfolio. For one thing, it's interesting later to look back over your career and see how styles have changed and also that you've become more experienced. If you are pursuing a client in some specialty field, you can look through your samples and find related work, even though it may not be useful for your primary book. Save all your samples!

## YOUR PORTFOLIO

Portfolios are not as much a part of self-promotion as they used to be. Thanks to the Internet, you can present yourself without having to meet to show your portfolio. If you have a Web site, potential clients can find you from anywhere in the world. They might be looking at your online portfolio while they're speaking to you on the phone.

Still, you need to have a portfolio for those occasions when it is requested. You can carry your portfolio with you to jobs, too. You might have an opportunity to present it toward the end of the shoot day to the art director or photographer, if they have not recently seen it.

Art-supply stores are good places to look for portfolio cases. Usually black, they needn't be expensive or any particular style. A good choice has removable sleeve-style pages that can be added and rearranged. Choose a portfolio that will accommodate standard printer paper or larger, so that all your printouts and tears will fit into the pages.

Pagination is a process of designing "spreads" and deciding what goes where. A spread is a set of two facing pages; even though different pages are printed together for collating later on, a catalog is designed in spreads. You can design your portfolio by looking at facing pages. (Many stylists may not think of this.) I spread my samples out on the floor and rearrange them until I find the most complementary pairs of pages.

A large image might look good next to a small detail from the same shoot, with a border of white space around it. Two similar shots from different projects can make good neighbors. You can build themes and create a flow of the subject matter in your portfolio. These concepts will help you when planning out your Web site also.

You should periodically revise your portfolio to include new work. Add tears and images from tests. At the same time, you can remove samples that have become dated or don't represent your newer skills. By using removable pages you can change your presentation depending on the client. You may be presenting it to an athletic-wear catalog; in that case, you can pull sports samples from your files to emphasize related experience.

If you are represented by an agency, your portfolio will be an important part of the agency's promotion and there will be a standard portfolio binder that they use. It's your responsibility to keep the agency supplied with new portfolio work.

## Mock-ups of Editorials

A good creative exercise is designing a "mock-up" of an editorial story. Even if you haven't styled for a magazine, you can have a portfolio piece that looks like a magazine page, as long as you are honest that it is a mock-up. You might collaborate with a graphic designer who could use an attractive portfolio addition.

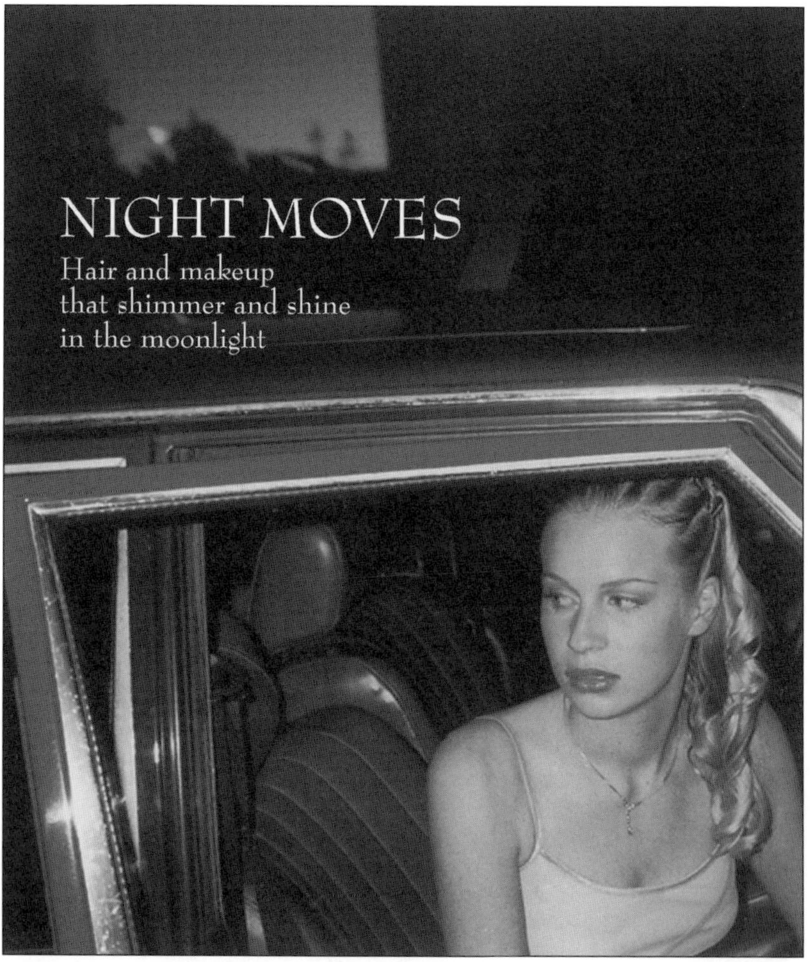


A snapshot was the inspiration for this mock-up of a magazine story with headline. *Photographer:* Susan Linnet Cox. *Copywriter:* Nan Gage. © Susan Linnet Cox

I took a photograph of my daughter getting into a red Mercedes on prom night that I thought looked like it was right out of a magazine. I scanned it at a high resolution so I could print it large and asked a copywriter friend to help me with a heading for the "page." She wrote, "Night Moves—Hair and makeup that shimmer and shine in the moonlight." I applied it to the image in Photoshop using an attractive font and "reversed" the type, printing it white against the dark background.

If you don't already own Photoshop software, it would be helpful to purchase Adobe Photoshop Elements, a less expensive version. You can resize, add text, and even fix flaws in this useful software program. When you receive images from photographers, they will most likely arrive in a TIFF or JPEG format, which can be resized and reworked in Photoshop.

In assembling my portfolio, I had the challenge of conveying the various roles I had played on different shoots. Sometimes I was not the stylist but had found the locations, built props, or booked the models. I decided to divide the portfolio into five sections marked with side tabs. They are labeled Fashion & People, Clothing Off-Figure, Products, Sports, and Prop Design & Production. I explain to clients that the samples in the last section include various contributions but not necessarily styling.

If you have samples of projects you worked on as an assistant, be very careful how you present them. If you are present when your portfolio is being reviewed, you can state that you were the assistant. Otherwise, you should label the portfolio pages with your role in the shots.

## YOUR WEB SITE

Your own Web site is a wonderful tool for promoting yourself as a stylist, whether you are discovered and booked through it, or only use it to display your work. Essentially it serves as a portfolio, a biography, and an open door to contact you, all in one place.

You'll need to start with a domain name for your site. You can go to *www.networksolutions.com* or other Web services to see if the name you want is available, and then purchase it. The full Web site address (or URL) will include "http://www.," then your domain name, followed by ".com". Your domain name may be your own name or your business name. You may purchase hosting services at the same time you buy your domain name, or you may want to work with a Web designer on hosting options. The domain name is yours for as long as you decide to pay for and renew it.

There are now easy, do-it-yourself Web-design options you can select along with hosting. The number of pages displayed on your site is limited, but this may be a perfect way to start. It can help you avoid the problems of finding a cut-rate designer.

The days of setting up your portfolio on a group site are gone. To appear professional you must have your own domain name and not be nested with another site. However, there are useful resource sites related to the photo industry where you can display your portfolio. Just be sure to have your own site to refer visitors to.

## Find a Web Site Designer

Finding someone to design your Web site is sometimes the most difficult part of building your site. I strongly recommend going with a professional and paying for his or her services, not the free or low-ball services of a friend or acquaintance…and here's why. Let's say your designer friend is starting out and needs more experience. He or she offers to work for free or a low price. Perfect, because you don't want to spend a lot at the start. But if you don't like the style of your new site, it's awkward to say so. You put up with it; at least you now have a site. Things go well for a while until you want to make some changes to the original design. Your friend has become busy with other projects, and since you're not a priority client, your site is on the back burner. You wait and wait, and end up paying someone else to revise the site.

I went through this myself, with three parties working on the site, and I still wasn't satisfied. I paid the original designer her full price to get the look back on track, then studied both HTML Web design and Dreamweaver software at a community college so I could maintain the site, add new images, and make other changes.

## Map Out Your Site

Plan your site by making a diagram, with the home page (called the "Index") at the top, and lines connecting it to the other pages on the site. The pages are linked by buttons or tabs on each page, so you can navigate around the site no matter where you are.

The first tier of pages after the home page may include a portfolio, a biography or other background information, and contact information. These pages can link to another level of pages, perhaps enlarged views of your work. (This is a way to show your portfolio online.) Every page on the site should have an internal link to get back to the home page or to any other page easily. A copyright line is usually placed at the bottom of each page to discourage illegal use of the images.

It's also important to give a credit to the photographers who shot the images you are using, after you ask for their permission to use them for self-promotion. Links to their sites would probably be appreciated, and if they link to your site, you will have more exposure.

There are other decisions to make about the look of your site, such as the colors, type font, images to display, and where you want the navigation buttons or bars. My original designer created a logo, a purple background for the navigation list, and graphic buttons, but a simpler design can work as well and would be easier to revise. The most important attribute is the ease with which a viewer can move around the pages and view your work.

As with my portfolio, I faced the challenge of presenting my varied specialties. One page, Services, provides a list of all the services Cox Productions offers. Under Services, I decided to include a page for each of the following: Product Styling, Wardrobe Styling, Props, Art Direction, Production, Graphic Design, and Casting. Each of those pages features some small examples (called "thumbnails") of work I've done. The thumbnails, when clicked, connect to another page with a full-sized image and a credit for the client and photographer. I added comments from someone I've worked with (known as "testimonials") for each category to emphasize my experience.

Some of the pages listed below are other pages on my Web site. Some are basic to many sites; others are unique to mine. There are "Locations," where I show a sampling of local backgrounds to attract clients to shoot in San Diego; "Career Workshops," where I promote my workshops and help publicize this book; "Meet Susan," which has a brief biography and a photograph, so people will know who I am before we meet; and "Client List," which lists some of the clients I have worked for—in my case I also listed the service I provided, since I do more than styling. Finally, and very important, is the "Contact Us" page, with my office and cellphone numbers and a direct link to my e-mail. I posted recommended sites on the Contact Us page, although you could have a separate page for links to others. This is a service to the visitor but also a good way to build good will with other professionals and more exposure for your site.

## Promote Your Site

The site design should include a good title for each page and "meta tags" that help your site be found on the Web. Meta tags are words or phrases someone might typically type into the search bar of a search engine when looking for a stylist. Be sure your designer builds these invisible tags into the structure of the site.

*Searchwebservices.com* describes the tags this way. "The keywords meta tag lists the words or phrases that best describe the contents of the page. The description meta tag includes a brief one- or two-sentence description of the page. Both the keywords and the description are used by search engines in adding a page to their index. Well-written meta tags can help make the page rank higher in search results."

You might use combinations of words or phrases like "styling, stylist, fashion styling, fashion stylist, wardrobe, catalog styling, editorial stylist, Minneapolis, Minnesota." This would be a good start to describe a regional stylist. Experiment on your own by searching for other stylists and see what words and phrases get results.

Most search-engines have a page where you can submit your site's information to their index of sites. This way, you have a better chance of being at the top of the first page of search results, rather than on page 10. When submitting your information, you may have to enter a description of the site, so have this information available for you to copy and paste. Gradually the visibility of your site will spread, but never stop looking for directories and resources to add it to. Alternatively you can pay for search submission services after researching them carefully.

*Shoots.com, workbook.com,* and local film commissions are among resources offering free listings for freelancers, including stylists. Resource Advantage (*www.rasource.com*) is an example of a targeted subscription directory; formerly free, it now charges a fee. Just reading the categories is interesting. As your site moves around in cyberspace, you may find yourself listed on directories that you don't even know of. It is essential to ask new clients how they found your site.

Remember, your site must provide a way for clients to contact you, preferably an e-mail link and your phone number. Your street address is optional: you may or may not want to post your home address. If your e-mail address changes or you move, remember to change your contact information on your site as well as with other resources where you have posted your information.

## BUILDING YOUR RÉSUMÉ

When my daughter was a teenager working on her self-esteem, I used to encourage her to write a résumé. As she developed a sense of who she was, I figured that putting her accomplishments down on paper would increase her confidence. She didn't do it then. But now she's greatly skilled at describing her qualifications. Building a résumé is a gradual process of understanding who you are.

I have finally reached a point in my career when I rarely need to use my résumé. As clients started to find me from my Web site, I gradually had less and less call for a portfolio and a résumé. However, the résumé is still important as your career develops, and a necessity when job-hunting.

Spend some time looking back at your experiences, whether learning or work, and make some notes. It will take a while for a good résumé to take form, and thanks to computers, you can add to it at any time. Your résumé should be an ongoing project. Update it when you have more expertise or a new address.

One important element to add to your résumé in this business is a "client list." Clients can simply be listed, or you can describe briefly what kind of work you did for them, whether it was wardrobe styling, assistant stylist, or preproduction. Most of the time, you will have been hired by a photographer to style a campaign for his or her client. But unless it's a well-known photographer, that won't carry much weight or show the type of project you worked on. In such cases, it's fine to list the end client. And just who is the end client? Remember the brochure for the grocery chain from chapter 8? The grocery chain, Publix, was my end client—technically, the advertising agency that represented Publix hired the photographer, who, in turn, hired me.

Add to your client list often. You'll be happy to know that eventually you may have so many you won't remember them all.

If you work as a styling assistant on a project, you need to be clear about that. It's not fair to the stylist who hired you to imply that you were the stylist. This is where listing your role on the project comes in.

There are many books available on writing résumés. In a creative field like photography, you have a little leeway in designing yours. The standard style is always acceptable, but you can be more artistic than someone applying for a job as a legal aide, for example.

The résumé sample on page 192 is of wardrobe stylist Pippi Robben, who is very creative. I like it and was motivated to read it when she sent it to me as an e-mail attachment. It shows that she likes clothing and is able to illustrate her own concepts. I'd be very likely to hire her if I were looking for a film or video stylist. She lists her clients and the jobs she did for them, helping her appear quite experienced. One thing that could be improved, though, is its readability. The font she used is stretched out, and overprints the illustration, making it hard to read. It's to Pippi's credit that I was interested enough to try.

My traditional style résumé on page 193 appears less interesting at first glance. It concisely lists job descriptions, publishing information, education, and a brief client list. Only the most recent ten years of job history need to be included; I recently omitted my earlier experience and condensed the résumé onto one page. The client list is on a separate page.

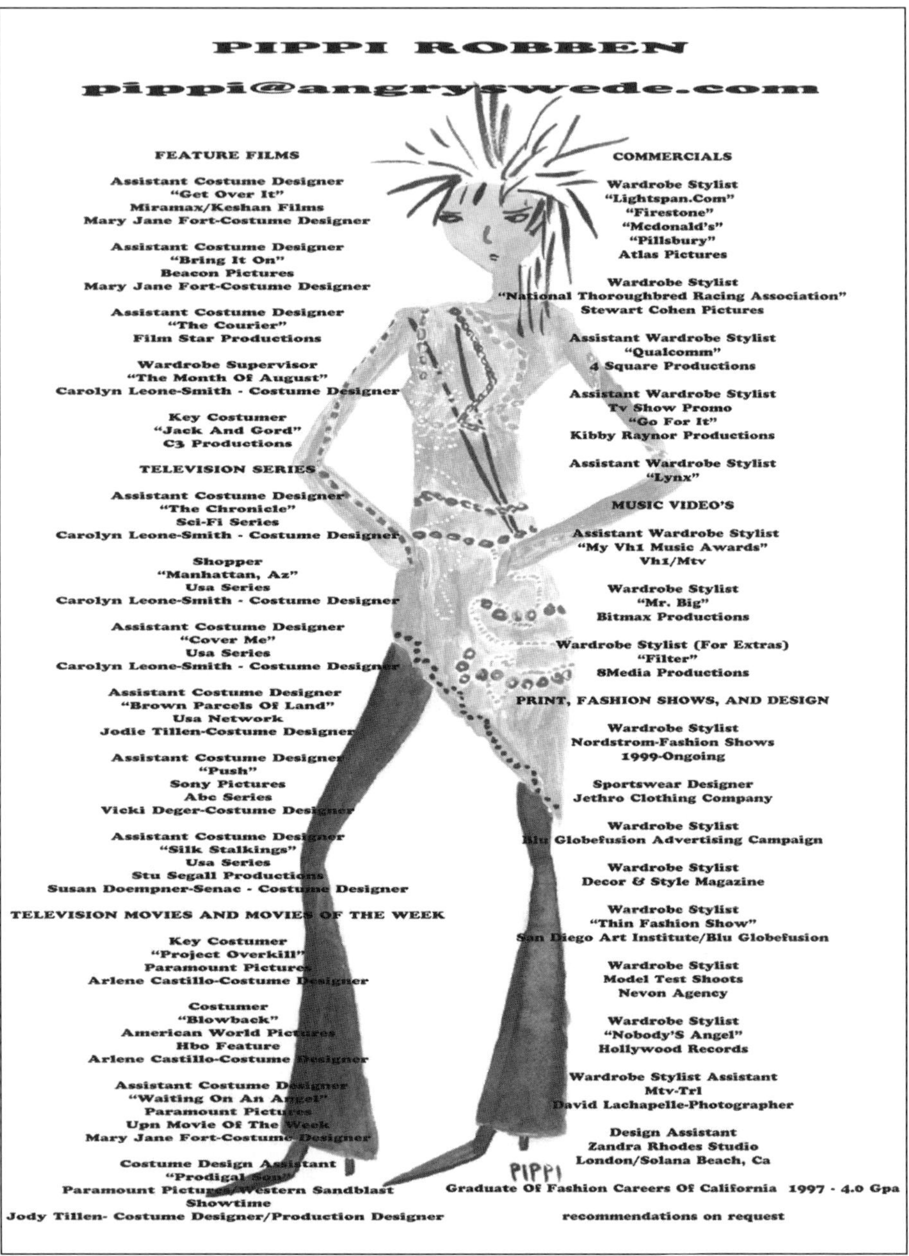


*Résumé courtesy of Pippi Robben

You may find your style someplace between the creative and traditional résumé. What is most important is the content: your qualifications consisting of experience and education.

**Susan Linnet Cox**
**Street address**
**Email address ~ Phone numbers**
**www.coxproductions.com**

## PROFESSIONAL EXPERIENCE

**Cox Productions; 1994–present**
**Photo Shoot Production and Styling; Career Workshops**
Projects incorporate photography art direction, photo shoot production, styling, and design of catalogs and other print materials. Services provided are location scouting, casting, wardrobe and product styling, and prop styling. Provide training for college interns. Present career and styling workshops to students nation-wide including hands-on styling experience, career exploration, and business practices.

**Norm Thompson Outfitters; Portland, Oregon, 1989–1994**
**Art Director, Photography; Graphic Designer**
Produced and art directed photo shoots of fashion and products for major catalog company, both on location and in studios. Hired and supervised crews of photographers, stylists, and models. Developed budgets. Edited photos. Monitored color separation and printing of finished pieces. Analyzed sales results with other marketing team members to provide marketing database. As design director for targeted marketing program, introduced recycled paper and soy ink as corporate standards. Designed catalogs for all divisions (Norm Thompson, Solutions, The Primary Layer and Early Winters). Team member in developing company-wide recycling program.

## PUBLICATIONS

Author of *Photo Styling: How to Build Your Career and Succeed,* Allworth Press, New York, NY

## EDUCATION

Computer Graphics, UCSD, University of Oregon

Bachelor of Fine Arts, Kent State University, Kent, Ohio

Pre-College Design Program, Carnegie-Mellon University, Pittsburgh, Pennsylvania

Portfolio review and references upon request.

Visit me at www.coxproductions.com.

*Résumé courtesy of Susan Linnet Cox

## SELF-PROMOTION, YOUR OTHER HAT

Unless you are represented by an agency, you are in charge of your own marketing. No one but you is going to remind people that you are here. When you're working you are, in fact, promoting yourself, by your professionalism, your personality, and the quality of your work. But that is not enough. You need to find new work.

### Business Cards

These are the most basic of all marketing materials. Business cards are small and easy to carry and you should never be without them. Gone are the days when you had to order a large quantity of business cards from a printer. The printing would invariably be completed just before finding that you are moving or changing your phone number. Now you can make your own business cards on your home computer.

If you want to print your own, purchase business-card paper that snaps apart, creating cards that look professionally printed. There are templates you can download to set up the layout. An eye-catching design could include a small photo of your styling work.

### Comp Cards and Leave-Behinds

The cards that models use are known as "comp cards." They are printed on heavy paper known as card stock and are half the size of a standard piece of paper. They're printed on both sides, with the model's name and a head shot on the front, and other photos, the model's sizes, and the agency information on the back.

The cards are sent out by agencies when clients request a selection of talent for a project. You can also use comp cards, whether you have an agent or are independent, by leaving them behind with potential clients or at the end of jobs. These "leave-behinds" serve as a reminder of you and your work. Mailed in medium-sized envelopes, comp cards will not need extra postage. They may end up in a file of possible stylists for the future or, if really attractive, on a bulletin board. By making sure yours contains helpful information and is attractively designed, you can reduce the probability that it will end up in the wastebasket. There are printers that specialize in affordable comp cards.

### Special Promo Ideas

When I was represented for a short time by a model agency that handled stylists, I ordered five hundred high-quality comp cards. I had paid for them myself, and when I left the agency, I didn't want to waste them, even though the agency's information was on the front and back. I could have printed stickers on my home computer to cover it with my own contact information. I decided, however, when I had some marketing time on my hands, to convert the cards into magnets.

There is magnetic printer paper on the market that is thin enough to fit into your home printer. Some are sized to fit business cards, but there are also full size sheets that can be cut into various sizes. For my magnet promo, I printed my name and Web site onto the lower part of business-card magnets, then cut up the small comp-card images using a paper cutter and glued them onto the magnets. I tired of this fastidious process pretty quickly but plan to do more some day. I did have the pleasure of seeing one of my magnets on the file cabinet of a local photographer.

Any clever ideas you may have for self-promotion can only help your business by showing off your creativity.

## Postcards and Other Mailings

My favorite promotional pieces are postcards, useful for both mailings and leave-behinds. They can showcase one example of your styling work or a group of images. Your name and Web site should be on the front, and the back should contain more information and a clear area for the address and postage. I suggest some open space also where you can write a note by hand. Postcards under a certain size use lower postage than the regular letter rate, so if you're doing a large mailing you can save money.

Find a printer that specializes in postcards and can provide postal specifications to you. A good one is Modern Postcard (*www.modernpostcard.com*). Most printers will provide graphic-design services, too.

Mailing lists can be purchased for a reasonable amount. One good source is the Workbook, *www.workbook.com*, which can break down lists by a number of characteristics and regions. You can gather your own contact list for mailings by visiting Web sites of local—or national—photographers, ad agencies, and catalog companies.

Remember the clients you've worked with during the year by sending holiday greetings at the end of the year. You can buy cards or make your own with holiday images that you've styled. As always, be sure to add your contact information and credit the photographer and the client.

## Free Listings Versus Advertising

There are many sites on the Internet that list crew resources. They generally offer free listings as well as more-visible paid listings. An inexpensive paid listing on some of these sites may be a good way for you to receive exposure. You can do some Web research and find out what's best for you. One example is *www.rasource.com*, described in the discussion on promoting your site; there are many other options in cyberspace.

Free listings, of course, are best. One example is a site maintained in San Diego by Chrome, a local photo lab. The site, *www.sdprolist.com*, is a resource for finding photographers and other creative professionals in the area. Search for similar services wherever you're based.

Placing paid ads in trade magazines for photographers or art directors can be effective, but I try to save expenses by finding free Web resources. Look for sites like that of *Create* (*www.createmagazine.com*) that focus on the local or national creative industry.

An important place to be listed, and even to advertise, is your local or state film commission's directory, both printed and online. This may be the first place clients look for crew resources, whether they are traveling from out of town or are local.

## Self-Promotion Between Projects

Your projects wind down, the returns have been made, you've invoiced the clients, and you're starting to ask, "Will I ever work again?" Now you can really get to work. You have some down time and it's your opportunity to promote yourself. Do it now while the satisfaction of your most recent styling project is still there. Here are some suggestions about how to use that time.

- **Plan a test shoot**. Call a photographer you want to work with to plan a collaborative project. Get some ideas and concepts, and brainstorm together. Since it will take a while to pull the test together and coordinate your schedules, you're free to work on some promotional materials, maybe do a mailing.

- **Design a mailing**. If you have design skills or design software, you may be able to create a postcard or other mail piece. If not, you might suggest an exchange with a graphic designer who could use a styled photograph for self-promotion. Some printers provide in-house design.

- **Update your résumé**. Remember to put the most recent clients on your client list. Revise the description of your skills and experience.

- **Add to your portfolio**. Include new tears from recent projects. Scan them and add to your Web site. Take some time to look at your portfolio as if you haven't seen it before.

- **Make contact with your peers.** If you are out of jobs, perhaps there's a regional slump in the market. Maybe it's seasonal: after a couple years, you'll learn to expect these trends. If so, others in the field are going through a slow period. It is a good time to e-mail or call photographers who are in the same boat. They may be interested in planning a test shoot, and will remember you when the next job comes up.

- **Learn new software.** Add to your computer skills by taking an inexpensive or free software class at a community college or adult-education program. You can learn a Web design program so that you can maintain your own site. A desktop-publishing program can help you to create your own business cards, postcards, résumé, and note cards, even if you don't have a graphics background.

  You might learn a business-management program for creating invoices, doing estimates, and recording your income and expenses. Find out how to use a scanner to copy your styling work for your Web site or portfolio.

- **Do some cyber research.** Explore the Internet to find out how your site is ranking. See how other stylists are promoting themselves through their sites and the types of work they are presenting. Find organizations, blogs, and sites that provide styling suggestions.

- **Join professional organizations.** ASMP (American Society of Media Photographers) and APA (Advertising Photographers of America) are photography organizations. Local chapters have regular meetings that you can attend and where you can meet the local photographic talent. Look into business groups in your area that focus on marketing, such as DMA (Direct Marketing Association). Introduce yourself to potential clients who will be interested to learn what a stylist does.

- **Work on your business.** Enter receipts into your accounting software, organize your outstanding invoices so you know what's due and when, file your most recent job envelope, pay bills, get organized, and be ready for the next flurry of work.

- **Update your kit.** Add any new items you've come up with and restock anything in low supply. Have your kit clean, organized, and ready for the next job.

## SELLING YOUR TALENTS

If you are feeling overwhelmed by all this discussion of marketing yourself, you're not alone. Selling yourself is one of the hardest things to do: just ask any artist who creates something from the soul and puts it out there for critique. Marketing yourself may take some practice, or you may really enjoy it. Remember that a model or actress goes to about forty castings for every role she gets. A rejection is just a bump in the road on the way to your destination.

Agency representation can take care of much of the marketing for you. However, you must first market yourself to an agency before you are represented. After being told by two Los Angeles agencies that I needed new samples in my portfolio, but not having a clear understanding of what they wanted, I decided to stay on my own. Rather than pursuing these agencies after having promoted myself for several years, I determined that I can trust myself to sell my skills and talents better than anyone else.

In the next chapter, we'll explore some business practices and organizational techniques that should help you run your styling business smoothly. More information about the agency option is also provided.

# chapter 12

# The Business of Styling

**T**HIS CHAPTER IS PROBABLY NOT ONE MOST READERS WILL read first. In fact, you may put it off—or not read it all. It may seem as exciting as paying taxes, which we will talk about in this part of the book. The information here is important, however, and mastering it can make attending to this part of your styling career much more pleasant. Actually, one of my favorite parts of my work is invoicing; the sooner the invoice is mailed to the client, the sooner I will be paid for my work. I can never understand procrastination about this final aspect of a job.

## YOUR STYLING RATE

Determining your styling rate is not easy. It's awkward asking other stylists, who may be your competition, what their day rate is. It's not professional and in fact may be considered illegal restraint of trade! When I started styling, I had the advantage of my photography and art-direction background. I'd been hiring stylists for catalog projects, so I knew the going rate. I started at that rate, then $350 a day, and after a year or two started raising it.

You can get a feel for acceptable day rates in your area by talking with art directors. If you're having a comfortable conversation, it's all right to ask what they usually pay. When you assist a stylist you can ask, in a friendly, non-threatening way, what rate you might think about working up to.

## Comparing Rates with Your Peers

I had an excellent opportunity to compare my rate with other local stylists a few years ago. The Affiliate Chapter of the San Diego APA (Advertising Photographers of America), a group of makeup artists and stylists, became active and held several meetings. It was a unique opportunity to meet many of my peers whom I wouldn't have met otherwise, since we all work independently.

Most of them were makeup artists, but there were a couple of other stylists. Normally we might be vying for the same work. In one meeting we discussed the local rate, which is comparable for makeup artists and stylists. Actually, it is illegal for such a professional organization to set rates: it's known as "price fixing" and it's a violation of the Taft-Hartley Act. We were careful to avoid stating that this is what local rates *should* be. We did, however, agree that it is good for the local industry if experienced professionals charge a rate we are worth. I realized that the $600 rate I had recently started quoting was what others were charging too. After that I felt confident that my rate was fair and that I should be consistent with it.

Makeup artists might be a good resource for comparison rates in your area. Sometimes rates for makeup artists are a little higher than for stylists—I don't know exactly why, as stylists work as hard, or harder—but you can get a reference point.

## Quoting Your Rate

When I am asked for an estimate, I am now comfortable quoting my daily rate. Whether the shoot is on location or in a studio, the rate for one day's work is the same. However, if there is hesitation on the part of the client when I state my rate, I offer to work with their budget—within reason—but such negotiation rarely occurs with experienced clients.

If you are asked to do a longer job of five days or more, you can be flexible with your rate. The extended work period is worth the concession. You might also feel a lower-paying job is worth doing, for experience or for tears.

Often food styling rates are a little higher than other styling rates. This is partly because of higher kit and learning costs, but also because food stylists understand the demand for their professional skills. Remember your skills, experience, and value to clients when determining your own day rate. And remember it is only a starting point in negotiating for work you love.

You won't jump into styling at the top end. At the same time, you don't want to undercut the profession by offering a budget rate. Later when you're more experienced, you'll appreciate the professional standards you've helped maintain. Continue assisting and practicing your skills until you are confident that you can do the work.

## Regional Rates

As you would expect, there are variations in rates depending on where you live. Rates in New York, Chicago, and Los Angeles are higher than other cities. But the differences are not huge.

The type of businesses in your area has an affect on styling rates. There may be a large advertiser or a publisher in a medium-sized city, like Target stores in Minneapolis or *Better Homes & Gardens* in Des Moines, Iowa. This increases respect for the profession and the rates accordingly. Some areas pay comparable rates for commercial and editorial (magazine) styling; in others there is a greater difference.

Regional rates for assisting vary, too. If you are asked to assist, the stylist will usually tell you what has been budgeted, generally between $150 and $350 a day.

## Day Length

In the photography field, a ten-hour day is the norm, and the day rate is based on it. After ten hours you may charge an hourly rate plus 50 percent (divide your day rate by ten hours and add half of that figure on for your hourly overtime rate) but it's important to inform the client first. You might state that the day is getting close to ten hours, ask how much longer you'll need to work, and mention your overtime rate. This may subtly create an end to the day; but if not, you will be comfortable charging the extra amount.

If the day ends early, say eight hours or less, and you have been booked for a full day, you will still charge your full day rate.

Some shoots are planned for a half-day. Working a half-day prevents you from accepting a full-day shoot, and you're unlikely to be booked the other part of the day. Therefore the half-day rate is more than 50 percent of your normal day rate, up to 75 percent. Often the shoot will go longer than expected anyway and you can, with your client's understanding, charge your full-day rate.

## Production Rate

I do a good bit of production for clients, involving location scouting, booking models, and arranging permits. I may work a couple of hours calling model agencies or applying for film permits; half a day holding a casting; or six hours scouting locations. I record these hours and when they accumulate to an eight-hour day, I consider that a full day, and bill the client accordingly at my usual daily rate.

This honor system seems to be acceptable to my clients. I explain it to them before beginning the job and provide a client agreement, as described in the following section. I could provide my notes on my job envelope if questioned but that has not happened.

## Compensation for Travel

If you are asked to travel to a distant location for a shoot, you might charge a half-day rate for the time spent traveling. This is really a matter of negotiation between you and your client. Perhaps you could inquire whether they usually pay for travel time.

It's not such hard work, being flown to a location, but you certainly can't book any other jobs for that day. This is the approach an agency would take in negotiating travel time if you are represented. The value of work lost by a professional stylist while traveling is considered.

If you're driving to another city, the same considerations apply to your time. Most likely you won't charge travel time but your client will agree to compensation for mileage. This compensation is also important when you're doing a lot of driving for prop shopping. You can use the IRS mileage rate as a reference amount. The mileage rate is an amount that the Internal Revenue Service allows as a deduction. It is calculated to include gasoline as well as wear and tear on your vehicle. You should keep a record of all mileage driven for your business, both for billing purposes and as an income tax deduction.

"Per diem" is a daily amount calculated for living expenses during business travel, including hotel and meals. If these expenses are coming out of your own pocket, you can deduct them as a business expense. Your client may pay for your hotel room and provide an additional amount for your morning and evening meals. When you receive this compensation the amount may be considered part of your income, showing up on a 1099-MISC form, so be sure to deduct these expenses. (More about the 1099 form follows in the section on taxes.) Visit *www.irs.gov* or talk to your accountant about deductions for these expenses.

## Editorial Rates

The rate paid for magazine projects is generally lower than a commercial rate. For up-and-coming photographers, the opportunity to have photos published in a magazine can boost their careers. The images are more creative than commercial work, they may be displayed better (maybe a cover or a full-page spread), the printing is better, and the photographer's name is usually prominent. These jobs make great portfolio tears.

The same applies to the crew. Many magazines list them in small type near the gutter, some more prominently. You can look for these credits to learn more about editorial work. You'll see the stylist, prop stylist, or food stylist listed, along with agency names if they are represented.

Sometimes local magazines request editorial styling for no fee at all. It may be worth it to acquire tears. Depending on the project, the experience may be valuable enough. I recently was asked to do styling for a regional bridal magazine for free. I accepted because I'd always wanted to see what it's like to style wedding gowns.

## Flat Fee

A few years ago, a unique wardrobe styling project came my way. It was unique in that I agreed to a flat fee for styling and for wardrobe costs, something I have done only a few times. I was asked to style the participants in a series of exercise videos for people with health problems, whose capability for movement is limited. It's a good program and the creator was financing the project from sales of her earlier videos. I agreed to accept a flat fee for the project. By dividing the figure she offered, I was able to calculate my day rate for a set number of days, a styling assistant for the most intense days, and have a certain amount left for the wardrobe shopping.

Working this way usually reaches a balance point where the more work you are asked to do, the more it eats into the budget, so that your day rate starts going down. That happened in this case. Then, of course, it's time to bring it to the attention of your client. Maybe there is more available in the budget, or perhaps your investment of time can be scaled back.

Naturally, I was motivated to keep the wardrobe costs low and return as much clothing as possible. The clothing the video participants wore to work out in was not returnable, but I had found some great bargains. And working in a television studio was fascinating for me.

When I've accepted a flat fee, I have done it for a higher purpose, one I consider similar to a pro-bono project. I produced a video for a children's health center and was glad to do it, both for the sake of the program and because I had the opportunity to learn about video production and editing. My entire fee went to the videographer, Carolyn Springer, who herself charged a lowered rate for the project.

## ESTIMATING PROJECTS

This is a challenging aspect of working for yourself. If it's any consolation, estimating is hard for most creative, self-employed people. At first you may tend to estimate low so the quote will sound better, or so you'll be more likely to get the job. With experience, and when you have prior projects to refer to, it gets easier.

If you've established your day rate, you're halfway there. The next challenge is determining the number of days needed for preproduction (organization, planning, prop shopping) and postproduction (returns and other aspects of finishing a job). If preproduction is to include casting, location scouting, permits, travel arrangements, you'll need to estimate how much time that will take. All that will be in addition, of course, to shoot days.

I've found that the number of preproduction days can amount to as many as six days for a complex project. A starting point, in fact, could be to take the number of shoot days and add on the same number for preproduction plus two days for concluding the project. Your client agreement can state that if you work fewer days you will only bill for that number: that way, you're covered if the time does go longer than you anticipate, which it usually does. The client-agreement form described on page 206 can be adapted for use as an estimate. Simply substitute "Proposal" or "Estimate" for "Client Agreement" as a heading. The remaining information is the same as that included in a written estimate.

When a project is going to require you to do significant prop shopping, it's appropriate to request an advance, which could be a check delivered to you at the beginning of the job. Rather than investing your own money or credit in the client's project, an advance can help with the up-front expenses. You should negotiate this in your early conversations about the project, to allow your client time to request the check. The advance should be noted in your agreement, and later credited toward the payment due to you in your invoice. (See the sample invoice on page 210.)

## CLIENT AGREEMENTS

After discussing a job and agreeing on your rates, it's a good idea to present a client agreement. This is a contract that clearly spells out the details that have been discussed—or possibly omitted, if you forgot to state your terms for mileage or other expenses. It clearly helps to have a description of the project, what your duties are, and your terms for payment, in a written form.

The two samples on pages 206–207 are available for you to copy or adapt. Create a basic format in your word-processing program, which can be customized for each job. Provide the agreement to your client before beginning the project and ask to have it returned to you with a signature. It can be faxed to you, mailed, or delivered upon starting the project.

I don't always manage to get my signed copy of the agreement. Presenting it to the client clarifies my terms, though it might not hold up in court. If your client is new and the project is complex, it's especially important to present the agreement and have it signed. When you have any doubts or reservations about the client, or have had payment problems in the past, be sure to get a signed original agreement.

An agreement isn't always needed for a simple studio project with no expenses or other complications. But it would be a better habit to write one for each job, spelling out your terms.

## Hold or Booking?

It's important to understand the difference between a "hold" and a confirmed "booking." If a client inquires about your availability and puts you on hold, also known as "an option," the project is either unconfirmed or several stylists are on hold for it, allowing the client to make a choice later. When you're on hold and are offered another project, explain that you are on hold but will see what you can do. It's possible that the first client has changed the dates, delayed the shoot, or chosen another stylist (so you are no longer on hold).

Don't pass up any other work because of a hold, and don't assume that you are working until you hear more. It's not real until you have a confirmed booking.

# CLIENT AGREEMENT

To: _______________________________________________________________

Date: _________________________________

From: Susan Linnet Cox/Cox Productions

**Project Description**

_______________________________________________________________

_______________________________________________________________

_______________________________________________________________

_______________________________________________________________

**Project Notes**

_______________________________________________________________

_______________________________________________________________

_______________________________________________________________

_______________________________________________________________

**Rate & Payment**

Rate for location scouting and production is $____ per day, based on hours accumulating to an eight-hour day. Styling rate is $____ per day (up to 10 hours). Half-day rate is $____ (up to 4 hours). In addition, long distance phone calls, cell phone usage, mileage, and other expenses will be billed. Billing is net 30 days unless cash expenses are needed; in which case an advance will be requested. Please sign below and return agreement prior to project.

______________________________________

Signature

______________________________________          ____________________

Name/Title                                                                    Date

Thank you,

**Susan Linnet Cox**
**Cox Productions**
**www.coxproductions.com**
**[Street address and phone number]**

*Client agreement courtesy of Cox Productions

# LETTER OF AGREEMENT

To: ________________________________

## Re: Business Policies

I've prepared this memo to clarify my business policies. Since time is usually of the essence at the beginning of a project, this memo is to prevent any confusion or mis-understandings that may arise after a job is completed. Please understand that if you have concerns with any part of these policies, I am happy to discuss them with you before we get started and to modify as necessary to reach agreement. Nothing is set in stone, as I am aware there can be unusual circumstances that require a change in the usual policies. I'd just like to know of any concerns before we get started.

**Terms:** Invoices are due upon receipt, and become overdue and subject to a finance charge of ____% per month, ______ days after the invoice date. New clients are expected to provide ______% of the estimated fee before or on the date of services. C.O.D. payment is required for out-of-town accounts unless other arrangements are made.

**Expenses:** Receipts will be furnished with expense report upon request. If expenses are billed on the invoice, there will be a ______% mark-up charge. To avoid this out-of-pocket fee, a client may provide a cash advance against the estimated expenses prior to the beginning of the job.

**Props:** Props will be rented whenever possible, to keep costs to the minimum. If rented from my collection, the rental fee is ____% of the replacement cost, unless other arrangements are made. If purchased, the props are the property of the client, and may be taken by client after shoot, if desired.

**Rates:** $____ for a ____ hour day or $____ / hour, with consulting/preproduction time figured for all time spent on the job. For example, loading and unloading car and travel time are included. Partial days are figured on an hourly basis. For a multiple-day or out-of-town project, I am happy to supply an estimate for services and expenses on a project basis if you wish.

***All quotes are subject to modification if there is a change-order to the project.***

**Cancellation fee:** A fee of ____% payment is required for any jobs cancelled within ____ hours of a shoot, unless another client fills the time. Any expenses incurred on a cancelled job are the responsibility of the client.

These policies are reviewed annually and are subject to change.

AGREED,

________________________________      ________________________________

Client Signature                          Date

________________________________

[Your signature]
[Your name, and/or business]

Please note any exceptions here:

________________________________

________________________________

________________________________

*Client Agreement from *The Tweezer Times*, Back to Business issue, January 2004

## JOB ENVELOPE

Years ago, when I started my own graphic design business, I received some good advice from a mentor. This experienced professional designer suggested job envelopes as a system for keeping track of all the details of a project from start to finish. I ordered a large quantity of nine-by-twelve-inch envelopes with a side opening. I had them printed with my company name and spaces for recording job details.

With five hundred printed, I still had some left when I left the design business for my full-time job with Norm Thompson. When I later started Cox Productions, I developed a cover sheet that is taped onto these envelopes to record information for my current projects.

If I am going to work in a studio for only a few days, I don't use a job envelope; they're needed when a project involves multiple roles, such as preproduction planning, prop shopping, model booking, etc.

### The Job Sheet

As soon as a project becomes a confirmed booking, create the job envelope. I fill in the client and project information, the project dates, and important phone numbers on the job sheet (see example). The side opening allows easier access to the contents; the client and project names at the side make it easy to file alphabetically, so I can access and refer to prior jobs.

As I'm working on production jobs, with sporadic tasks here and there, I write down my hours every day. Sometimes it may be one or two hours, sometimes a full day. When I'm contacted later about a similar project, I can refer to this job and see how much preproduction time it took, how many days on location, and for returns. Whether you charge for time spent in meetings depends on the client.

### The Contents

Once, it's been started, I never leave my office without the envelope throughout the course of a production project. It gets pretty beat up. It is handy to have all the information with me, especially contact phone numbers. Inside are printouts of e-mails, layouts, shopping lists, and miscellaneous jots. There's even room in the job envelope for a tablet of ongoing notes. At the end I tear off the pages and leave them in the envelope.

Also inside is a smaller envelope for receipts. They are all there in one place when it's time to do returns. On the receipt envelope, I write down the date, amount, and method of payment for any purchases. This step isn't really necessary since the receipts are inside; I just like to have the extra documentation.

This is my technique; you will probably establish a system that works best for you. The important things are organization, having your job information accessible, and keeping track of each project for invoicing and future reference.

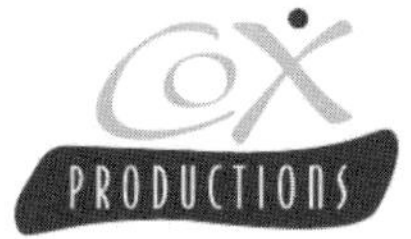

Full Production Services • Product Styling • Wardrobe Styling
Props • Art Direction • Graphic Design
www.coxproductions.com
Address
Telephone • Cell number • E-mail address

Client _______________________  Date started _______________

Project _______________________  Project date _______________

Rate _______________________  Advance _______________

Description _________________________________________________

_________________________________________________

| Date | Work | Hour |
|------|------|------|
|  |  |  |
|  |  |  |
|  |  |  |
|  |  |  |
|  |  |  |
|  |  |  |
|  |  |  |
|  |  |  |
|  |  |  |
|  |  |  |
|  |  |  |

Expenses _______________________  Mileage _______________

*Job sheet courtesy of Cox Productions

# INVOICING

As I've stressed, it's important to create an invoice as soon as a job is finished. Receiving payment for your work can take anywhere from a week to several months depending on the client's payment cycles. Clients who pay the next week are rare and, naturally, you love to work for them. Typically you'll receive payment in about one month. Some ad agencies and magazines work on a sixty-day cycle. That's a long wait and it helps if you expect it. Try to find out about the typical payment cycles at the beginning of the project.

Your invoice should display your terms of payment at the top. Mine states "Net 30 days" and shows a late-charge percentage. I've tried putting C.O.D. (cash on delivery) in the terms section but it didn't seem to speed up the process.

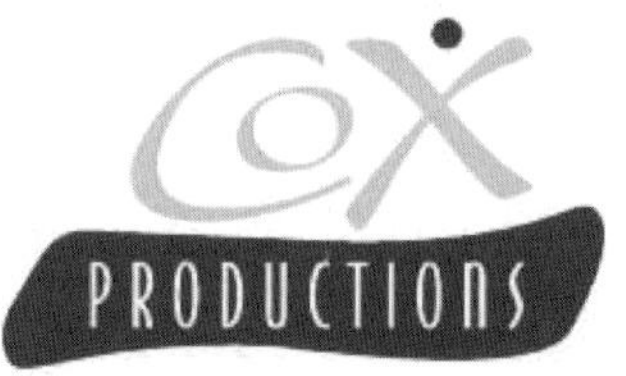



**My Address • Phone Number • Cell Number**
**www.coxproductions.com**

Date: ___________________________________

Invoice #: _______________________________

Client: __________________________________

[Client's Name and Company]

_______________________________________

_______________________________________

[Client's Address]

Project: Styling and production for ___________________________

Terms: Net 30 days; Late charge: .015% per month, 18% annual

| Date | Description | Amount |
|------|-------------|--------|
| Jan. 24–28, 2006 | Five days product styling @ $600/day | $3,000 |
| Jan. 31–Feb. 3, 2006 | Two and a half days production and location styling @ $600/day | $1,500 |
| Jan. 21–Feb. 3, 2006 | Expenses (see attached) | $245.45 |
| Jan. 20, 2006 | Advance received | ($500) |
| | **TOTAL:** | $4245.45 |

30 Days: ❑   60 Days: ❑   90 Days: ❑   120 Days: ❑

Invoice sample courtesy of Cox Productions

## Who is Your Client?

When a photographer calls you to work on a project, you need to determine whether you'll be invoicing the photographer or the end client. I have worked both ways. It does get uncomfortable when the photographer waits to be paid before paying your invoice, and a late payment can affect your working relationship. When that happens, arrange to bill the client directly for future projects.

Some photographers may mark up your rate when presenting their own invoices. In that case, it's important to be aware of the rate that was charged if you later work for and bill the client directly.

During the workday be sure to get the exact billing information for your client, including address and project name. I have received invoices from people who had done freelance work for the huge cable company Cox Communications; they sent them erroneously to Cox Productions.

## Billing for Expenses

When invoicing your client for your expenses, you will provide a breakdown of the expenses, whether or not you've received an advance for them. You'll also need to provide the original receipts; the client will need the originals for its tax records.

The following page shows the format I use for expenses. It was created in word-processing software with tabs set for the four columns. I list the date of the purchase, the store, item, and amount. The same categories are listed for returns and items I keep. The result at the bottom is the expense total for the shoot. This amount would be entered on the invoice.

# EXPENSE LIST

Date: _______________________
Client Name: _______________________
Project Name: _______________________

| Date | Provider | Item | Amount |
|---|---|---|---|
| 10/22/06 | Vons | Groceries, snacks, water | $78.97 |
| 10/22 | Vons | Ice | 2.36 |
| 10/22 | Thrift Store | Props | 12.82 |
| 10/23 | Encon | Gas | 57.53 |
| 10/23 | Starbucks | Coffee, snacks | 23.65 |
| 10/24 | Vons | Snacks, water | 36.38 |
| 10/24 | Vons | Ice | 2.14 |
| 10/26 | Ralphs | Snacks | 13.84 |
| 10/26 | Ralphs | Ice, water | 10.02 |
| 10/26 | Starbucks | Coffee, snacks | 25.35 |
| 10/27 | Starbucks | Coffee | 13.90 |
| 10/28 | Vons | Snacks, water | 13.25 |
| 10/28 | Music Rentals | Guitar rental | 16.16 |
| 10/28 | Tiki Land | Props rental | 75.00 |
| 10/28 | Marina | Location fee, sailboat | 500.00 |
| 10/28 | My Bank | Bank fee, cashiers ck | 7.00 |
| 10/29 | Coast Surf Shop | Surfboard rentals | 180.00 |
| 10/29 | Rental Studios | Studio rental | 300.00 |
|  | Miscellaneous | Tips, valet parking | 4.00 |
|  | Miscellaneous | Tips, Palm Springs | 23.00 |
| **Total** |  |  | **$1,412.37** |

| Mileage | Miles ($0.485 cents/mile) | Cost |
|---|---|---|
| 10/20/06 | 18 | $8.73 |
| 10/21 | 22 | 10.67 |
| 10/22 | 48 | 23.28 |
| 10/23 | 22 | 10.67 |
| 10/24 | 40 | 19.40 |
| 10/25 | 21 | 10.18 |
| 10/26 | 90 | 43.65 |
| 10/27 | 66 | 32.01 |
| 10/28 | 106 | 51.41 |
| 10/29 | 65 | 31.52 |
| 10/31 | 40 | 19.40 |
| **Total** |  | **$260.92** |

*Expense list sample courtesy of Cox Productions

## Keeping Track

Since the client needs to have the original receipts, you should make copies of them for your files. The process of returns, billing, and then making copies of receipts slows down invoicing by a day or two after the conclusion of a shoot. This is another reason to get started on invoicing as soon as possible.

For your own records, staple the receipt copies together with duplicates of the invoice and expense list, and file the packet in a special folder. This "Invoices" folder should be kept where you can regularly check on your unpaid invoices. You can keep track of what is owed to you and on what date, and follow up when it becomes past due. When your check is received, staple the stub to your copy and file that in another "Paid" folder for your accounting records.

## Following Up on Your Invoice

Like getting calls from new clients when you're going on vacation, this is another ironic aspect of the styling business. Often when I call a client to follow up on a late invoice, the check is in my mailbox the same day. The check really *was* in the mail. I don't mind laughing my way through this situation.

Sometimes it's not so simple. The due date has passed, the invoice hasn't been paid, and you're getting frustrated. Start with a cordial call to your client—let's say it's the art director—who will offer to check on it. You may get an answer, even a date that the check will be cut.

You can check with the photographer to see if his invoice has been paid; you may both be in the same boat. If they've previously paid on time, the company may be going through a delayed accounting period for some reason or other. You hope it's not serious financial problems.

You don't want to show your frustration to your client yet. This may be a valuable future relationship. A second call or an e-mail is appropriate. Then re-submit your invoice with one month's late charge added. Unless the company has gone bankrupt (something I have not experienced in all these years), you eventually will be paid.

## The W-9 Form

Another scenario is calling a client about a late payment, being referred to accounting, and finding out that they need you to sign a W-9 tax form. Required of individuals/sole proprietors, corporations, and partnerships, this is a signed statement of your Social Security number (or Federal tax

ID number), name, and address. When this happens I wonder if they were just waiting for me to call to initiate the process, but instead I simply ask them to fax me the form, sign and return it, and receive payment. (You can also download the W-9 form at *www.irs.gov/pub/irs-pdf/fw9.pdf.*)

This usually happens at the end of the two-month waiting period for magazines and agencies. You could probably avoid this tired situation by calling the art director or accounting department to follow up on your invoice shortly after submitting it. Ask if they need you to send them a completed W-9 form.

## BANKING AND CREDIT CARDS

Ideally you should keep your business finances separate from your personal money. As soon as you become a professional stylist, you should establish a business checking account and separate credit card.

### Business Checking

If you are working under your own name as opposed to a business name, like Cox Productions, you could deposit checks for your styling work into your personal account. It's better, though, to have a separate account for your business. This account should be used exclusively for business expenses and to pay yourself.

When you receive an advance for prop shopping, it's much easier to keep track of it this way. Use the business account to pay business expenses such as storage-space rent and cellphone bills. You can transfer money to yourself if your accounts are linked online, like giving yourself a paycheck. You could also go through the process of writing yourself a check, making a special ritual out of it. This is known as a "draw" on your business.

If you do use a business name, you may need to apply for a business license and establish a business name to open the account. Check with your local government or your bank to find out about these requirements. You will then be able to deposit checks made out to either your business or your own name.

### Savings Accounts

One of the wisest things I ever did was to open a savings account tied into my business checking account. By setting up an automatic monthly transfer of a specified amount to the savings account, I am able to set aside money for a rainy day, a late invoice, or a month without work. While the interest paid on savings accounts is small these days, it's a convenient way to save. And you can later open a more profitable retirement account when you have accumulated enough.

## Business Credit Cards

It's important to make prop purchases using either a credit card or debit card. If you make your purchases with cash or check, you'll have to wait for store refunds. Using your own credit to make purchases for a client is a difficult issue (even more complicated if you're married and your credit is tied to another person's).

When you expect a job will require a large investment in prop spending, you should request an advance to alleviate the risk to your own credit, as discussed previously. You can use your credit card knowing you already have the advance to pay the balance.

It can be to your advantage to have a credit card that earns airline-mileage points. Though a considerable amount of your purchases will later be returned, you will accumulate mileage on the purchases you do not return. Many business people who have reimbursable expenses use such a mileage-earning credit card.

I have learned one lesson the hard way: Pay the full balance for each job charged on the credit card as soon as you receive payment, no matter how much you'd like to hold onto the income and make payments gradually. In addition to avoiding interest payments at sky-high rates, you will need the available credit for the next project.

## TAXES

When you are a full-time employee, your employer deducts taxes from your pay, and sends them to the appropriate government agencies. Depending on your income and deductions, at the end of the year the taxes paid is sometimes less than what you owe, resulting in a refund to you. Social Security tax is also deducted from your pay but the employer matches it, and sends the combined amount to Social Security. That amount stays in your fund for retirement.

## Self-Employment

But you are self-employed and running your own business. Your federal and state income taxes and Social Security are your responsibility. You are responsible for filing your own taxes, IRS Form 1040, along with IRS Schedule C (Profit or Loss From Business), which is a statement of your profit or loss and the expenses for running your business, and Schedule SE (Self-Employment Tax). The process really motivates you to keep all receipts for business-related expenses.

Visit *www.irs.gov/businesses/small* to view an array of resources provided by the IRS for the self-employed, including business workshops.

The IRS 1099-MISC (miscellaneous income) form currently must be filed by any business paying you $600 or more in a calendar year. Near the end of January of the following year a copy is sent to you and another filed with the IRS. In this way, your earnings are recorded and must match with what you claim you earned when you file your taxes. Likewise, if you pay anyone else, like a styling assistant, $600 or more, you are responsible for filing a 1099-MISC form.

## Your Accountant

I am a photo stylist, not an accountant, and I don't presume to tell you what expenses are deductible from the point of view of the Internal Revenue Service. The best advice I can give is to have an accountant as an advisor for these financial questions, and to assist you with filing your taxes.

When I owned my plant store in the 1970s, I amazed friends and myself by filing my own business taxes. After a lifetime of math-phobia, it was an unlikely adventure. I actually recorded all the business income and expenses in a ledger book with a sharp pencil and totaled them on an adding machine. Now I don't have to bother with this challenging exercise, since computer software makes my record keeping much less complicated. Financial software such as Quicken is easy to use and you can categorize and total your expenses.

Working with an accountant, you can provide a detailed list of your expenses—or pay the accountant more for the convenience of handing over your receipts. As part of your income tax, you'll be filing a Schedule C, which is a business profit and loss summary. You will have business use of your car and possibly a part of your home. You will need to list and describe equipment purchases. The tax-filing process is complex and accountants know what deductions are valid.

Here are some business expenses that you *may* be able to deduct from your income. You should save all your receipts from these expenses as documentation. Some are obvious, but others you may not have thought about. Again, please confirm them with your accountant:

- Computer equipment and software
- Office furniture
- Office supplies
- Cellphone usage (or the portion used for business)
- Mileage (record all mileage used for business in a small calendar kept in your car), OR actual auto expenses (ask your accountant which is better)
- Reference materials (books and magazines)
- Materials for your kit
- Marketing expenses (like Web design, printing, postage)
- Props purchased for your own styling use
- Testing costs
- Legal and professional fees
- Portion of utilities, home phone, rent, or mortgage (based on the size of your home office)
- Bank fees, check printing
- Professional organization dues
- Travel expenses for work-related travel
- Career workshops and related travel
- Meals and entertainment (partially deductible; note who was entertained on receipt)
- Health insurance payments and medical expenses (partially deductible)
- Donations of cash or materials

## Quarterly Payments

Generally the federal and state government expects a self-employed person to make quarterly tax payments. These are an estimated amount based on the previous year's income. Your accountant can help you set up this filing process.

## BUSINESS LICENSES

Whether a license is required for running your business is a local matter. Check with your city or county government offices for the requirements for establishing a business. You are probably operating a home-based business, and depending on where you live, a license may not be required. Still, you need to know.

If you use a name other than your own name for your styling business, you may need to file a fictitious business-name notice in a local newspaper. Particularly in California, you will need this in order to open a checking account under that name. If you receive checks made out to your business name, you would not be able to deposit them otherwise. Find out about business-name procedures in your area by searching for "business licenses" and your state on the Web.

While you can use your own Social Security number, it's helpful to have a Federal ID number for identifying your business. Apply for it by logging onto *www.irs.gov* and filling out a form. It is more secure than supplying your Social Security number to clients when completing W-9 forms.

## PROVIDING YOUR OWN BENEFITS

Benefits are one of the biggest differences between regular employment and self-employment. In addition to regular paychecks, retirement accounts, paid vacation time, and sick days, health insurance has become an important issue for American workers.

### Health Insurance

Despite great fears about it, individual health insurance coverage in the United States is not so hard to find, if you are healthy. By doing some research you can locate information on a variety of policies available. It will take some time to compare deductibles, co-payments, and what services are covered, but it can be done. The rates depend on your age, so when you are in your twenties or thirties you should easily be able to afford your own health insurance. Insurance for the self-employed can still be found when you're older but may be more expensive.

While some professional organizations offer membership in group policies, I haven't found the rates are much different from what you can find on your own. You might look at those policies, then look at some major insurers like Blue Cross/Blue Shield and Kaiser Permanente, and other insurance companies when making your decision. Many smaller insurers may provide comparable plans.

### Business Insurance

As a stylist, you are working as an independent contractor without an actual place of business. The photo studios or clients you work for have their own business-liability coverage, so you shouldn't need this type of insurance. (These are the same policies that were discussed in chapter 4, amended to cover locations.)

And you shouldn't need to carry worker's compensation; make sure that your health-insurance policy covers you if you are injured while working. But do check with an insurance expert for information in your state.

When you hire an assistant you might avoid the responsibilities of an employer, and some paperwork, by having the assistant bill the client or photographer directly.

## Retirement

When you are old enough to retire, Social Security may have changed a great deal. As it is, your retirement income is based on the amount you have contributed to the system. The more years you've put in as a well-paid employee, or a self-employed person with a profitable business, the more you'll be eligible to receive.

There are many options, however, for you to contribute to individual retirement accounts. If you start contributing to these accounts when you start your freelance career, and keep up your good habits, you should be able to accumulate a decent retirement income.

There's no official age when you can't work as a stylist anymore. I keep wondering how long I'll do this. Though the work requires strength and stamina, I think it's very healthy work, both physically and because of the pleasure of being a stylist. One forty-something stylist styles her hair in an orange Mohawk to maintain a youthful impression, which may extend her career.

# AGENCY, STAFF, OR FREELANCE

Agency representation can take care of many business details that could be overwhelming. If the business of styling seems too much for you, an agent can take on the burden of finding clients, quoting rates, estimates, negotiations, invoicing, and collecting payment. The percentage of your rate paid to the agency for this benefit may be well worth it, unless you're the most independent sort of person.

## How Agencies Work

A styling agency is in business for the purpose of finding you work, from which it takes a percentage in order to stay in business. The agents' incomes, marketing, and overhead are all paid through the commissions taken on placements.

Generally, a 20 percent commission is taken from the stylist's rate, and the client pays an additional fee of 20 percent of the rate. Since the client will be paying more when booking through an agency, experienced and professional-quality styling work is expected. Plus the client gets the service of having the details managed by a professional agent and knows a qualified stylist will arrive on the job.

Styling and makeup agencies expect their talent to be exclusively represented by them. It's agreed that all of the stylist's work is to be channeled through the agency. The stylists are not allowed to book jobs independently or through another agency, except an agency in another region or country. The agency takes charge of scheduling work, keeping a calendar for the stylists, with a comprehensive idea of what they can and cannot do time-wise. With years of experience and many stylists on their rosters, agents can realistically project a good schedule, and they negotiate travel compensation.

Many model agencies will also represent stylists, often in a more casual way. The stylists' comp cards may be sent with models' cards to potential clients. Generally you are not asked for an exclusive agreement with model agencies, and this is a good place to start in smaller markets.

## Connecting with an Agency

According to Doni Miller, an agent with Art House Management in New York, "We like to see a strong portfolio that shows a lot of range and different styles. When you have a strong body of work to show a potential client, the better chance of getting your stylist the job. You never really know what the client wants to see, so the better portfolios usually get the job."

Unless your portfolio is pretty amazing, you may first have to meet with an agency and then develop some new imagery for the agency's specific market—the agents will know what their clients are looking for. An agency may suggest some shots you can add to your portfolio to better represent yourself to the agency's market.

## Benefits of Agency Representation

The agency takes care of every aspect of the stylist's professional life, from the previously mentioned calendar to billings. The rate is negotiated so you don't really have to discuss money with your client. Expenses may be arranged through the agent or directly with the stylist. The agency will invoice the client and make sure payment is received, and then it'll pay you. Your agent knows what type of work is marketable and can advise about your portfolio and promotional materials.

Ann Fitzgerald is a Boston-based stylist who joined other stylists in forming the Team Agency in 1986. Ann says being represented by an agency is essential: "Financial issues never need to be discussed between the stylist and client, you don't need to show your book as often, and you can recommend your agency friends for jobs if you are already booked, and vice versa. It is also nice to have that bond with other stylists, especially since we spend so much time searching for the elusive prop, and time prepping alone. It's great to feel comfortable enough to call someone up for a resource if you need to."

## Drawbacks of Agency Representation

In spite of the helpful career management, there is no guarantee that you will have plentiful work through an agency. The jobs depend on the marketplace as well as on your own skill and professionalism. And there is a Catch-22 in that you need to have quite a portfolio in order to be signed on with an agency, and by the time you have that much work, you may have already established your freelance career.

Even with agency representation, you are still responsible for filing your own taxes and acquiring your benefits. You can expect to pay for your own promotional materials too. All these details should be clarified when signing with an agency.

Agencies understand the styling demands of clients in different parts of the country and know the market. But you'll be informed about this too, once you network and do research.

## Agencies Representing Assistants

A good time to learn about agency representation is when you're learning the styling profession and working as an assistant. Some agencies do represent styling assistants; some don't, but will list you as a resource for professional stylists looking for an assistant. The stylists will refer good assistants to each other.

At this point in your career you can do some research into local agencies and develop your own opinion about a relationship with an agency. While you build your own portfolio, talk to stylists you assist and determine how you feel about marketing yourself, or what agency representation can do for you.

## Stylists on Staff

Full-time positions for photo stylists are few and far between. While most stylists are hired on a freelance basis, some larger retailers and catalog companies maintain their own photo studios and employ stylists. This can be a very good situation for the stylist who desires some stability and prefers not to spend time on marketing and business. (I told the story of one staff stylist in chapter 3.)

## An Independent Spirit

An independent spirit and strong motivation to succeed are a plus, if not a requirement, for a freelance stylist. In spite of the workload of testing, promoting yourself, managing your business, *and* styling, you do have freedom. You can work a part-time job, take a vacation, or pursue other interests at the same time.

chapter

# Your Styling Kit

**C**OMPARED TO WHAT IS REQUIRED FOR MANY PROFESSIONS, your investment in your styling business is small. First, without expensive schooling you won't have student loans to pay off, like an attorney or doctor does. You don't need to rent an office since you can usually manage your styling business from home. You needn't acquire the camera and computer equipment a photographer does. What you *do* need is a well-planned styling kit so that you have everything you might need on a shoot. The recommended equipment listed later in this chapter is fairly inexpensive and can be accumulated gradually.

Your kit, combined with your styling skills and creativity, are your most important assets as a photo stylist. This chapter provides suggestions for useful tools for all stylists and sources for finding some unusual ones. While you are assisting and building your business you can gradually build your kit.

## KIT INSPIRATIONS

Keep your eyes open for kit contents. Some useful—and affordable—items can be found in dollar sale bins at grocery and drug stores. I found a miniature whiskbroom and dustpan set, a spray bottle, containers for pins, and children's barrettes this way. I love the items at the checkouts

223

at the retail chain the Container Store. This is where I find silver cleaning cloths, clear museum gel, and the tiniest bottles of Goo-Gone.

When a professional carpet cleaner left small white Styrofoam blocks under the furniture in my house, I gathered them and added them to my styling kit. They work well for positioning items, especially on a white set. Photographer Michael Christmas has a box of children's wooden blocks. In assorted shapes and sizes, they're invaluable for styling. When covered with cloth tape, they do not slip or move.

Another thrilling find was pet-conditioner spray. I had a bottle on hand one day because my dog was modeling and I tried spraying it on the outside of a glass lemonade pitcher for moisture. It stayed in place longer than water and looked exactly like cold condensation. Now it's part of my kit.

Your kit is an individual as you are. It will take time and experience to complete. Some items you think you're carrying for no reason; then one day, you'll be glad they were there. I have a roll of magnet tape that I've never used, but someday, I'm sure it will be needed.

## THE CONTAINER

The kit that holds your styling supplies is as important as its contents. The toolbox or tool bag should be something that you like—it will become your companion. It should be easy to access and comfortable to carry. Choose one with a shoulder strap if you think you'll carry it on location frequently.

You can shop at hardware or building-supply stores for a durable container. It should be just big enough to fit all your supplies, with a little space to spare. One stylist found a combination step-stool and toolbox that also comes in handy for use as a seat while she works on wall styling.

My own basic kit is a toolbox with small compartments on the top for small things like pins, a removable tray inside with compartments where I keep my tools, and a large bottom area that holds bigger things like safety goggles, tape, lint roller, and my small bottle of degreaser. I keep everything in its place and always know where each item is—typical organized stylist behavior.

For fashion or wardrobe styling, you'll need a portable mini-kit to carry on your body, like a fanny pack or shoulder bag. When you're moving around between the wardrobe and the model, you need to have your tools handy. This may be a secondary wardrobe kit in addition to your larger complete kit. Some stylists keep their scissors on a string around their necks, and clips and safety pins attached to their clothing.

## Multiple Kits

More than one kit may be needed for different types of styling. No need to carry all your wardrobe supplies, like lint rollers, hairspray, and clothing clips, if you're going to be styling shoes on a beach. Or the window cleaner, furniture pads, and lemon polish that you'll need for room styling when you're working with a model. You can store extra supplies you don't always use in see-through bins so you can pull them for special projects. These could even be brought to locations, just in case.

There are some basic items that all stylists will use. And some very specialized kits, as you have seen in the earlier chapters. Essentially, as a stylist, you need to have on hand *everything* that you might possibly need to get your job done.

## BASIC STYLING KIT

Following is a list of basic items for photo stylists. You may not use them all and you will want to add your own items. Keep an ongoing list of items you think of. Often, you'll be working on a shoot and discover something you wish you had, or a great gadget the photographer has that you want to add to your kit.

| ITEM | DESCRIPTION, USE |
| --- | --- |
| ❑ Scissors, small and sharp | For clipping threads and removing labels; use only on fabric |
| ❑ Scissors, bigger | Use on everything but fabric; clean with degreaser after using for tape |
| ❑ Degreaser | Cleans off labels or anything sticky; find a small bottle |
| ❑ Rag(s) | For wiping products and sets, use with window cleaner or water |
| ❑ Window cleaner | For shining products and surfaces, cleaning dishes without water |
| ❑ Paint brush | For dusting small items on set |
| ❑ Quilt pins | For pinning fabric; yellow heads, one- to two-inches long |
| ❑ Corsage pins | Also used for adjusting, lifting; like quilt pins but longer |
| ❑ Pliers, needle nose | For bending wire, grab things |

| | | |
|---|---|---|
| ❑ | Screwdriver *or* Combination tool | Find a screwdriver with changeable heads or use the combination tool with many tools in one |
| ❑ | Wire cutter | For cutting heads off pins, cutting wire |
| ❑ | Safety glasses | Always worn when cutting heads off pins |
| ❑ | Wire, thin | Forms edges of off-figure clothing, lots of other uses |
| ❑ | Monofilament | For suspending objects; also known as fishing line |
| ❑ | Carpet tape | Many uses; double-sided, sturdy, white tape; or use one-sided |
| ❑ | Tweezers | To hold or adjust small items; long ones are useful |
| ❑ | X-Acto knife *or* Box cutter | Cutting and trimming; be sure to cover and have extra blades (the box cutter may be more convenient; it's retractable but less precise) |
| ❑ | Weights | For balancing or weighting objects; divers, weights or flat stones |
| ❑ | Styrofoam or wood blocks | For raising and lifting objects; may be from carpet cleaners |
| ❑ | Permanent markers | For touch-ups; black, brown, and other neutral colors |
| ❑ | Spray bottle of water *or* Wrinkle release product | For spraying wrinkles out of clothing, moistening products or sets; Water works as well, but spray bottle's nozzle may be better |
| ❑ | Lint roller and refills | For removing lint from fabric |
| ❑ | Putty | For holding objects in place; removable with more putty |
| ❑ | Hand sanitizer | For keeping hands grease-free |
| ❑ | Sewing kit | For mending; small kits you find at hotels are good |
| ❑ | Basic first aid | Antiseptic, bandages, aspirin, etc. |

You can usually count on photographers having "gaffer's tape," a strong black fabric tape, along with lots of other tape. Ask the assistant for it. They will generally also have on hand: trash bags, tools, putty, blocks or bricks for lifting items in the shot, foam board, clamps, and C-stands for suspending items from above.

One photographer I worked with even supplied the exact tools I needed for applying dewy moisture to the outside of a moisturizer bottle. He had a long, oversized hypodermic needle and a bottle of glycerin, which I used to carefully place the droplets.

## VARIATIONS FOR STYLING SPECIALTIES

Depending on your styling specialty you'll need additional items for your kit. In each chapter are some suggestions to add to your basic kit for styling specialties. If you do all types of styling, I'd recommend having a basic kit plus several kits that you can customize for each type of project. I keep a plastic bin of extra supplies on hand and customize my kits when needed. The only exception to the basic kit is food styling; your food styling kit is extensive but it's all you need. (The specialized kit described in chapter 9 duplicates many of the supplies in the basic kit.)

### Styling Supply Sites

Browse these Web sites to find unique and specific items for various styling specialties:

#### Fashion and Wardrobe

- *http://wardrobesupplies.com*: Many varied wardrobe supplies

- *www.camerareadycosmetics.com*: Professional makeup palettes

#### Product

- *www.gotputty.com*: Source for earthquake putty, same as photographers' putty

- *www.improvementscatalog.com*: One of many sources for clear museum gel

#### Food

- *www.thestylingstore.com*: Assorted professional food styling supplies

- *www.trengovestudios.com*: Food styling special effect supplies, acrylic spills, ice cubes

- *www.foodesigns.com*: Complete food styling kits available for purchase

## RECOMMENDED EQUIPMENT

The items listed here are a financial investment in your professional career. When you're starting out, you might invest in this equipment one piece at a time, just as a photo assistant purchases cameras and lights gradually while working with a professional photographer. The initial cost of starting your photo-styling business is really rather small. Your first needs are a kit, a portfolio, a home office, and some hands-on experience.

Many photo studios will already have rolling racks, steamers, and irons, but always make sure before the shoot day. If you have your own iron, you'll be familiar with its settings, and know the surface is clean, so you may want to take it with you, rather than rely on a hotel or studio iron.

Having your own rolling rack does elevate you to a more professional level and you will really need it. When I've done preproduction work, I have even been able to rent mine to crews, whether I'm styling for them or not. The same applies to the steamer. I charge a reasonable figure, like $25 to $50 a week. This way you might eventually get your investment back.

I purchased a mannequin, a male torso, for a shirt-styling job. I rented the mannequin to that client. I thought I'd get more use out of it but haven't used it again. Still, I like having it, and may have a need for it again someday.

### Equipment Basics

**Rolling Rack** is essential for hanging, organizing, and transporting wardrobe. An adjustable and collapsible metal rack available at retail supply stores, this is your most valuable piece of equipment. You can organize wardrobe on it at home, transport garments to and from vehicles, and take the rack on location. Bottom bars can carry boxes and your kit. The extensions on either end carry purses, belts and other items. A rolling rack is known as a "rail" in Britain.

**Steamer** is a styling basic for preparing most clothing, fabric, even vinyl (with caution.) Be sure to purchase a professional-style steamer at a retail supplier, having a removable gallon bottle and valve top to avoid drips and spills. Hand-held and travel steamers are not adequate for use on photo shoots. I suggest saving the box your steamer comes in to pack it for traveling.

**Iron and Ironing Board** are used for crisp pressing. Shirts, and fabrics needing more than steam, may be ironed. Purchase a sturdy, high-quality steam iron, which you keep in clean condition. Test fabric first, iron on the wrong side of fabric, and use a cloth or tissue paper over delicate fabrics and screen prints. Some silks cannot withstand the moisture from a steamer or steam iron. Most hotels and studios will have an iron and board on hand, but check first. A ham, which is a rounded cushion for ironing curved areas, helps with pressing fine garments.

**Plastic Hangers** with swivel tops keep garments in good condition. These can be purchased at store fixture suppliers. Hangers can be hooked together for grouping outfits. Have shirt hangers as well as clip style skirt/pant hangers on hand. After using these, you'll come to detest wire hangers, like the Joan Crawford character in *Mommie Dearest.*

**Rack Dividers** are helpful for dividing wardrobe, by model, shot, or day. Like size markers in stores, they can be marked to help with organization. These can be placed on the rolling rack or on individual hangers.

**Tagging Gun** is used to replace hang tags that have been removed. It's available at store suppliers for a nominal amount, with a lifetime supply of plastic strips. Be sure to keep track of the store price tag, as well as extra buttons and other tags. Label them with a sticky note or place in envelopes so you can attach them to the right items.

**Clothing Rod** allows you to hang and transport wardrobe in your car. Adjustable shower rods work well and can be suspended from back seat hooks or handles. You can use permanent plastic tie-downs or small bungee cords to attach a loop.

**First Aid Kit** is always a good idea. A basic first aid kit is something you may some time need to have on location. Keep it stocked with a supply of bandages, antiseptic, alcohol wipes, and aspirin.

**Computer** is a requirement for managing your business. It is essential to have word-processing and accounting software, and an Internet connection. Use the computer for managing projects, writing client agreements, billing, record keeping, and producing promotional materials. Naturally, there is a world of information out there on the Web; you should have your own site, and maybe even maintain it yourself. (We discussed marketing yourself through the Web in chapter 11.)

## KIT FEES

Some makeup artists charge a kit fee in addition to their day rate, because of the high cost of the makeup used. Generally stylists don't charge this fee; the materials used in an average workday don't amount to much expense. Materials needed for specific projects can usually be purchased for that particular job and deducted as expenses. Examples may be boxes, ribbons, and double-sided tape used for wrapping gifts.

Food stylists for still photography do not generally charge kit fees either. Requested items for specific shoots can be purchased when food shopping and added to the expenses. However, it is standard practice in video and television to charge a kit fee of about $75.

## TRAVELING WITH YOUR KIT

Your styling kit is filled with dangerous objects, which could arouse suspicion at an airport; you certainly wouldn't want to take it through a security checkpoint. When you're traveling by air, plan on shipping it ahead or checking it in. Packing it in another suitcase with the wardrobe or other supplies will give your kit some extra cushion and keep the contents from spilling out.

It is important to keep your passport up to date. You don't want to miss an opportunity to work in the Caribbean or France because you have to wait several weeks for a passport. Even with the expedited, "emergency" service, it can take days to get one.

Passports are valid for ten years, so the investment of money and time acquiring yours is dispersed over a long period of time. Don't wait until you need one. Keep it in a safe place, like a safe deposit box at a bank, so you'll know where it is when you need it. Or a fireproof safe at home can provide instant access on weekends and holidays. And check the expiration date. Nothing is as upsetting as learning the night before a trip that your passport is expired!

Even our neighbor Mexico is about to change travel requirements for U.S. citizens. When you accept a job that requires travel to another country it's a good idea to verify the visa policy, since acquiring one may take weeks or months. If you're a citizen of a country other than the United States, know your country's travel and visa rules and restrictions, so you can confidently accept a job requiring international travel.

While you try to be prepared for any event on the go, sometimes you have to solve problems as they come along. A large stone might keep your rack from rolling downhill. Rope might be tied between two trees if no rolling rack is available. The trunk of your car might be where snacks are served and the interior may be the models' changing room.

## YOUR OWN KIT LIST

The kit lists in this book are guidelines to get you started, not an absolute rule. Your own kit will grow and evolve over time as you individualize it. No two stylists have the same items in their kits, just as no two styling jobs are ever the same.

I hope you enjoy the process of building a kit. There is a unique thrill in finding an item like my miniature whisk broom and dustpan set at a dollar sale or discovering clear museum gel. When adding to your kit is that much fun, you know you're meant to be a photo stylist.

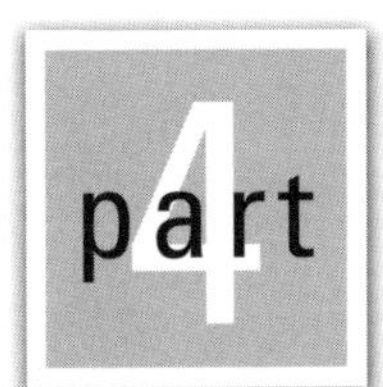


# Photo Styling for Models, Art Directors, and Photographers

# The Model's Perspective

**A**S A MODEL, YOU WILL FIND THAT EVERY PHOTO SHOOT IS different; crew, wardrobe, location, background, and purpose are all variables. What is consistent is that you are presenting yourself to the camera in whatever manner is needed to create the image.

Through the years I have worked with photo shoots in many ways. Currently a photo stylist, I have been a catalog designer, photo art director, model agent, and a model. Having been on both sides of the camera, and behind the scenes as an agent, I have a unique perspective on your career choice as a model.

## A MODEL'S FUNCTION

Your role as a model is to be the human presence in a photograph. From birth, infants like to look at faces; that recognition is developed early. As we grow, we continue to enjoy looking at other people.

### Selling Fashion Clothing

In magazines, the fashion editor researches the latest designs, plans and produces the shoot, and creates a visual story with models. Fashion advertisements feature specific lines of clothing and may show the model in a full-length pose or just show a hint of the clothing.

While a trend has developed of showing clothing off-figure in catalogs and magazines, most clothing is still photographed on models. Catalog customers can see how the garments fit the figure and other details such as pockets, button plackets, side slits, and collar styles that can be shown by an effective model.

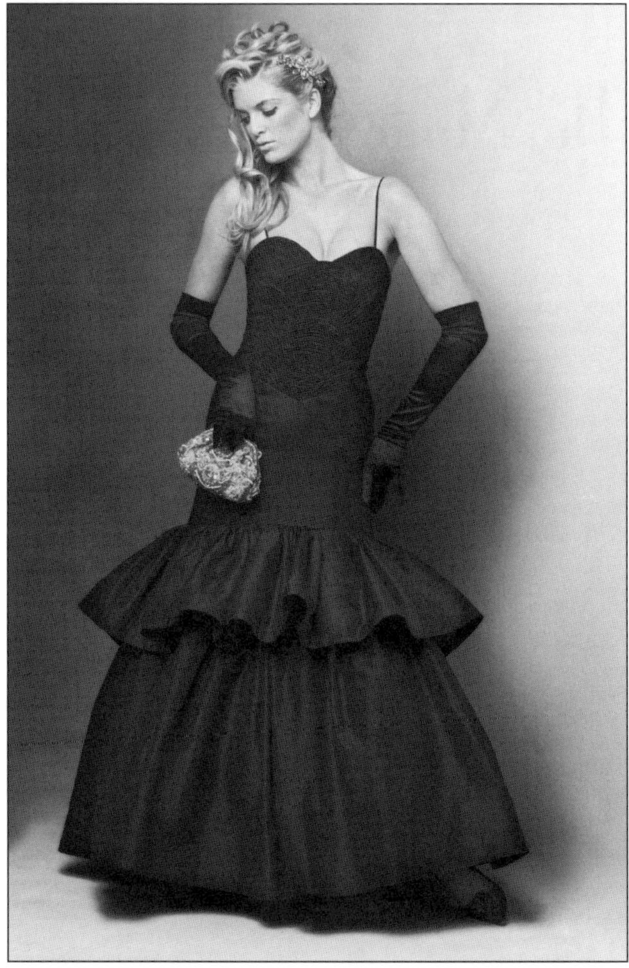

Classic 1950s-style fashion with a modern twist. *Photographer:* Tim Mantoani. *Art director:* Cindy Cochran. *Styling:* Susan Linnet Cox. *Hair and makeup:* Claire Young. © Tim Mantoani

## Selling Other Products

In advertising photography the model may be interacting with a product such as a cleaning product, car, or food. Your wardrobe is not the feature and should not distract from the featured product. Again, the human element is important for engaging the customer.

A lifestyle shot depicts real-life situations and people for an advertisement, other print media, or stock photography. Or the talent may be enhancing a lifestyle concept for a specific company or brand. A scenario that tells a story is being created. The stylist is dressing the talent so as not to distract from the implied activity.

As a model, you may receive assignments in media other than photography. Runway modeling and public appearances at trade shows and other events are some examples. Fit models are hired to try on new clothing for merchandise buyers. The fit model is selected because she is a standard size and proportions for that client's merchandise; it may be a regularly scheduled job.

You may have the opportunity to audition for commercials or music videos. Classes in acting for television will give you experience in this type of casting, and help you to be expressive.

## THE HAPPINESS EFFECT

Elsewhere in this book, I describe how the mood of the photo shoot invariably ends up in the model's face. I call this the "Happiness Effect."

Any tensions among the crewmembers or stress caused by outside factors, like locations and weather, no matter how hard you try, show in your face. The effect may be subtle and most people wouldn't know, but to the art director it is there. On the other hand, the comfort level created by a crew working well together, when everything is going smoothly, results in a happy, relaxed model. Conversations and humor can play a big part in creating a pleasant appearance.

Years ago when I was a catalog art director, I regularly worked with a beautiful model named Lonnie Partridge. Lonnie, along with the assistant photographer and the male model, got seasick while we were doing a shoot on a small cruise ship in the Caribbean. Being a professional, she heroically continued to work. It was fascinating to see her nauseated state between rolls of film vanish when the camera was on. She appeared to be enjoying the cruise of her life but the usual sparkle in her eyes was missing. Looking back at those images I can see the tension; but maybe it's only because I know the real story.

## AT THE PHOTO SHOOT

As you already know, modeling is harder work than most people think. They know the day rate for top models is high and think they are being paid to be beautiful. In reality, the preparation for this career takes work, dedication, and patience. And the photo shoot can involve very long days, holding uncomfortable positions in ill-fitting shoes, and red-eye flights to other jobs—and that's when you've become successful!

## Roles of the Crew

The crew on a fashion or lifestyle shoot is working together to create a photograph, which will either feature you or include you as a sort of prop for a lifestyle shot. (Their duties are described fully in chapter 2.) These are the ways they specifically relate to you as a model.

**Photographer** is, of course, the person behind the camera. The rapport between you and the photographer will happen when the camera is rolling. This is the person who really sees what the shot will be.

**Assistant Photographer** helps the photographer by setting up lighting, caring for the cameras, and carrying equipment on location. Reflectors to bounce light at you and scrims that soften sunlight are held by the assistant.

**Art Director** determines the shots that will be taken and is responsible for approving the look of the photographs. The art director will be looking carefully at you and other aspects of the photo. I recently realized that as an art director, I was smiling and mimicking what I wanted the model to do, without even knowing it.

**Client** works for the company financing the photo shoot and is often less experienced with shoots. During the early steps of setting up a shot, the model's dress may not have been adjusted by the stylist and the lighting is not yet refined. The client might jump the gun and draw these problems to the crew's attention.

**Stylist** is the person who makes all elements of the photograph look the way the client needs, from making sure the products and props are at the shoot, to adjusting the fashions and prepping the clothes when there isn't an assistant stylist.

**Assistant Stylist** may be hired to help the stylist perform multiple tasks, such as steaming the wardrobe and handing you garments to dress in. You can return them neatly on their hangers to the assistant or the stylist.

**Makeup Artist** is generally the first person you will have contact with, taking up to an hour to prepare you at the beginning of the shoot. The makeup artist also makes sure the model continues to look good. On set, he or she will smooth stray hair, mop shininess with a sponge, touch up makeup and lipstick, and change hairstyles between shots.

**Talent or Model** is you, the person being photographed. The generic term talent can refer to a professional model, child, famous person, or lifestyle actor. As a model, you are the one the camera is focused on.

## Digital Photography

In the studio the photos will almost always be shot digitally. On location the photographer may use digital or traditional film. Before digital photography was the norm, there was a different rhythm to the shoot. Once the Polaroid was approved, the shooting began. Often, the first roll of film was just for warming up. The model could hear the automatic winding of the camera and the see the lights reset and flash. Experienced models built a series of moves based on this cycle.

With digital photography the flow is interrupted—the model is often left standing alone while the crew looks at the monitor. I thought this was a problem until I talked to newer models. Model Jolie Benoit says models prefer digital photography since there is instant feedback on the shoot. They appreciate looking at the monitor to see how their poses are working, whereas with film the models would rarely see the final images.

I worked as a stylist on a shoot for a muscle-building supplement that featured an athletic couple in bed together covered by a sheet. The photographer, the art director, and I were repeatedly startled when the woman kept jumping out of bed—nude—to run over to the monitor and view the shot.

## Production Schedules

Due to printing and production schedules, most photo shoots happen anywhere from two to six months ahead of the season. Catalogs may shoot holiday books in July and summer books in February. Magazines shoot from two to six months ahead of the issue. This can result in some pretty uncomfortable work for the model. I remember models wearing wool coats one sunny summer afternoon and being powdered frequently for shine. And there are always stories of models freezing in bikinis.

You can expect to feel too hot or too cold—that's part of what you are being paid for. Remove wool coats during shooting lulls, with the stylist's help to prevent wrinkles. Have a warm sweatshirt or jacket nearby to cover up with when you're cold—again being careful to prevent wrinkling.

## Working with the Stylist

The person who will greet you at the shoot, look out for you during the shoot, and may well have booked you, is the stylist. The stylist will be physically close to you during the shoot helping you look your best. Clipping, pinning, adjusting the hem, and lint rolling, all involve the stylist "going in" and approaching you on set.

The stylist can be as important a contact for you as the art director or the photographer. Recommendations from the stylist can improve your career. The stylist may ask you to test in the future if you work well together. These collaborations can be helpful contacts and be great for your portfolio.

The stylist will love you if you rehang the wardrobe on the hangers, turned right-side-out, and bring it back to the stylist or assistant. It's that easy. It's just a matter of awareness of others; if you don't treat a stylist like she is there to pick up after you, she will continue to respect the hard work you're doing in front of the camera and with all those wardrobe changes.

Tags and labels on garments should not be removed except by the stylist. You might find tags on the hangers that identify the item. Try to rehang the right garment on the right hanger, and let the stylist know if there is confusion.

When you are given wardrobe to put on, that's all you're doing. Put the items on but don't finish dressing by completing all the usual details such as tucking in shirts, buttoning cuffs, putting on shoes, or fastening your belt. The stylist will want to attend to these, possibly in a different way. Avoiding wrinkles in garments that have been meticulously prepared is much appreciated.

On some lifestyle shoots the stylist may request that you bring wardrobe items. Most models like clothes and don't mind bringing some of their own to a shoot. This helps with the wardrobe budget, provides options, and assures that they will fit. The stylist will provide a list to the agency. Don't feel obligated to purchase any items

## Dos and Don'ts of Dressing

* Do wear shoes easy to step out of, and have a warm, open-front jacket or sweatshirt.

* Don't tuck in shirts or button all the buttons.

* Do stay wardrobe-ready after you are dressed for the shot.

* Don't wrinkle your wardrobe by folding your arms, sitting down, or bending over.

* Do let the stylist put on your shoes and belts.

* Don't stretch garments over hangers, or get makeup on clothes.

* Do hang clothes and return to stylist.

* Don't forget your personal jewelry if you've handed it to the stylist for safekeeping during the shoot.

* Do keep a sense of humor and enjoy what you're doing.

you wouldn't normally wear, but if you can share some of your own wardrobe for the day, the stylist will appreciate it. And there are some basics you should always have, like undecorated jeans and generic white sneakers.

The same type of lifestyle shoot may involve a request for you to do your own makeup. In a beauty or fashion shoot there should always be a makeup artist, but if you're not shown closely the expense may be saved. Keep your makeup light and natural and bring it with you to the shoot for touch-ups.

## Photo Shoot Etiquette

Professionalism is your priority. Beyond that, you can enjoy the company of the crew during the shoot. Greeting everyone upon arriving to the shoot, saying thanks for lunch, signing vouchers, and saying goodbye to all at the end of the day are all part of the model's day and an opportunity to express your appreciation of the crew.

Follow-up notes are always nice. One model I worked with took the time to make cards with group crew photos attached, which I have saved.

Tell your agent if you have a bruise, scrape, injury, or a weight or a hair change. Let the client know this when you arrive at the shoot, in case a busy agent forgot to mention your black eye. Maybe they can dress you in sunglasses instead of sending you home. This actually happened on a shoot I worked on, and we were naturally irritated with the agent. Fortunately it was an outdoor shoot and the sunglass option worked.

# FOR NEW MODELS

While it doesn't take long to learn the ropes, you're pretty much on your own at a photo shoot. The stylist, photographer, and other crewmembers are your allies; they want you to be an effective model so great shots can be accomplished. The photographer will direct you, but it's all right to ask questions. Do you want me to turn this way? Do my feet look funny in this position? Should I try walking in again and starting over?

Ask the stylist questions when you're getting dressed about who's who, what kind of look the clients are after, and what the photos will be used for. And don't be afraid to admit you haven't modeled much before—a good crew will help you out if they want to succeed at their own jobs.

## How to Look Like You've Been Modeling for Years

Certain tendencies reveal an amateur or a new model at the shoot. These tips can help you look seasoned and experienced, and speed up your career tremendously.

**Know how to dress in wardrobe**. Put on clothes carefully so they don't wrinkle; the stylist will take care of the details. Don't tuck in shirts. The stylist will put on your shoes (really!), belt, hat, scarf, and other accessories.

**Stay camera-ready**. Once you're in wardrobe, don't fold your arms across your waist, sit down, bend over, tie your shoe, or anything else that will cause wrinkles. The stylist has worked hard to steam or iron the apparel.

**Come prepared**. Wear your own slip-on shoes rather than walking in prop shoes; put them on when you get in front of the camera. Bring a warm jacket if the weather is chilly. Pack a model bag with the right undergarments.

**No need to freeze**. The 1800s are over and cameras are faster. Nothing makes you look less experienced than staying still after each frame is shot. Move around unless instructed to stay put; sometimes changing foot position improves the drape of clothing.

**Don't help the stylist adjust your clothing**. Avoid the tendency look down when the stylist comes in to give your clothes a tug; it changes your position from what the stylist is trying to fix. The stylist can do it without your help.

**Experiment with poses**. Practice in front of a mirror at home. Look at your test shots, whether film, proof sheets, or digital images. Watch other models who are working with you and study photographs in catalogs and magazines.

**Work the merchandise**. Remember, it's not about you; it's about what you're selling. If it's apparel, learn some moves. Work with the features of what you're wearing.

**Stay on your mark**. This is a focus point the photographer has established, possibly marked with tape. If you are walking in the shoot, the moment when you are over the mark is when the photographer will snap the shot.

## KEEPING FIT

While you may have gaps between bookings, a regular part of your job is to stay in shape. A gym membership is a must because you need to have your body ready to model. Fortunately, the current style for models is healthier with less call for bony thinness. Some agencies focus solely on athletic models.

Your eyebrows should be kept waxed or plucked. Your hands and feet should be kept in good condition. Before a booking have a manicure and a pedicure, if your feet are going to be showing, with natural polish or neat French nails. Many makeup artists will have polish remover, but it's safer to keep your polish neutral. You may receive specific instructions about manicures for a booking.

If you expect to be modeling swimwear or lingerie you should maintain an even tan. As the makeup artist later in this chapter suggests, visit a tanning booth but don't get a spray-on tan as it can streak. (She also has important advice about hair color and roots.) You can apply some self-tanning lotion to touch up tan lines in a pinch.

When underwear, lingerie, or any revealing clothing is being modeled there must be a "closed set." This means that to respect the model's privacy, no one other than the crew can come and go. For these shoots, you should know this in advance and agree to them. Be sure to have a bikini wax. Don't use a razor, even though it may seem like an adequate shave. I'll always remember viewing some underwear shots with the color technician at a catalog. After looking through the loupe at a greatly enlarged image, he exclaimed, "She should get a new razor!" And I had to agree with him.

Keep tattoos to a minimum. Ask your agent before getting new ones; they may or may not be detrimental to your marketability. It's hard to predict whether they will limit your work as an older model in future years. While tattoos can be covered with makeup, this is time-consuming and large areas can't be covered effectively.

Body piercing, too, should be considered carefully. I styled one model who had pierced nipples. I didn't notice until we were on set and felt uncomfortable about asking her to remove the rings then. There were visible bumps in the final shot and I always regretted my reluctance, though she herself should have had the foresight to remove them.

Male models must keep up on grooming by getting regular haircuts. Makeup artists frequently will trim stray hair, brows, and necklines when needed. Shave before the shoot unless requested not to.

## WHAT AN AGENT DOES

After leaving a senior art-director position, I spent a year as model agent. I wanted to see what that aspect of the photography industry was like. While there were things I liked about it, it was one of the most difficult jobs I've ever had. Though they stay on the phone all day at the agency, booking agents work diligently for each assignment and feel disappointment when the models don't work—at least I did.

Making my role even more challenging was that my own daughter was one of the models I represented, but it was probably worse for her having her mother as an agent. What I loved about it was getting to know the young models, promoting them with potential clients, and sharing the excitement they (usually) felt about their careers.

Agency representation takes care of many business details, which could be overwhelming if you tried to manage your own modeling career. What's more, most clients won't book a model who isn't represented by an agency. Rarely would a valid client look at Internet listings for models, and then only at legitimate agency Web sites. It's an assurance that the models are professional and at least somewhat experienced. And it's definitely safer for the model.

## How Agencies Work

A model or talent agency works to find you bookings for which they can take a percentage in order to run the business. The agents' incomes, marketing, and overhead are all paid through the commissions taken on bookings.

From the model's rate a 20 percent commission is taken; the client pays an additional fee of 20 percent. The model therefore receives 80 percent of the established rate after the commission, and the agency receives 40 percent.

Your booking agent may send you on many castings before you get a job. Sometimes there are "call-backs," or second castings. Be brave and patient—some day it will happen. I've heard the average for actors and models is forty castings for every job. That seems like a lot of work that you don't get paid for; your belief in your career makes it worthwhile.

This is the part of modeling that eventually became too much for my daughter; it's challenging to keep your ego intact with rejections, in spite of your successes. She is now happily working with small children who have developmental disabilities.

Having a part-time or flexible job while building your modeling career helps take the pressure off. When you do get a booking it may be a month or more until you're paid. You'll need another income.

Model agencies expect to represent their talent exclusively. The agency takes charge of scheduling, keeping a calendar for the models and managing their work schedules. The model may not book jobs independently or through another local agency, but may have an agency in another region or country.

## The Mother Agency

Most models start with representation in their home areas. This primary agency is called the "mother agency." But models can also be represented by agencies in other cities, or on each coast. These agents must check with the mother agency for availability. There's always a delay before agencies can confirm the client's model choice; after clearing the schedule with other agencies, they also talk to the talent directly before confirming a booking.

## Connecting with an Agency

Most agencies have restrictions about how and when they will view prospective talent. Find out when there is an open call, whether you can drop in, or make an appointment. Wear natural makeup and be yourself.

If you want to be a model, approach several agencies before you have any photos taken—certainly don't spend any money on photography at this stage. When an agency accepts you, the agent will tell you what looks are needed; chances are they'll be softer and more natural than what you would have provided. The agent may suggest a photographer and stylist for you to test with.

## Benefits and Drawbacks

The agency takes care of nearly every aspect of your professional life, from your calendar to billings. Rates are negotiated so you don't have to discuss money with your client. Agencies invoice the clients and make sure payments are received, before paying you. Expenses like travel, cab fare, and manicures can be negotiated and added to your invoice. Be sure to keep the receipts.

Agents are particularly skilled at negotiating with clients to assure you receive the best rate. In addition to a day rate, extra payments for usage of your images beyond the original agreement are your agent's responsibility. Most often related to television commercials, usage can apply to commercial print jobs as well. Compensation for your time traveling to and from jobs is negotiable, as it is considered time lost from other jobs.

A good agent advises you about your portfolio and promotional materials, and helps you to develop your career. Your responsibilities are filing your own taxes and acquiring your benefits, such as health insurance. (The information for stylists in chapters 11 and 12 applies to your modeling career, too; there you'll find guidance for managing your career as a business, from marketing to insurance and taxes.)

You can expect to pay for your own promotional materials (but they're tax deductible). All these details should be clarified when signing on with an agency. Read your contract carefully. In no case should you pay any money to an agency when you sign up. And there should be no *required* classes or training that you have to pay for. The agency may *suggest* some workshops, however, that would be helpful, such as runway modeling.

## Paperwork

A voucher is a triplicate form that you fill out and present to the stylist or art director for signing at the end of your workday. A packet of vouchers will be provided by your agency. Complete your hours worked and the agreed rate and sign it; the art director fills in the billing information and signs it. The stylist may be authorized to complete the voucher instead.

Remove the client's copy, keep your copy, and deliver the first page of the signed voucher to your agency as soon as possible after the booking, along with receipts. It might be faxed or scanned, with the original following by mail. The project can't be billed until the vouchers are submitted. Your agent shouldn't have to call and remind you. Keep your voucher copies in a file so you can keep track of your unpaid and paid jobs.

During the shoot you will be presented with a model release form to sign. Its purpose is to convey the right to use your image to the photographer or client. Ask your agent for advice on signing releases; there may be exceptions, such as stock usage, that you'll want to understand. It's better to know ahead of the shoot if there are any usage limitations, rather than slow down the shoot with a call to your agency.

# YOUR MODEL BAG OF TRICKS

The items listed here should be kept in a bag you always take to shoots. Keep it packed and ready to go. Some are undergarments you'll need to wear so the clothing fits best. The sweatshirt and slip-on shoes will keep you warm and comfortable between shots. Wear or bring a button-up shirt so you don't have to pull your clothes over your head after makeup.

## Model Bag for Women

❑  Vouchers

❑  Zip-up sweatshirt, or warm jacket

❑  Slip-on shoes

❑  Button-up shirt (for makeup)

- ❏ Bathrobe (if shooting lingerie)
- ❏ Nude-colored seamless bra
- ❏ Nude thong or full underwear to waist
- ❏ Nude body suit
- ❏ Panty hose
- ❏ Bra lifts, also known as push-up enhancers (if needed)
- ❏ Small stud earrings
- ❏ Basic jewelry
- ❏ White T-shirt
- ❏ Jeans
- ❏ Generic white sneakers

## Makeup Kit for Women

- ❏ Brush
- ❏ Hair spray
- ❏ Ponytail elastics
- ❏ Foundation
- ❏ Powder (or use combination product like MAC Studio Fix)
- ❏ Neutral lip color
- ❏ Mascara
- ❏ Makeup remover for later
- ❏ Moisturizer for elbows and knees
- ❏ Neutral eye shadow

## Model Bag for Men

- ❏ Vouchers
- ❏ Zip-up sweatshirt, or warm jacket
- ❏ Slip-on shoes
- ❏ Button-up shirt (for makeup)
- ❏ White T-shirt
- ❏ Jeans
- ❏ Generic white sneakers
- ❏ White and dark socks
- ❏ Watch

## Grooming Kit for Men

- ❑ Hair gel
- ❑ Brush
- ❑ Powder (or use combination product like MAC Studio Fix)
- ❑ Rechargeable shaver (for touchups)
- ❑ Vaseline for lips
- ❑ Makeup remover for later
- ❑ Moisturizer for elbows and knees

### Suggestions from a Makeup Artist

These beauty suggestions are courtesy of San Diego makeup artist Mary Erickson. Most professional models know from experience what needs to be done before a photo shoot. If you do not have a lot of modeling experience, the following list will help you with a healthy appearance. The more of these guidelines you follow, the better your shots will be.

- Avoid the following items seventy-two hours before your photo shoot (they can give you oily skin and swelling):

  - Red meat

  - Alcohol

  - Caffeine

  - Spicy foods

  - Retin-A and alpha hydroxy creams (these cause skin peeling that shows with photo makeup)

- Drink lots of water. Carry it with you everywhere you go, and keep sipping.

- Exfoliate your skin at least once a week and also the morning of the shoot.

- Have your brows professionally shaped and keep them up by plucking strays every few days. Makeup artists pluck strays but may not have time to shape your brows.

- It is a good idea to carry your own mascara. Some makeup artists use mascara with the same wand on several people, which can spread infection very quickly. Unless you know the artist only uses disposable wands, it's safer to bring your own.

- Dark roots look even worse in photos. Refresh your hair color a few days before your shoot. If you do not color your hair, try a toner a shade lighter than your hair to make it shine. If you need a trim, do it before the shoot.

- Fingernails and toenails should be one length, well-manicured, and the polish should be colorless or French, unless the shoot calls for color.

- If you are asked to arrive makeup-free, all traces of makeup should be gone from your skin. All eyeliner and mascara should be removed. Your face should be clean and product-free when you arrive.

- Do not over-condition your hair before a shoot. Your hair must be dry before you arrive.

- Avoid dry lips by putting Vaseline on your lips before bed and the morning of your shoot.

- For body shots (when lots of skin shows), be sure you get rid of tan lines by visiting a tanning booth a few times.

- Don't have a spray-on tan; it looks orange in photos and looks streaky most of the time.

- If you are a woman with facial hair, you need to have it waxed before the shoot. Peach fuzz will show up on your skin; in fact, it will look worse in photos than it does in person.

- Get rid of body hair, anywhere and everywhere it could possibly show. Waxing is best.

- Bring strapless bras, nude undergarments, and tube tops.

- Wear loose, comfortable clothing to the shoot; clothes and socks that bind will leave marks.

## Web Resources

There are many Web sites directed toward modeling, and not all of them are safe places for you. Use the Web to research model agencies, communicate with other professionals, and learn about the profession. But be very careful about marketing yourself through the Internet and accepting work from individuals without going through your agency. A few sites for communicating and learning are:

- *www.talentnetworks.com*: Online talent and styling resources, articles, and chats

- *www.theagencyforum.com*: Education for aspiring models by professional models

- *www.themakeupartist.com*: Makeup artist Mary Erickson's site with resources

- *www.coxproductions.com*: My own site which offers workshops for stylists and models

## IMAGE DECISIONS

Unless you are paying for your own portfolio shoot, it's best not to comment on how you want to look. On a commercial shoot leave the decisions on styling, makeup, and hair to the professionals you're working with; they understand the look the photographer and art director are working toward.

When wardrobe is selected for you to wear, keep in mind that the art director has to select items that work for the market. Even though you may feel stodgy, mature, or out of style try not to be emotionally involved with the choices. You're just playing a role.

There are other factors in the project beyond your taste, such as color shifts, lighting, backgrounds, and lens filters. Even when the shoot is a collaboration or test there may be technical aspects the crew understands best. But a test is one opportunity for you to express yourself and get the images you and your agent want for your portfolio.

# The Art Director's Perspective

**T**HE ART DIRECTOR IS AS CRUCIAL TO THE PHOTO SHOOT AS the photographer and stylist, though the art director is less physically involved. While responsible for creating the concept and bringing back the best photos possible, the director's role at the shoot is essentially one of supervision.

## ART DIRECTOR DEFINED

This job title is subject to many interpretations. In an advertising or design agency it may mean a person who manages projects and supervises designers. But when a graphic designer is given the responsibility of attending a photo shoot, the designer is serving as an art director. The role is quite different from the daily work of designing printed campaigns in the office.

As an art director your job is to ensure that the right photograph is being produced. To do that you need to understand the goal of the photo. Is it to intrigue people, to shock them, to make them hungry, or to sell them dancewear? To achieve your goal, you are overseeing both the technical aspects and the aesthetics of the image. You are also the supervisor of the entire project: the crew, the talent, the location, and after the shoot, bringing back the digital files.

Catalog companies that consistently produce photography may have a full-time photography art director on staff. This was the job I moved into at Norm Thompson after having been hired as a graphic designer. I had earlier designed printed work with photographs as a freelance designer, and had hired photographers, but hadn't supervised shoots this intensively. I accepted the offer to try art directing a fashion shoot in Miami to see if I liked it—and I did. For the very first shot, I knew where I needed to be—behind the photographer's shoulder—and felt completely at home. Art direction is not always so easy, however.

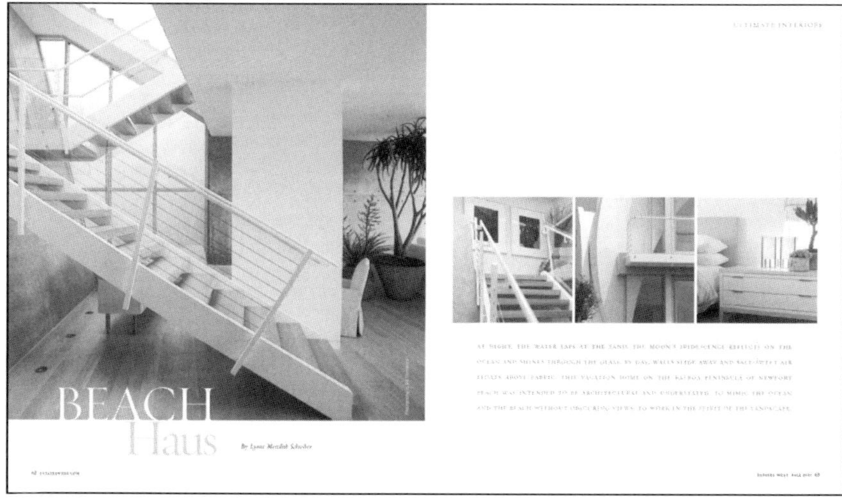

Featuring a home in a magazine requires thorough attention to every detail and viewpoint as well as design skills. *Art director:* Caitlin Beier. Courtesy of *The Boulders*, published by Media That Deelivers, Inc. © Media That Deelivers, Inc.

Magazine art director Caitlin Beier contacted me soon after receiving her bachelor of science in design and graphic design. She wanted to learn more about the photo-shoot aspect of her new career. Soon after, she was offered a job as an art director for a group of luxury magazines based in Arizona. Here is what she has to say about editorial art direction:

*Magazines are a bit different than other projects because of tight deadlines and constantly changing issues. For a monthly publication, one week a month is actual shooting. However, planning for these shoots can be done weeks, days, or even months ahead of time. For example, if there are two unrelated stories that are based on, let's say a beach, they will be shot at the same time, even if one set of photos will sit for six months until the issue is in production.*

*Most concepts for magazine shoots come from perusing other magazines, national and worldwide, ripping out tear sheets, looking through books, and just getting inspired by different ideas. Also, it is really important to have a great photographer and stylist who will bring their own ideas to the shoots.*

## LEARNING HOW TO ART DIRECT

The role of the art director can be daunting, as many graphic designers walk into a photo shoot unprepared in terms of education. According to Caitlin Beier, "Unfortunately, more often than not, programs in design give you a solid background in design techniques and history but focus very little on real-life scenarios, like photo shoots, irate clients, and short deadlines."

The subject of photo direction may not even come up in interviews for agency positions, according to many art directors I have talked with. Either it's assumed that you know how to manage a photo shoot, or there is no expectation that you will later direct shoots. You may be on your own when it comes to developing the skills for art direction.

Art direction for photography may receive casual mention in graphic design classes. Perhaps it will receive more attention in the future if students request it. Otherwise, your best opportunities to learn about art direction may be on the job. Attend photo shoots any chance you get. In the studio or on location, soak up information. Pay attention, notice the result of small changes made by the crew, and ask questions.

### Photography Classes

Taking photography courses can be very helpful. Hands-on experience with composition, depth of field, focus, apertures, light readings, and lighting will take you a long way toward understanding art direction. Rather than learning gradually by observing and listening, you will understand technically what the photographer can accomplish.

One art director I worked with, however, had a hard time holding back and annoyed photographers by handling the camera and giving too much instruction. His photographic background should have been set aside enough to allow the photographer to make decisions. A balance between knowing how your image can be created or refined, and taking over the process, is a critical part of your job.

Studio-lighting techniques are rarely taught in basic photography classes. San Francisco-based art director Mike Coyne studied photography in design school but didn't learn enough about lighting techniques. He says, "When there is something off about a photo, whether it be mood, detail, or style, it usually comes down to lighting. And it's all a mystery to me. I wish I had a better grip on the process so I could communicate what I'm going for and what they need to change."

You can find a studio-lighting class through local community colleges or art centers or learn by attending photo shoots. You will need to listen to every word exchanged by the photographer and assistant, ask questions, and watch what they are doing. An internship in a photo studio would be a wonderful opportunity to absorb this information. You'd also get to learn how the business operates. There are estimates, scheduling, invoicing, material purchases, and countless other details involved in studio management, which all indirectly affect the art director.

## Collaborations and Testing

It doesn't seem to be done often, but why not test with a crew developing its own portfolio projects? (Read more about collaborative projects in chapter 11.) These creative collaborations are assembled by photographers, stylists, makeup artists, and models to give themselves an opportunity to be creative, develop concepts, experiment, and make great additions to their portfolios.

As an art director you could contribute by developing a mock-up magazine layout and print a finished printed piece for all crewmembers. In the process of adding to your own portfolio, you would have a chance to actually direct a shoot with your collaborators, learning far more than you would in a classroom.

## Visual Elements

Our vision works quite differently from the camera. The human mind can edit extra material out of a visual field; the camera lens does not. The next time you're in beautiful neighborhood, see if there are, in fact, any telephone wires, signs, or damaged pavement that hadn't caught your eye on first glance.

In a preview, whether it's Polaroid or digital, be alert for any distracting juxtapositions in the background. Horizontal lines shouldn't cross behind the model's head, neck, hips, or any point that catches the viewer's eye or makes the body look wide. Watch for vertical items too, like a palm tree coming out of the model's head shown here. When you, the photographer, and the stylist are looking at a preview shot, unwanted elements will be obvious that you may have overlooked. Note that the stylist still has to improve the clothing and that the model is not really modeling yet. The preview is for overall composition.

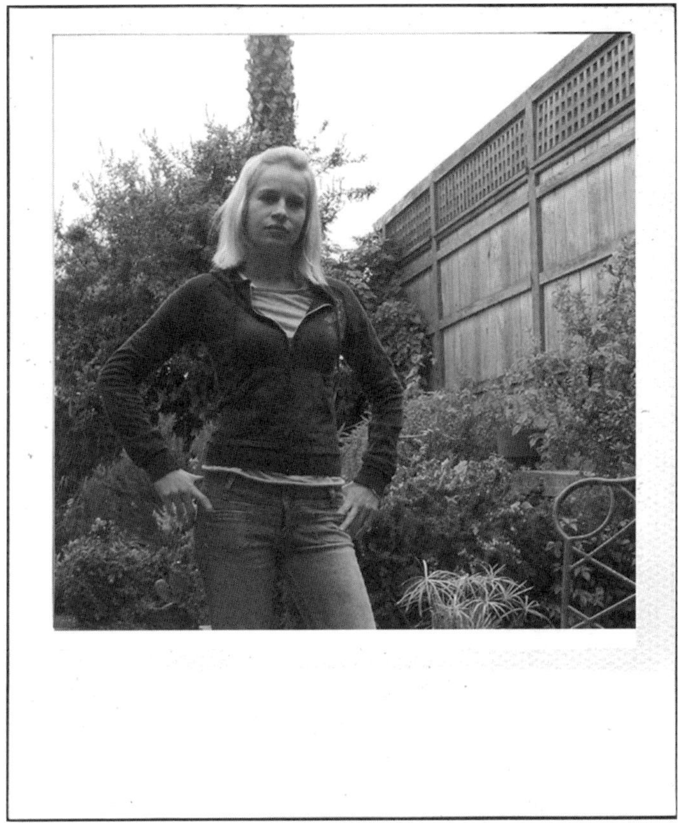

A Polaroid preview shot. Notice the disturbing element of a palm tree above the model's head. Fence and foliage effectively draw the viewer's eye to the model. Contrast between the model's sweatshirt and background could be improved for a better shot. © Susan Linnet Cox

Another phenomenon of our vision is how we see the photographs on a two-page spread. If an image on one page contains the same visual clues of a particular location (a certain setting, such as a beach, or a color scheme) as the other, it is implied that the other photos were taken at the same location.

The same thing can be accomplished in a feature story that continues over a number of pages. Of course, designers also build a visual story with colors, layout items, and photographic style, but the viewer may add unseen interpretations to the images.

## PRODUCTION ROLES

As an art director you are likely to have production responsibilities too. In addition to selecting a photographer, you may hire other crewmembers and models, and organize the entire project.

Alternatively, a stylist with production skills can help organize the project for you by casting the talent, finding locations, acquiring permits, arranging meals, and buying or attaining props. If you are needed at your office, you may not be able to allocate the chunks of time required for these tasks. It's nice to know that someone who knows the big and small details involved in a photo shoot has handled them for you.

(The many aspects of producing a photo shoot are discussed in chapter 4. Unless you've directed many location shoots, there will be tasks described there that might surprise you.)

## Organization Is Crucial

Like the other players in the photo shoot, you must be highly organized. With the budget and the responsibility for bringing back the shots you need, you can't afford to miss any details. If you're directing a shoot for a catalog, you'll need to have all the products pulled and labeled. Bring layouts, shot lists, and photo references.

Arrange a preproduction meeting with the photographer and the stylist, at least several days before the shoot. The stylist will ask questions you may not have thought of. You'll be sure that the team understands your vision for the shoot and how they can help achieve it. If it's a location shoot, the practicality of certain locations can be discussed, as well as who will arrange permits.

There may be propping ideas that come up during this meeting, and there should be time built into the project for them to be acquired, found, purchased, or rented by the stylist. If the shoot involves products rather than concepts, be sure the team gets to preview them and arrange for getting them to the shoot.

## The Budget

The budget for the shoot, of course, is your responsibility. And photo shoots are expensive. It seems like every minute costs so much; that's why the time needs to be used efficiently and organization is important. What appears to be down time is sometimes necessary preparation. The timing of lighting, set changes, steaming garments, and applying makeup must be coordinated so they can happen at the same time.

You may need to provide advance checks to the photographer or stylist to cover expenses; certificates of insurance may have to be quickly processed through your company.

A limited budget for a shoot may require that you serve as the stylist in addition to being the art director. If you work for a young company with little photography experience, shoots may be done on a shoestring. I can sympathize with clients facing thousands of dollars in photography costs while they start to market their products.

Reading the earlier chapters on styling specialties will provide you with some techniques to do the styling yourself. But you can set up a difficult precedent by fulfilling both roles at once. Your focus is diverted from watching the entire project and the look of each photo if you're involved with the minute details a stylist deals with. Later, as the shoots grow more complex, the expectations for you may not evolve. It may be hard to decide when to budget for another crewmember, especially if you are willing to do it all. But when the art director is overwhelmed by location shoots and cannot keep track of the project details, it is time to take the step.

## THE PHOTO SHOOT

At the shoot, your primary focus is on the shots. The crew has been hired to make them happen. You monitor the process, the shot list, and the schedule. Even though you are in charge of the project, your job is to observe, watch the shot, answer questions, and approve the shots. Be on top of things—but with a good crew they largely may run themselves.

### Watching the Shot

I have worked with many art directors in my years as a stylist. Having been an art director myself, I understand their responsibilities. The progression from art direction to styling is not a typical career path, but seeing stylists doing their jobs I felt the hands-on work would be very satisfying. In fact, I learned to be a stylist by observing their techniques. Sometimes I had found it hard to say what I wanted and had to hold back from doing it myself. This can be one of the most challenging aspects of art direction for some—it can be easier to just make the change than to formulate the words.

For other art directors, the shoot seems to be a chance to catch up on paperwork and make phone calls. From a couch in the corner of the studio, they let the crewmembers do their thing. While this trust is flattering, the art director is not involved and perhaps is inexperienced.

Keep in mind that what you are seeing varies greatly with the slightest change in position. From this spot, notice how the tiniest movement to the right and left, or up and down affects what you see; be sure you are accurately viewing the shot before you make composition comments.

Observe how a higher camera view will change the shot. A line running through the background of a shot will fall higher in the frame from that angle—if the horizon goes behind a model's hips and makes her look wide, raising the camera will put it behind her torso and be more flattering. If you want less background and more sky, a lower camera view will work.

Mike Coyne says one of the most challenging aspects of directing is "seeing easily overlooked things like a telephone pole coming out of someone head." If you don't catch them at the shoot, you'll certainly notice later—and regret it. Remember, our brains filter out details that the camera sees.

## The Photographer

You and the photographer work as a team to create the photos. The more technical elements are the photographer's domain, but he will have a great deal of interest in the aesthetic look of the photo as well. The photographer will make the shot happen; you give input and approve it.

You may need several regular photographers on your roster for various styles of photography. Someone who shoots incredible still lifes in the studio may not be so great on location. And a fashion photographer clearly has a different set of techniques—and equipment—than a food photographer. Architectural photography is a specialty with unique skills in lighting and in capturing large interior spaces and exterior building facades without awkward perspective shifts.

Don't touch the camera or lighting equipment. The photo assistant handles all that. The photographer may let you look through the camera, but don't do it without asking—it's not your turf. The photographer will probably be shooting digital, and you will be able to view the images on the screen together. Of course, you're careful not to touch the monitor.

## Clients at the Shoot

Often with agency shoots there is a client representative present. The clients attend because of the importance and expense of photo shoots, and also because it's interesting. While you are the one directly in charge of the shot, you will need to get their feedback to be sure the photograph is what they want. It's a chain of command involving diplomacy.

## The Stylist

The stylist works hands-on with everything in your shot, with the techniques, materials, and kit to accomplish what you visualize, if it's physically possible. Preproduction communication is valuable if there are props or special materials needed, such as art paper for a background or a fresh-cut Christmas tree. The stylist may give you ideas about props and presentations as well as unanticipated aspects of the shoot, such as snacks and water for the crew, location permits, and transportation.

## Talent and Models

When there is talent in a shot, the project is much more complex. Schedules are coordinated so each person's expensive time is used effectively. You might stagger call times so you don't pay talent to wait while another person is getting makeup. Or maybe that time can be used for the stylist to fit the wardrobe.

## Makeup Artist

A makeup artist is needed when models' faces are shown. If you hire "real people" as talent, they may not have the on-camera skills that models and actors have and may not have good skin or hair; you should hire a makeup and hair stylist. I've seen the buck stop at makeup many times; the blame for slowing down the shoot always falls on the makeup artist's shoulders. Be sure to work into the schedule the length of time this step can take. Sometimes the stylist can do the makeup for simple lifestyle shots.

## The Parents of the Crew

Often it seems like the photographer and art director, regardless of gender, are the "mom and dad" of the crew. With a sharp eye on the budget and schedule, this pair keeps things under control. These "parents" are watching over other crewmembers to make sure the shots are done on schedule, bringing conversations back to the project, and monitoring the costs.

I recall one shoot in particular when I booked an Italian makeup artist who was like a happy child. To protect the innocent, we'll call him Sonny. When I noticed that the model needed powder or had a loose strand of hair, he would be gazing at the sky in the other direction like a young Little Leaguer in the outfield. "Sonny. Sonny? Sonny!" I'd say and finally get his attention.

Though you sometimes will feel like a stern parent, it's part of your job to ensure that the crewmembers are doing their jobs, and to communicate ways they can improve.

## DIRECTING THE STYLIST

At the beginning of the shoot day, be sure to communicate to both the photographer and stylist as much information as possible about the shoot. They need to know the goal of the shoot and the photographic style you have in mind. Be clear on props and show them similar examples and any resource material you can provide. They'll need a complete shot list so time can be allotted for each.

Each photograph develops gradually. In setting up a shot, the stylist may place items to get an idea of the camera's viewpoint before beginning to style them. While the photographer and assistant set up lighting, further styling will be done. The image is perfected this way. Be sure you aren't jumping ahead and critiquing the work before it's completed. A client will often do that, but the art director should know better.

As the art director, you are watching the shot come to life, and if you see something you want to change you can ask the stylist directly. Or you can consult with the stylist to see how something can be improved or changed.

## FINDING A STYLIST

Next to the photographer, the stylist is your most important ally on a photo shoot. The photographer has a great deal of creative input in setting up the shots, interpreting the style you are after. Stylists have the skills to make everything in a photo have the appearance you need. They serve as your hands in attending to each detail within the image. While the art director may have a vision, it is the role of the stylist to make that vision come to life.

Sometimes it's hard to put into words the subtle changes you would like the stylist to make. You'd rather jump in and do it yourself. But remember that your role is to step back and watch the process, looking at the big picture. When you find a stylist who sees what you see, who says, "Yes, I just noticed that too, and I'll do such-and-such to fix it," who brings just the props you had imagined, you have found the right stylist. A good working relationship makes the shoot move smoothly and, as a bonus, increases the shot count.

How do you find this person? As an art director, you will be most likely be found by stylists. Postcards and other mailings will come to your office; save them for later review. Agencies representing stylists will contact you by phone or mail, hoping to present their portfolios. Local stylists may request a meeting to show their portfolios. You'll see if you have rapport and if the portfolio matches your needs.

All these contacts are worthwhile, if only for future projects. The style may not be what you're looking for now, but next month a project may come up that's a perfect fit.

Photographers will have recommendations and may even hire the stylist for you. If you're shooting in another geographical area, use your photographer as a resource or do a Web search for local stylists. Film commissions will provide a thorough list of crew resources.

It's a good idea to keep several stylists on your list for specialties and availability. You can't always count on your favorites being available unless you book far ahead. You'll need to work with different stylists for different types of projects. Food, wardrobe, or off-figure stylists have skills which help with some shoots more than others. Techniques used for off-figure styling are challenging even for many stylists. (Uses and background of these presentations are described in chapter 7.)

## THE MOOD OF THE SHOOT

Back at the office a week after a fashion shoot, I would look at transparencies through a loupe to see them closely. I searched for the best six to ten shots, cut them apart, placed them in a protective sleeve, and then brought in the buyers from various divisions to select their favorites.

In the best shots the clothing looked good, and this was the most important element. If many features such as length, side slits, pockets, buttons, and fabric were visible, that helped make a strong shot. And in addition to good makeup and hair, there was the model's expression. She might be looking at the camera or away, but there had to be a genuine look of happiness. I call this "the happiness effect." No matter how skilled a model is at smiling, any stress or tension going on in a model's life, or among the crew, shows on her face.

### Tsunami on Maui

The first morning of directing a shoot in Hawaii, on the island of Maui, I was checking in with the fashion stylist and discussing the outfits we would shoot that day. The assistant stylist ran into the room stuttering as though she'd never heard of this, "there's a suam—sunani—tsunami— there's something coming!"

We turned on the television and sure enough, a tsunami was coming. There had been a moderate earthquake off the shore of Japan that morning, and a tidal wave was expected to work its way across the Pacific Ocean, potentially headed for Hawaii. It was predicted to make landfall on the Marshall Islands in about an hour; then we would know more about what to expect. This was when I realized the scope of my responsibility to the crew *and* to the catalog project we were there to work on.

It seemed there might be time to get a couple of shots accomplished before the announcement would be made—we needed to do about twelve shots a day to be on schedule. We went to the beach outside the hotel and did a couple of easy shots. That kind of anxiousness, as I've said, tends to show up in the model's face, so we concentrated on small insets. Watching the television news helped me decide that the safe plan was to evacuate to the higher center of the island.

A couple of outfits were brought along in case it all blew over and we could either shoot on the way up or down the mountain. I had seen a restaurant along that road when we scouted locations that would make a good background. But the photos we took there on the way also revealed tension. I wondered if I wasn't being ridiculously focused on getting shots done.

The crew made its way to a small mountainside village in the middle of the island in two vehicles and waited it out with many others in a restaurant there. I was even more aware by this time of the need to protect the crew from danger but was also thinking about my family and how anxious they must be to know if I was in danger. I finally found an available pay phone (this was before cell phones were common) and called my husband at work. He hadn't heard about the imminent tsunami and wasn't worried about me at all. With that out of the way, there was nothing to do but wait until the threat was cleared, which took most of the afternoon. On the second day we resumed our shooting schedule, making up for lost time.

## An Unhappy Model

On another shoot, to keep up with our schedule, the crew was trying to finish one more shot before lunch. Sometimes easy shots turn out to be hard ones, and this wasn't going smoothly. Instead of being his usual professional self, the male model suddenly burst out "You are such a control freak!" to the photographer. The photographer had been rather exacting on that shot. I wanted to crawl away instead of taking charge. I didn't, of course. We broke for lunch and a chance to resolve the crew tension. The image that we finished after lunch, though, wasn't much better—the model didn't look happy.

# WRAPPING UP THE SHOOT

As the art director, your responsibilities extend beyond the actual shoot. In most cases you are representing the financial and legal interests of the client. If a stylist needs an advance for initial prop or wardrobe expenses, or insurance certificates for location permits, this will be your responsibility. Larger agencies and magazines employ photo buyers or photo editors who handle these details.

## Billing and Follow Up

During the shoot, be sure to provide billing information to the freelance crew. They'll need to know where to send their invoices and what job reference to use. Do what you can to see that the invoices are processed quickly. Clients who pay early become favorite clients. All of us would put working for them ahead of the ones with a long, uncomfortable wait.

At the end of the shoot day, if you are working with models—or a stylist with an agency—you'll be presented with a voucher. This is a statement of the work that was done, the hours, rate, and travel expenses. You can complete the billing information, make sure the voucher matches the conditions you and the agent have agreed to, and sign it. Agencies will bill the client based on the voucher.

Invoices from the stylist and photographer will likely include documentation of their expenses, including receipts. Review them and be sure they match the terms you agreed to before passing them on to accounting.

The stylist, photographer, and models all like to see the finished product when it's printed, so make arrangements for them to follow up and ask for samples or tears. You might receive a cordial follow-up note from the stylist after the shoot. If you valued the work, be sure to keep the stylist in mind for future projects—it's better to work with a stylist who knows your communication style and your photographic needs.

## Achieving a Comfort Level

As art directors gain experience with photo shoots the process becomes more comfortable, especially when an effective support team is in place. Creating the image you are after can be very satisfying. There's nothing like receiving the final image from the photographer and placing it in a piece you have designed.

chapter

# The Photographer's Perspective

COUPLE OF YEARS AGO I REGISTERED FOR A CLASS IN STUDIO lighting at an art center. Though I'd been in the photo industry as a catalog art director and a stylist for over twenty years, I wanted to learn more about technical aspects of photographic lighting. Most of the concepts presented in the class were what I'd already observed, but it was great to be more involved with the lights, reflectors, and sync chords.

What surprised me in the class was meeting photographers who didn't know about stylists. I'm accustomed to working with commercial, fashion, and architectural photographers who know the value of working with stylists. These class members were shooting weddings and portraits and did everything on their own, from carrying equipment to marketing.

## UNDERSTANDING STYLING

While you can save money by going it alone, there are many occasions when a stylist is needed. It's important to understand when and how to hire a stylist, to achieve the high-quality photographs you need for a commercial client or for complex productions. If you read the earlier chapters of this book you will get to know how stylists develop their skills and what they can accomplish on a shoot.

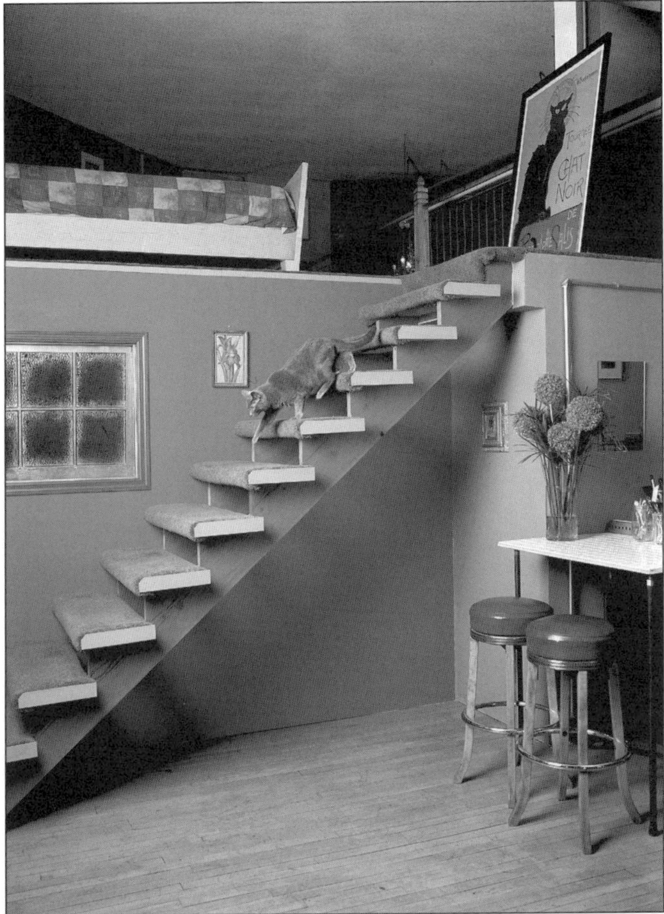

A production shot like this requires working with a stylist. Building the set, adding props, and working with a cat are too many aspects to handle alone. *Styling:* Colleen Heather Rogan. © *Milwaukee Magazine*

Many stylists excel in all areas of styling. Others are specialists in one aspect or another. This is especially the case with food stylists who are well trained in culinary arts and food marketing in addition to having the skills required to make food look attractive under the camera.

## Styling Fashion, Wardrobe, and Off-Figure Apparel

It's obvious that a photographer would need to work with a stylist for fashion photography. Editorial fashion is an opportunity to create beautiful magazine pages. Stylists for these features (also known as editors) have the inside knowledge to select and source the fashions.

Catalogs that market apparel may not be cutting-edge fashion, but they do provide a great deal of work for photographers and stylists. Intense shoot schedules with a goal of showing the best features of the merchandise require a team including stylist and makeup artist. In the studio or on location, they work with you to complete complex projects. The stylist is responsible for dressing models and refining the fit of the garments while the photographer assembles and lights the shot.

For lifestyle photography, the stylist dresses the talent in generic items so as not to detract from the featured product or concept. The effect should be just enough that the clothes enhance and do not distract. Shopping for or pulling together a wide selection of garments, the stylist eliminates one more concern for you. The stylist can often maintain hair and makeup and deal with shiny faces during lifestyle shoots.

At the end of the shoot, the stylist makes returns of unused items while you are busy with images and wrapping the business aspects of a shoot. It helps the budget when a professional knows how to shop economically and return extra items to stores.

The goal of most off-figure clothing presentations is to create a casual look. Techniques range from showing natural-looking folded items to imitating gestures of the human body, all of which is much more difficult than its relaxed look implies.

## Styling Products and Props

Stylists are valuable for product photography also. When there is the challenge of making a handbag strap drape in midair or when props are needed, a stylist has experience and resources that save time and money while greatly enhancing the shots. Often a background surface needs to be selected, as well as props that will give a sense of scale and create interest.

Shoe styling involves standards for showing specific details of footwear. A stylist works on sets and backgrounds while arranging the shoes in gravity-defying positions. Working on a much smaller scale, jewelry photography is improved by a stylist. The stylist presents and positions spotless items in a variety of arrangements, while the photographer carefully controls the tiniest reflections.

When an assignment includes food presentations, the need for a professional food stylist is apparent to photographers. With a unique kit and specialized skills, food stylists have the qualifications to make prepared food appear fresh and delicious under studio lights. Usually a stand-in is created so the photographer can set up the shot while the final dish is perfected. A prop stylist may be hired to work in conjunction with the food stylist to enhance more complex shots.

Architectural photographers, skilled at lighting and shooting a large area without awkward perspective shifts, literally see a bigger picture than many other commercial photographers. Assembling furniture, rugs, curtains, and other props that make a room look like home are the stylist's responsibility.

Many projects for an architectural photographer/stylist team are advertising images, including kitchen cabinets, appliances, windows, window coverings, or grills. The product is the star and, as with wardrobe, the set is styled to enhance it. Editorial projects for home magazines involve a similar attention to detail. When special props are needed, stylists know obscure sources for renting props, and how to track them down. Many a stylist appreciates the challenge of building and creating props.

Easily overlooked elements can take away from a great photo, while careful propping suggesting a lived-in space can pull the entire room together. With a large-scale project, it's beneficial to have the extra set of eyes and hands on the set.

## Advantages of Hiring a Stylist

- Photographer can focus on photography.

- Another "eye" is watching the shot and sharing responsibility for details.

- Hands-on member of the crew helps transport merchandise and holds the occasional reflector.

- Wardrobe and prop shopping by an experienced stylist saves time and money.

- Construction or rental of hard-to-find props expands your resources.

- Return of unused clothing and props after the shoot helps the bottom line.

- Preproduction duties, such as locations, permits, meals, RVs, and travel can be taken care of.

- Casting, booking, and coordination of talent may be handled by stylist.

- More professional impression to client; shows that the photographer is not an amateur but an experienced professional, understanding the scope of photo shoots.

### Working with the Art Director

When a capable stylist is on the shoot, the photographer is free to concentrate on creating the shot the art director is after. Communication with the art director proceeds while the stylist is taking care of the "small details" such as fitting the clothing, building cumbersome stacks of towels, or suspending items in mid-air.

## PRODUCING PHOTO SHOOTS

Typically stylists have a full set of production skills in their repertoires. Stylists accomplish many aspects of photo shoots before, during, and after the shoot days; this allows the photographer to concentrate on creating the photograph. (Chapter 4 provides in-depth descriptions of these production tasks.)

Most photographers also handle production duties. How much to attend to yourself and how much you can delegate to a stylist/production manager depends on the client, the timeline, the complexity of the shoot, and especially your schedule. Hiring a local stylist may provide a resource for an out-of-town crew. Equipment rentals, studio rentals, photo labs, local assistants, and delivery services, as well as your everyday location needs like permits, can be found with the help of the local stylist.

## WORKING WITH A STYLIST

When interviewed about the styling needs of the photographers she represents, Charlene Nevill of Vis-à-Vis agency in San Francisco, explains their universal preference for working with a stylist:

> *All of the photographers I represent would choose to work with a stylist whenever possible, and they only work without one when there's not enough money in the budget to hire one or more. For people and lifestyle shoots, stylists are almost always necessary for wardrobe, grooming, and props. If it's a product shoot, it depends on whether additional props are needed, how many, how difficult it is to source them, and how many shots need to be done in one day.*
>
> *Whether the stylist is needed only to shop and drop—or to be on the set as well—depends on the complexity of the job and whether it's for an ad agency, for an annual report, or for editorial. For advertising, it's almost always expected that stylists will be part of the production, while for an annual report or an editorial shoot, it depends on the subject and the client.*

## Studio Managers and Spouses

When a photographer has a full-time studio manager, many styling projects are included in that person's daily responsibilities. Preproduction duties and logistics are probably at the top of the manager's list, along with estimates and billing. Simpler prop shopping, lifestyle shots, and basic product styling can be accomplished without hiring freelance stylists. However, complex projects may be better assigned to a professional stylist while the studio manager manages the day-to-day business of the studio.

High-profile photographers like David LaChappelle work with a full-time stylist. Collaborating on extravagant background scenarios requires a more intense work relationship than the typical freelance one.

Often the spouse of a photographer falls into the role of stylist. I have been contacted several times by women who want to learn about styling because they find themselves assisting their photographer husbands in these duties. While most stylists discover the career unexpectedly, this is a natural alliance. Of course, this can put a strain on some relationships, but I have seen it work successfully—though not yet with a female photographer and a stylist husband.

One such team was a favorite for product photography when I worked for Norm Thompson. The couple came together to meet with the art directors and review the shot list and layouts. Then they took care of the shots in their studio, bringing back film precisely matching what we wanted.

Experienced photographers want to work with the best and most experienced stylist the budget will allow. For lower budget or editorial jobs, the investment could be balanced by working with a fresh trainee who has gained experience assisting a top-level stylist.

## WHEN TO DO YOUR OWN STYLING

Budget constraints are the most common reason for shooting without a stylist. Most photographers would prefer to have a professional handle the products and props so they can concentrate on the many technical and creative aspects of the shoot.

But sometimes that isn't possible. The budget may not allow several hundred dollars a day for styling. It could be quite a shock for a new client who learns how much a photo shoot can cost. Many of them need to be educated about the advantages of a professional shoot and that may happen slowly.

I've been hired by a photographer who wanted to show his client—a skateboard clothing maker who typically shot with a small budget—how a stylist could improve the shots. He actually took my pay out of the studio's budget to demonstrate the improved look and increased volume of shots. The client loved the results and later starting booking stylists.

Some commercial projects don't require a stylist. Portraits and weddings rarely allow for a stylist in the budget and the customer wouldn't perceive the advantage. You don't need professional help with repetitiously setting products in the same position for clients' low-resolution Web site images. But when there are people, clothing, food, props, and production work, it's great to have a stylist's help.

## Doing It All

An example of a photographer doing her own styling is a young woman who signed up for one of my styling workshops. She had started out as an assistant in a retail chain's in-house photo studio. When another photographer was needed in the studio, she was handed a camera. I can't say if it's to her credit or detriment, but she was willing to do her own styling in exchange for the opportunity to *be* a photographer.

The shot-per-day volume was high, and this eager photographer managed to style and prop while keeping up on the shot list. She wanted to know how to style stacks, laydowns, and set up wall styling. I don't advise this kind of blind determination, though it saves the employer or client a lot of money. The photographer can accomplish simple and basic styling, but to maintain a professional appearance it's better to be a photographer, not a jack-of-all-trades. Reading the chapters on styling specialties will teach you some useful techniques. (Chapter 13 provides you with a basic kit for styling. These are the items I have found most useful for general styling projects. Many of them you may already have in the studio.)

## CHOOSING THE BEST STYLIST

The most important part of hiring a stylist for attending to shoot details, is hiring the *right* stylist. You want someone who takes care of duties independently, is quick, and is efficient. The stylist must be confident but able to take changes and revisions in stride without taking them personally. A pleasant personality is important in this working relationship.

Photo rep Charlene Nevill says, "In addition to the obvious—attention to detail, knowledge of the industry, experience doing his or her particular job, a great eye, and knowledge of design—it's important that a stylist is able to work well with the rest of the crew. Our clients not only expect great photography, they want to enjoy themselves on a photo shoot. How well the entire crew works together as a team can make or break a shoot. A sense of humor and willingness to do whatever it takes to get the job done also go a long way."

## Flexibility

San Diego-based photographer Greg Bertolini doesn't often get to hire stylists for his projects, but when he does, the trait he looks for is flexibility. Much of his work occurs in New York, and he hires locally for those jobs. On location, when he's most likely to hire a stylist, it's important for everyone in the crew to improvise and deal with changes. There are always last minute revisions to well-laid plans and the ability to solve problems is the key.

For example, a model may be asked to bring his own black shoes but they turn out to be combat boots. The stylist (if she didn't have the foresight to bring options) needs to quickly run to a store and purchase something appropriate "without tantrums." An art director may have a sudden inspiration for other props and, again, flexibility is required.

When Greg has a lifestyle shoot with male models, whom he finds don't always bring the best wardrobe items, he likes to wear a nice shirt that day, in case the model is unprepared. In fact, he keeps a small collection of items in the studio. There are black and brown men's shoes and boots, and a couple of dress shirts. He's in the process of adding several belts, ties, and white T-shirts, which are good for layering and obscuring hairy chests under dress shirts.

## Finding a Favorite

When you find a stylist you work well with, the relationship continues. You will suggest each other for projects whenever possible so the team can be efficient and familiar.

Finding that special combination is not always easy. Some ways to locate a good stylist include recommendations from other photographers and word-of-mouth reputation in your photographic community. Another option is hiring from an agency that represents stylists fitting the profile for that particular shoot. Source book directories and online searches for local stylists can produce good results.

While one favorite stylist is a comfortable fit, it's best to have two or three stylists on your roster as your stylist may be not always be available; rotate them occasionally to keep in contact. One may be better at hard goods and another at off-figure or wardrobe, and of course you'll need a food stylist for food shoots.

## COLLABORATION

A test shoot is a creative exercise and an opportunity to work with new stylists. At the same time you'll most likely produce great images for your portfolios. And you'll find out how well you'd work together on future commercial projects. Working in collaboration with stylists who have original ideas can expand your own way of seeing. You can learn from them and they can learn from you, no matter what the stylist's level of experience.

Your professional reputation as a photographer is underlined by every image you shoot. Along with the art director, you are best qualified to determine when having a stylist on your team will help your career. The collaborative trio of photographers, art directors, and stylists on commercial shoots can be the source of creative ideas and techniques for making those ideas come to life.

**index**

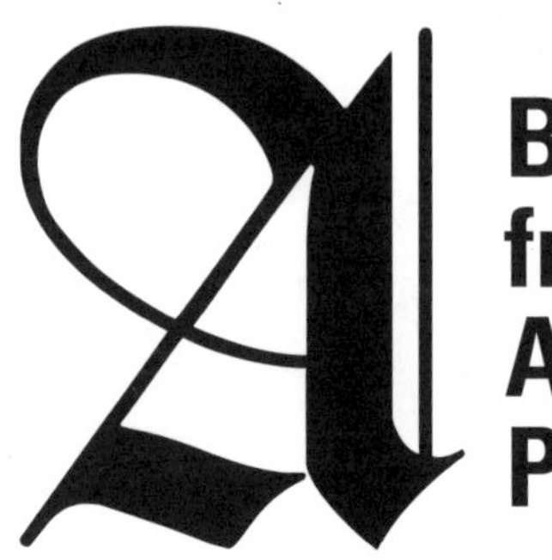

# Books from Allworth Press

Allworth Press is an imprint of Allworth Communications, Inc. Selected titles are listed below.

---

**Mastering the Basics of Photography**
*by Susan McCartney* (paperback, 6¾ × 10, 192 pages, $19.95)

**Photographic Lighting Simplified**
*by Susan McCartney* (paperback, 6¾ × 9⅞, 176 pages, $19.95)

**How to Shoot Great Travel Photos**
*by Susan McCartney* (paperback, 8½ × 10, 160 pages, $24.95)

**The Photographer's Assistant, Revised Edition**
*by John Kieffer* (paperback, 6¾ × 9⅞, 256 pages, $19.95)

**The Real Business of Photography**
*by Richard Weisgrau* (paperback, 6 × 9, 256 pages, $19.95)

**Starting Your Career as a Freelance Photographer**
*by Tad Crawford* (paperback, 6 × 9, 256 pages, $24.95)

**Photography Your Way: A Career Guide to Satisfaction and Success, Second Edition**
*by Chuck DeLaney* (paperback, 6 × 9, 304 pages, $19.95)

**Mastering Nature Photography: Shooting and Selling in the Digital Age**
*by John Kieffer* (paperback, 6 × 9, 288 pages, includes CD-ROM, $24.95)

**Creative Canine Photography**
*by Larry Allan* (paperback, 8½ × 10, 160 pages, $24.95)

**Business and Legal Forms for Photographers, Third Edition**
*by Tad Crawford* (paperback, with CD-ROM, 8½ × 11, 180 pages, $29.95)

**ASMP Professional Business Practices in Photography, Sixth Edition**
*by the American Society of Media Photographers* (paperback, 6¾ × 10, 416 pages, $29.95)

Please write to request our free catalog. To order by credit card, call 1-800-491-2808 or send a check or money order to Allworth Press, 10 East 23rd Street, Suite 510, New York, NY 10010. Include $6 for shipping and handling for the first book ordered and $1 for each additional book. Eleven dollars plus $1 for each additional book if ordering from Canada. New York State residents must add sales tax.

To see our complete catalog on the World Wide Web, or to order online, you can find us at
**www.allworth.com.**